IoT
Advanced Emerging Applications

IoT
Advanced Emerging Applications

Prof. (Dr.) Rajiv Chopra
CSE Department (DCE)
Gurugram, Haryana

Manakin
PRESS

CRC Press
Taylor & Francis Group
Boca Raton London New York

CRC Press is an imprint of the
Taylor & Francis Group, an **informa** business

First published 2026
by CRC Press
4 Park Square, Milton Park, Abingdon, Oxon, OX14 4RN

and by CRC Press
2385 NW Executive Center Drive, Suite 320, Boca Raton FL 33431

CRC Press is an imprint of Informa UK Limited

© 2026 Manakin Press Pvt. Ltd.

The right of Rajiv Chopra to be identified as author of this work has been asserted in accordance with sections 77 and 78 of the Copyright, Designs and Patents Act 1988.

British Library Cataloguing-in-Publication Data
A catalogue record for this book is available from the British Library

Print edition not for sale in South Asia (India, Sri Lanka, Nepal, Bangladesh, Pakistan or Bhutan).

ISBN: 9781041206910 (hbk)
ISBN: 9781041217169 (pbk)
ISBN: 9781003728641 (ebk)

DOI: 10.1201/9781003728641

Typeset in Times New Roman
by Manakin Press, Delhi

Manakin
PRESS

Preface

I am contended to endorse this preface in favor of my new book on *"IoT-Advanced Emerging Applications"*. Through this book, I had ample opportunities to gauge the potential of the IOT. IoT, today navigates the entire Universe. Right from conceptualizing the idea of the book, I have also demonstrated my articulation and creativity. Through the presentation of the same, the author evinced his prowess in research. In today's era of instant information gratification, we have ready access to opinions, rationalizations and superficial descriptions. Much harder to come by is the foundational knowledge that informs a principled understanding of the world. Essential knowledge books fill that need. This book synthesizes specialized subject matter for non-specialists too and engages critical topics through fundamentals of Advanced IoT. This book is NOT purely descriptive and definitional but also follows a flowchart and algorithmic approach. I have attempted to present the technical details in an accessible way.

The hallmark of human intelligence is the capacity to learn. It is no secret that creating robust and manageable programs is what this books aims at. Businesses, teachers and students can harness the transformative capabilities of IOT using this manuscript.

There are plenty of books on this subject in the market, so thanks again for choosing this one!!! Every effort has been made to ensure that it is full of useful information as much is possible.

Happy Reading,

Prof. (Dr.) Rajiv Chopra
CSE Department (DCE)
Gurugram, Haryana

Detail Contents

1 INTRODUCTION TO IoT

1.0 INTRODUCTION

Another name for Internet of Things (IoT) can be **"Connecting An Object to The Internet"**. There has to be an information flow that connects the defining characteristics of the **"Thing"** with the world of data and processing represented by the Internet. **"Thing"** is present object in real world. **This means that it can receive inputs from outside world and transform those into data which is then sent on Internet for collection and processing. For example,** just putting an Ethernet socket into a chair is not sufficient. Your chair might collect information about how often you sit on it and for how much time. **Also note that the presence of Things also means that it can produce outputs into your world with "Actuators".** Some of these outputs could be triggered by data that has been collected and processed on Internet. **So, your chair might vibrate to tell you that you have received an email.** This can be shown with the help of a simple equation also:

[Physical Object] + [Controllers, Sensors, Actuators] + [Internet] = Internet of Things.

$$[Hardware] + [software] + [Service] = [Things]$$

Doing this does not have any impact on the physical object. So, we now define Internet-of-Things as follows:

"The Internet of Things (IoT) is the network of physical objects i.e., devices, vehicles, buildings and other items embedded with electronics, software, sensors and network connectivity that enables these objects to collect and exchange data".

or

DOI: 10.1201/9781003728641-1

"The Internet of Things, also called as the internet of objects refers to a wireless network between objects, usually the network will be wireless and self-configuring, such as household appliances".

[*Source: Wikipedia*]

or

"Internet of Things can also be defined as an Internet technology connecting devices, machines and tools to the Internet by means of wireless technologies like Bluetooth, EIFI, ZigBee etc.".

or

"It is a system of web connected objects that are ready to gather and trade information utilizing sensors embedded on a system."

or

"IoT is a framework comprising of systems of sensors, actuators and keen protests whose reason for existing is to interconnect "All" things including regular and industrial components so as to make them shrewd, programmable and more fit to interact with people and each other."

Hence, amalgamation of the digital world and the physical world is the main objective of IoT.

1.1 VISION, DEFINITION AND CHARACTERISTICS OF IoT

IoT defines a system in which in which different things or objects are connected to the internet or any other object. So, here things may be any physical objects, persons or devices. Each of the connected object/ things are represented by a unique IP address. Objects can generate or capture data and transfer using sensors or other network devices. In other words, IoT is a concept of connecting any devices and objects to the internet. This includes everything from mobile phones, headphones, home appliances, lamps or any wearable device.

Present day companies are using IoT to operate more efficiently, better enhancement of services and improving decision makings. We have moved from Internet-of-People to Internet-of-Things now. IoT helps people to enhance their living style as well as to gain complete control over their lives. IoT permits smart devices to automate home, hospital, garden and transportation and many more. IoT enables companies to automate system and reduce their manpower cost.it also provides better service quality and service delivery.

In nutshell, we can say that IoT is mandatory for each and every industry as well as for the people. It touches every sector such as retail, finance, healthcare, manufacturing smart cities, agriculture, battlefield etc. Hence, IoT is one of the critical technologies to be used today.

By 2050, 2000 billion devices will be connected by IoT. It is our Internet that connects large number of devices or sensors of IoT. IoT is also known as Internet of Everything as it considers larger number of consumer electronic devices, home appliances, medical devices, cameras, sensors, mobiles and industrial IoT devices. **According to Ericsson,** up to 50 billion devices are expected to be connected. This will result in a 20 trillion market opportunity in less than 10 years. In 2025, estimates tell that IoT will have an economic impact with revenue generated.

Characteristics of IoT

1. **Interconnectivity:** Everything can be connected to the global information and communication infrastructure. When there is proper communication between "Things" of IoT platform, we can say that connectivity prevails. **Please note that this connectivity may be between things or server or things with clouds.** This connectivity is possible due to the network technologies like internet, WIFI or sensors only.

2. **Heterogeneity:** Devices within IoT have different hardware and use different networks but they can still interact with other devices through different networks.

3. **Things-related Services:** provides things-related services within the constraints of things such as privacy and semantic consistency between physical and virtual thing.

4. **Dynamic Changes:** The state of a device can change dynamically. IoT systems work in dynamic environments i.e., to collect the data from the environment, dynamic changes are made in the dynamic systems.

5. **Unique Identity:** Each IoT device has a unique identity and unique identifier. So, the names and addresses of devices connected to Internet of Things should be unique. Efficient and unambiguous addressing mechanisms should be deployed for devices connected to IoT. **Also note that the conversion and translation of addresses from one network to the other should take place efficiently.**

6. **Integrated Into Information Network:** IoT devices are integrated with information network for communication purpose. It will exchange data with other devices.

7. **Self-adapting:** Self-adaptive is a system that can automatically modify itself in the face of a changing context, to best answer a set of requirements.

8. **Self-configuration** consists of actions of neighbour and service discovery, network organization and resource provisioning.

9. **Intelligence:** An IoT system is smart and intelligent. It is so because it has a set of algorithms, computational techniques, software and hardware. It provides capabilities to the "Things" to respond in more smarter ways. **For example,** a door opens automatically when a person stands in front of it and closes when he lives. This is possible because of sensors that can detect the objects and take intelligent decisions immediately.

10. **Enormous Scale:** The number of devices that need to be managed and that communicate with one another will be at least in an order of magnitude larger than the devices connected to the current Internet. The management of generated data and their interpretation for application purposes will be more critical. This relates to semantics of data as well as efficient data handling.

11. IoT is regarded as the third evolution of information industry due to three reasons:

    (a) **Networking** becomes large as IoT interconnects large number of things in the physical world.

    (b) **Network Mobility** increases due to use of mobiles and vehicular devices.

    (c) **Fusion of Heterogeneous Networks** becomes deep and complex as different types of devices are connected to the Internet.

1.2 SOME BASIC TERMINOLOGIES RELATED TO IoT

1. **IoT Device:** It is an independent entity that is connected to web which can be identified and monitored from a distant (remote) area too. It performs identification, remote monitoring, sensing and actuating functions.

2. **IoT Ecosystem:** It is a collective system of components that empower organizations, Governance with the Govts. and peer customers to

associate with their useful IoT gadgets with additional components like remotes, dashboards, systems, entryways, investigation, information piling and security.

3. **Entity:** It includes organizations, Govt and customers.

4. **Physical Layer:** It is a layer that constitutes an IoT device which includes automating sensors and an administrative unit of systems.

5. **Network Layer:** It is a layer responsible for the communication via transmitting the information gathered by the physical layer to route across various devices.

6. **Application Layer:** It is the layer which incorporates the set of protocols **and the catalytic interfaces that devices use in order to recognize and talk to each other.**

7. **Remotes:** Empower substances that use IoT devices in order to associate with device components and control them with advent use of a dashboard.

8. **Dashboard:** It displays data of the IoT biological community to peer clients which empowers clients to control their integrated components in IoT world. This is termed as **large housed data on a remote.**

9. **Analytics:** A software framework that determines the information produced by IoT devices. This information may be used further.

10. **Data Storage/Database:** A storage where the information from IoT devices is stored. IoT generates a large amount of **local database and cloud database.**

11. **Networks:** It is a **web correspondence layer** that allows the person to speak with the devices and also all devices to speak to each other.

12. **Resource:** IoT devices used software components as resources for accessing, processing and storing sensor information. It also controls actuators.

13. **Web/Controller Service:** It sends data from the device to the web service and receives commands from the application for controlling the device. It acts as a link between the IoT device, application, database and analysis components.

14. **Analysis Components:** It is responsible for analysing the IoT data and generate results.

15. **Application:** Users use this interface for controlling and monitoring various IoT systems.

Let us Now Differentiate Between M2M, IoT and IoE.

Attibutes	M2M	IoT	IoE
Size	M2M is a subset of IoT	IoT is a superset of M2M	IoE is superset of IoT.
Key Components	M2M encompasses three key components such as 1. Devices, which generates or receives the data from other devices. 2. Communication, for efficient transfer of data among devices and gateway. 3. Application, to provide services to the end user requirements	IoT consists of four key components such as 1. Sensing or devices, for generating or receiving the data from other devices. 2. Communication, for transferring of data to Internet or between devices. 3. Storage services, for efficient storage of data into database or to cloud. 4. Application, to provide intended service	IoE consists of four key components such as 1. People, considered as end nodes connected to the Internet for sharing information and activities. 2. Things, are devices that generate the data or receives data from other devices. 3. Data, used for analyzing and processing of useful information to take intelligent decision and control mechanism. 4. Processes, allows people, data and things to work together to deliver value.
Communication Type	Point-to-Point communication exists between the devices	IP network exists between devices, by integrating various communication protocols.	IoE is a network connection of people, process, data and things
Internet Requirement	M2M communication may exist without the Internet	Devices in Iot require an active Internet in most of the cases	Devices and their application require active Internet.

1.3 CONCEPTUAL FRAMEWORK

We usually talk of four layers of IoT's conceptual framework. Fig. 1.1 shows the 4-layered conceptual framework of IoT.

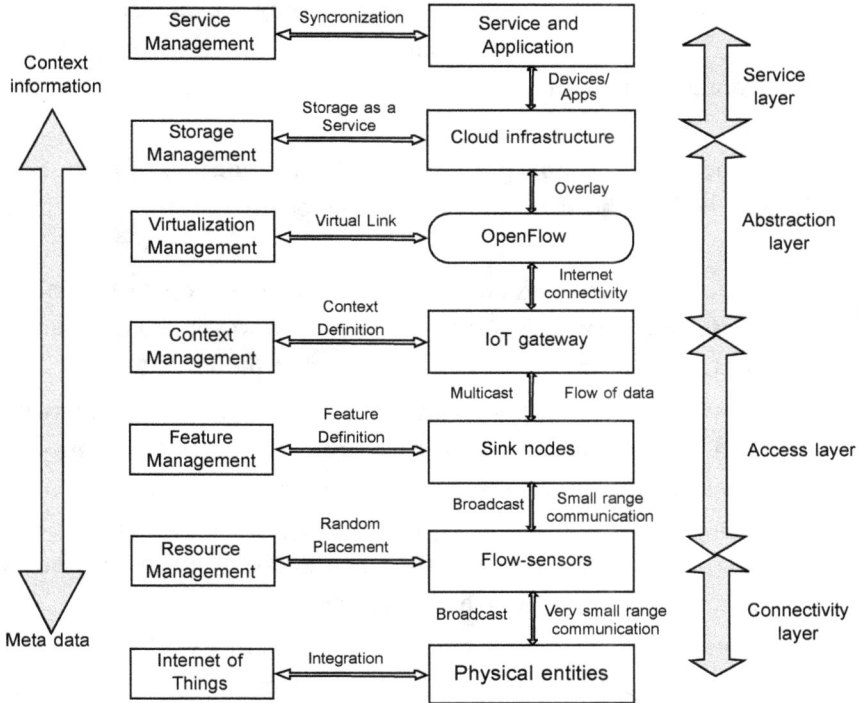

Fig. 1.1: 4-layered Conceptual Framework of IoT

Let us Explain This Layered Architecture:

1. The **Internet of Things** can be outlined in a universal network framework supported by regular and interoperable network protocols in which sensible and virtual "things" are incorporated into the communication network.

2. The **main task of this framework is to analyse and determine the smart activities of these intelligent devices through maintaining a dynamic interconnection among those devices.**

3. The framework will help to **standardize IoT infrastructure** so that it can receive e-services based on context information leaving the current infrastructure unchanged.

4. The active collaboration of these heterogeneous devices and protocols can lead to future **ambient computing where the maximum utilization of cloud computing will be ensured.**

5. This model is capable of **logical division** of physical devices placement, creation of **virtual links** among different domains, networks and collaborate among multiple application without any central coordination system.

6. Sensor network performs **gathering and consolidation of data.** Sensor devices collect the data and transformation of data is done through gateway.

7. **Communication management uses various protocols to transfer the data. Internet firewall is used** in between gateway and data processing system. Collected information is processed at the last stage.

8. **The Connectivity Layer:** This layer includes **all of the physical devices involved in the framework and the interconnection among them**. This layer also involves **assigning of low range networking devices** like sensors, actuators, RFID tags etc. and **resource management checks the availability of physical resources** of all the devices and **networks** involved in the underlying infrastructure.

9. **The Access Layer:** Context data will reach Internet via IoT Gateway as captured by the short-range devices in form of raw data. Access layer comprises topology definition, network initiation etc. **Also note that this layer will also include connection set-up, intra-inter domain communication, scheduling, packet transmissions between flow sensors and IoT gateway.**

10. **The Abstraction Layer:** A **virtual link** can be created among different networks and a common platform can be developed for various communication systems.

11. **The Service Layer: Storage management bears the idea about all sorts of unfamiliar and/or important technologies and information that can turn the system scalable and efficient.** It is not only responsible for storing data but also to provide security along with it. **Please note that it also allows accessing data effectively, integrating data to enhance service intelligence, analysis based on the services required and most importantly increases the storage efficiency.**

12. **The Storage and Management Layer:** It involves data storage and system supervision, software services and business management and operations.

1.4 ARCHITECTURAL OVERVIEW

Views are used during the **design and implementation phase of concrete system architecture.** A view is composed of **viewpoints** which aggregate several architectural concepts in order to make the work with views easier. Actually, the IoT reference architecture is **use-case and application independent.** That is why it is not compatible to the concept of views and viewpoints one-by-one.

Let us first of all discuss about the functional view specification.

Functional View Specifications

The following are the main features of functional view specifications:

1. Functional view describes the **system's run-time Functional Components,** their responsibilities, default functions, interfaces and primary interactions. **Please note that the functional view derives from the Functional Model and reflects the developer's perspectives on the system.**

2. It will need to be extended with all identified **new profile-specific functional components** including their interfaces and a **list of sequence charts** illustrating recommended usage of those components.

3. Fig. 1.2 shows the functional view of IoT.

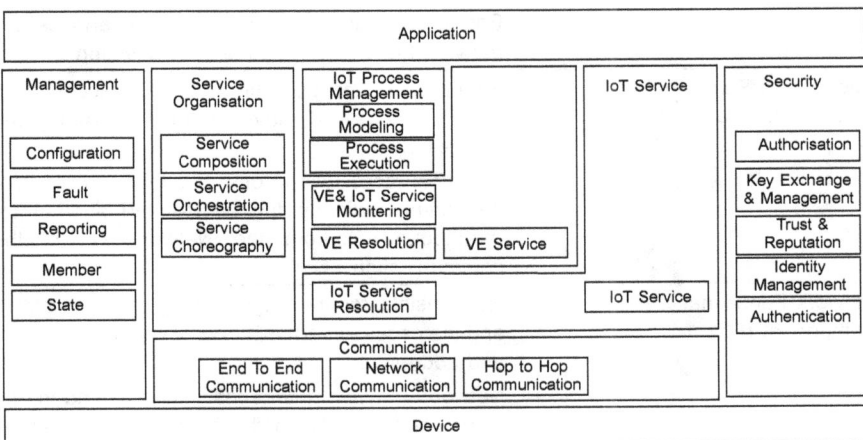

Fig. 1.2: Functional View of IoT

4. The viewpoints used for constructing the IoT functional view are therefore as follows:

   (a) The Unified Requirements.

   (b) The IoT Functional Model.

5. Once all functional components are defined, the default function set, system use-cases, sequence charts and interface definitions are made.

6. **Device and Application Functional Group:** Device functional components contains the sensing, actuation tag, processing and storage components. Application functional group contains standalone application.

7. **Communicational Functional Group:** it contains the components for end-to-end communication, network communication and hop-by-hop communication.

8. The following Table 1.1 summarizes it.

Table 1.1: Different Components of Communication

Communication Type	Description
End-to-end communication Functional Component (FC)	• Responsible for end-to-end transport of application layer messages through diverse network and MAC/ physical layers. • Used with mesh radio networking technologies like IEEE 802.15.4. • End-to-End functional component interfaces the network FC on the "southbound" direction.
Hop-by-hop Functional Component (FC)	• Responsible for transmission and reception of physical and MAC layer frames to/from other devices. • Two interfaces used: one "southbound" to/from the actual radio on the device and another for "northbound" to/from the Network FC in the communication FC.
Network Functional Component (FC)	• Responsible for message routing and forwarding and the necessary translations of various identifiers and addresses. • Network FC interfaces the end-to-end communication FC on the "northbound" direction and the hop-by-hop communication FC on the "southbound" direction.

9. **IoT Service Functional Group:** It consists of IoT service FC and the IoT Service Resolution FC. Various service implementations are

covered in service FC and serve resolution FC contains the necessary functions to realize a directory of IoT services that allows dynamic management of IoT service descriptions.

10. **Virtual Entity Functional Group:** The virtual entity functional group contains functions that support the interactions between users and **"Physical Things"** through virtual entity services.

11. **Process Management Functional Group:** It provides the functional concepts necessary to conceptually integrate the IoT world into traditional-business processes.

12. **The Process Modelling Functional Component** which provides the tools required for modelling IoT-aware business processes that will be serialized and executed in the Process Execution FC, which is responsible for deploying process models to the execution environments.

13. **Service Organization Functional Group:** It acts as a communication hub between several other functional groups by composing and orchestrating services of different levels of abstraction.

14. **The Service Orchestration Functional Component** resolves the IoT services that are suitable to fulfil service requests coming from the process execution FC or from users while the service composition FC is responsible for creating services with extended functionality by composing IoT services with other services.

15. **Service Choreography FC** offers a broker that handles publish/ subscribe communication between services.

16. **Virtual Entity Functional Group:** It provides functionality for the interaction of VEs with the IoT system, for **VE look-up** and discovery and for providing information concerning VEs. **The VE resolution FC** provides discovery services for associations between VEs and IoT.

17. **VE and IoT Service Monitoring FC** is responsible for automatically finding new associations based on service descriptions and information about VE's. the VE service FC handles entity services.

18. **Service FG:** It provides IoT services as well as functionalities for discovery, look-up and name resolution of IoT services.

19. **Security FG:** It is responsible for security and privacy matters in IoT A-Complaint IoT systems.

20. **Authorization FC** is used to apply access control and access policy management while the authentication FC is used for the user and service authentication.

21. **Key Exchange and Management (KEM) FC** enables secure communication ensuring integrity and confidentiality by distributing keys upon request in a secure way.

22. **Management Functional Group:** It is responsible for the composition and tracking of actions that involve other FGs.

23. **Configuration FC is Responsible** for initializing the system's configuration.

24. **The Fault FC** is used to identify, isolate, correct and log faults that occur in the IoT system.

25. **The Member FC** is responsible for the management of the membership of any relevant entity.

26. **The Reporting FC** generates reports about the system and finally, the state FC can change or enforce a particular state on the system by issuing a sequence of commands to the other FCs.

1.5 TECHNOLOGY BEHIND IoT

The **key actors** involved in IoT include Wireless Sensor Networks, distributed computing, big data analytics, security and communication protocols, web administrations, web, semantic web crawlers and search engines. Actually, **IoT is a Collection of Many Technologies and Devices.** Sensors, embedded systems, mobile Internet, security and protocols involving cloud storage/computing, all have become enabling technologies. In general, enabling technologies can be classified under one of the following categories:

1. Technologies that help in sensing (acquiring) of data.
2. Technologies that help in processing and analysing data.
3. Technologies that help in taking control action.
4. Technologies that help in enhancing security.

Let us Discuss Some of These Technologies Now

1. **Sensors:** Several real-time applications like air traffic control system, thermal power plant etc. need real-time data where there are strict time constraints. The input must be available within the strict time constraints else a disaster can occur. These inputs are brought into the system through these devices called as sensors. As the name only tells, that they sense the environment and retrieve data. **Please note that**

sensors are at the heart of an IoT application. These sensors may be analog or digital. **For example,** CCTV cameras, weather tracking system using temperature or moisture, vehicle health monitoring system to keep track of speed, pressure of tyre, vibration sensors to track the quality of buildings, water level monitoring uses sensors to measure its pH, chloride levels etc.

2. **Cloud Computing:** A market oriented distributed computing system consisting of collection of inter-connected and virtualized computers that are dynamically provisioned and presented as one or more unified computing resources based on SLA established through negotiation between service providers and consumers is known as CLOUD.

Full form of CLOUD is- **C**ommon **L**ocation independent **O**nline **U**tility provisioned on-**D**emand = CLOUD.

According to the recent reports, by 2050, 2000 billion devices will be connected by IoT. The purpose is to-

. Extract data →   Refine data → Model of ML →   Accuracy
  (using Python)   (using Python)

How is Cloud Computing Related to IoT?

As we know that data storage plays a vital role in IoT. And cloud has been found to be a popular option for data storage as it works on **sharing of resources principle.** Cloud provides effective and efficient medium for data storages. It provides everything as a service like **Infrastructure-as-a-Service (IaaS), Platform-as-a-Service (PaaS), Software-as-a-Service (SaaS), Testing-as-a-Service (TaaS)** and so on. In IaaS, we can choose virtual machines over physical machines. These virtual machines are available over internet and can be used on **"pay-per"** principle. Also, **a PaaS** provider hosts the hardware and software on its own infrastructure. Also in **SaaS,** the entire software application is now available on monthly, yearly subscriptions. That is why, it is also called as **Application as a Service.** Some popular cloud service providers are Amazon, Azure etc.

3. **Big Data Analytics:** Presently, there is a data deluge (flood). IoT is related to the collection of data from various sensors and handling it in a better way. However, one has to keep in mind the 5 **vs** **associated with big data- its volume, variety, velocity, veracity and**

its vulnerability. Volume of data is high and its variety is also high. But the term 'veracity' means data's accuracy. Data todays changes dynamically and is unambiguous. We need to handle this unstable data. Vulnerability refers to the ease which with the data can be attacked and stolen. This data is coming from sensors attached to security systems, sensors from weather monitoring systems, car navigation systems, water quality systems, data from industrial appliances, sensors from roads for traffic density and social media like tweets, photos uploaded etc. therefore, **when it comes to IoT, it is only data-related operations. So, data analytics is a technology to build bigger and complete IoT applications.**

4. **Embedded Computing:** Several embedded computing boards are available to design an IoT system today. For example, Raspberry Pi, Arduino, Intel Edison, Intel UP Squared IoT Development Kit. These kits are miniature devices. Furthermore, they are not very costly, around Rs 5000 - Rs 8000.

5. **Communication Protocols:** Protocols means a set of rules that are used for communication. Data exchanges occur through the protocols only. These protocols include addressing mechanisms, message formats, message security, routing, flow control, error monitoring, sequencing, synchronizations, retransmission rules and segmentation (breaking) of data packets.

6. **User Interfaces:** It is always desirable to have the best GUI for all devices. Same rule applies to IoT devices also. The end-user should be provided with either a mobile application or with a web application for this.

1.6 SOURCES OF IoT

There are several sources of IoT for data, for energy and many more.

In past, users have searched for information on the web. But IoT will seek for more machine-to-machine (M2M) searches which are automatically generated depending on location, preferences and local information. **For example,** Autonomous vehicles, will need to automatically collect data (such as traffic and weather information) from various sources without a user being involved.

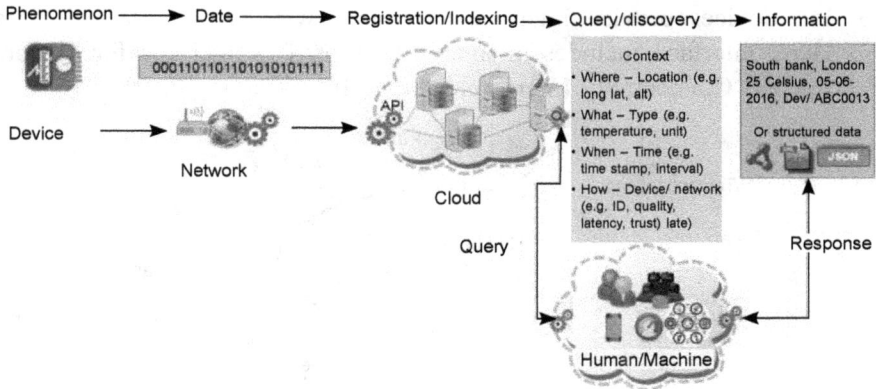

Fig. 1.3: Sources and Processing in IoT

1.7   DESIGN PRINCIPLES OF IoT

We understand the design principles of IoT from two perspectives:

    (a)   Physical Design of IoT.

    (b)   Logical Design of IoT.

Physical Design of IoT

1. IoT devices have a unique identity and they are referred to as **"Things"** in IoT. Device can perform remote sensing, actuating and monitoring. IoT devices can exchange data between them and process of send to centralized location for processing and storage.

2. The block diagram of IoT devices is shown in Fig. 1.4.

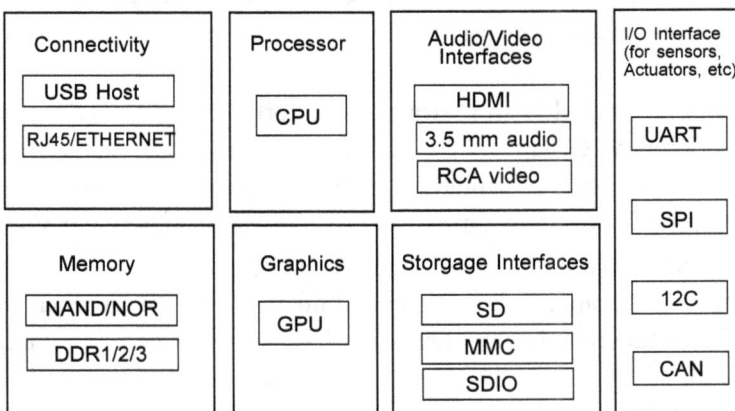

Fig. 1.4: Physical Design Block Diagram of IoT Devices

3. IoT devices provide interface to various wire and wireless devices. Here, interface includes memory interface, I/O interface for sensors, Internet Connectivity Interface, Storage Interface etc.

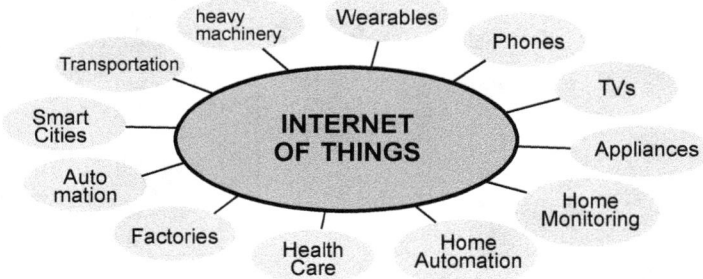

Fig. 1.5: IoT Devices

4. Using sensors, IoT collects various information like temperature, pressure, light intensity, humidity etc. some applications used cloud-based storage. Collected information is stored in cloud and transmitted to other devices.

5. Various types of IoT devices are smart clothing, smart watch, wearable sensors, LED lights, automobile industry etc.

Logical Design of IoT

1. Also called as the **Functional Model (FM) of IoT is** derived from **internal and external requirements.** Functional view is derived from the Functional Model in conjunction with **high-level requirements.**

2. IoT functional model identifies **Functional Groups** (FGs) i.e., the group of functionalities grounded in key concepts of the IoT Domain Model.

3. Functional Model is an abstract framework for understanding the main Functionality Groups (FG) and their interactions. This framework defines the common semantics of the main functionalities and will be used for the development of IoT—A complaint Functional Views.

4. The Functionality Model is not directly tied to a certain technology application domain or implementation. It does not explain what the different functional components are that make up a certain Functionality Group.

5. Fig. 1.6 shows the IoT Functionality Model.

```
┌─────────────────────────────────────────────────────────────────┐
│                          Application                              │
├┄┄┄┄┄┄┄┄┄┄┄┄┄┄┄┄┄┄⇕┄┄┄┄⇕┄┄┄┄┄┄┄┄┄┄┄┄┄┄┄┄⇕┄┄┄┄┄┄┄┄┄┄┄┄┄┄┄┄┤
┊            ┌──────────┬──────────┬──────────┬──────────┐        ┊
┊            │ Service  │Int Process│ Viertual │   IoT    │        ┊
┊ Management │Organisations│Managment│ Entity  │ Service  │ Security┊
┊            ├──────────┴──────────┤          │          │        ┊
┊            │                     │          │          │        ┊
┊            └─────────────────────┴──────────┴──────────┘        ┊
┊            ┌──────────────────────⇕──────────────────┐          ┊
┊            │              Communication              │          ┊
┊            └──────────────────────⇕──────────────────┘          ┊
├┄┄┄┄┄┄┄┄┄┄┄┄┄┄┄┄┄┄┄┄┄┄┄┄┄┄┄┄┄┄┄┄┄┄┄┄┄┄┄┄┄┄┄┄┄┄┄┄┄┄┄┄┄┄┄┄┄┄┤
│                           Devices                                │
└─────────────────────────────────────────────────────────────────┘
```

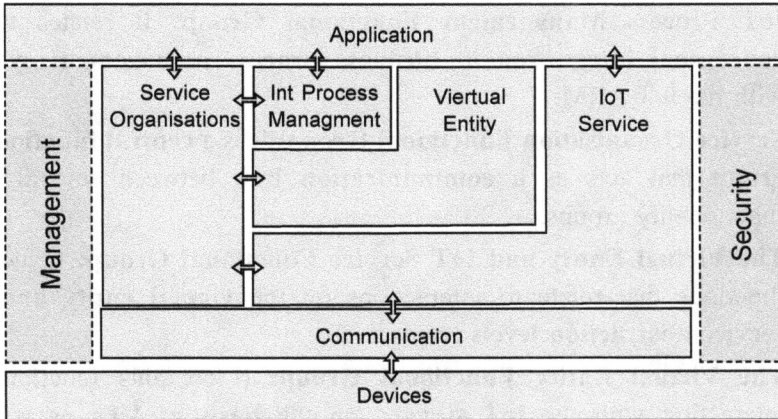

Fig. 1.6: Functional Model

6. The Application, Virtual Entity, IoT Service and Device FGs are generated by starting from the User, Virtual Entity, Resource, Service and Device classes from the IoT Domain Model.

7. **Device Functional Group** contains all possible functionality hosted by the physical devices. Device functionality includes sensing, actuation, processing storage and identification components, the sophistication of which depends on the device capabilities.

8. **Communication Functional Group** supports all of the communication used by devices. It uses wired and wireless technology.

9. **IoT Service Functional Group** Supports functions such as directory services which allow discovery of services and resolution to resources.

10. **Virtual Entity Functional Group:** It is related to the **virtual entity class** in the IoT domain model. Associations between virtual entities can be **static or dynamic** depending on the mobility of the **Physical Entities related to the corresponding Virtual Entities.**

11. **IoT Service Organization Functional Group:** To host all functional components that support the **composition and orchestration of IoT and Virtual Entity Services.**

12. Finally, **the management transversal functional group** It is required for the management of and/or interaction between the functionality groups.

13. **IoT Process Management Functional Group:** It relates to the **conceptual integration of business process management systems** with the IoT ARM.

14. **Service Organisation Functional Group:** It is a **central functionality group** that acts as a **communication hub** between several other functionality groups.

15. **The Virtual Entity and IoT Service Functional Group:** It includes functions that relate to interactions on the **virtual entity and IoT service abstraction levels** respectively.

16. **The Virtual Entity Functional Group:** It contains functions for interacting with the IoT systems on the **basis of VEs as well as functionalities for discovering and looking up services that can provide information about VEs** or which allow the interaction with VEs.

17. **Communication FG:** It provides a simple **interface for instantiating and for managing high-level information flow.** It can be customized according to the different requirements defined in the **Unified Requirements List.**

18. **The Management FG:** It combines all functionalities that are needed to govern an IoT system. The need for management can be tracked back to at least **four high-level system goals**: - **Cost reduction, attending unexpected usage issues, fault handling and flexibility.**

19. **The Security Functional Group:** It is responsible for **ensuring the security and privacy of IoT-A-Complaint system.** It is in-charge of handling the initial registration of a client to the system in a secure manner. This ensures that only legitimate clients may access services provided by the IoT infrastructure.

1.8 NEEDED CAPABILITIES OF IoT

Some of the needed capabilities of IoT are shown in Fig. 1.7.

IoT is a highly dynamic and radically distributed networked system. It is composed of a very large number of smart objects producing and consuming information. The main challenge associated with the IoT paradigm are as follows:

• Dealing with rapidly changing environment.

- Heterogeneity of devices forming the network.
- Lack of human capacity in managing those devices.

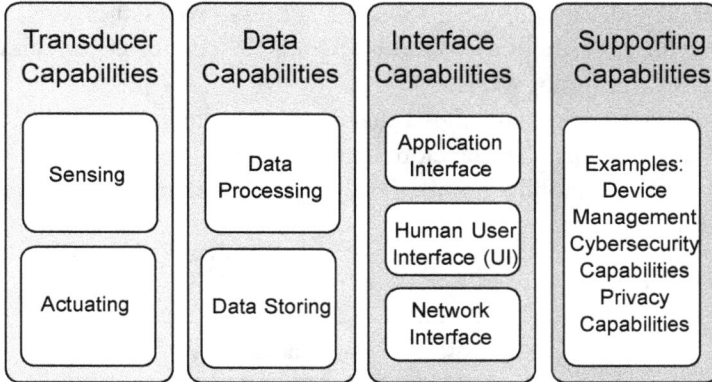

Fig. 1.7: Capabilities of IoT

Please note that these challenges cause increase in uncertainty at the design time about the operational context of devices in their run-time.

Working: The working of IoT can be explained as follows:

1. **Collect and Transmit Data:** The device can sense the environment and collect the information related to it and transmit it to a different device or to the Internet.

2. **Actuate Device Based on Triggers:** It can be programmed to actuate other devices based on conditions set by the user.

3. **Receive Information:** Device can also receive information from the network.

4. **Communication Assistance:** It provides communication between two devices of the same network or different network.

5. **Sensors** for various applications are used in different IoT devices as per different applications like temperature, humidity, proximity, force etc.

6. **Gateway** takes care of various wireless standard interfaces and hence one gateway can handle multiple technologies and multiple sensors.

7. **The Typical Wireless Technologies** used widely are LoWPAN, Zigbee, Zwave, RFID, NFC etc. gateway interfaces with cloud using backbone wireless or wired technologies such as WiFi, Mobile, DSL or Fibre.

   The main goal of IoT is to enable things to be connected anytime, anyplace, with anything and anyone ideally using any path/network and any service. It is the new revolution of the Internet.

8. Using IPv6 with its abundant address spaces, globally unique object identification and connectivity can be provided in a standardized manner without additional status or address processing.
9. Powerful new mobiles, wearable, foldable connected devices further feed IoT technology stack.
10. Cloud-based apps and those that rely on content stored in the cloud will increase as the development accelerates on the new Platform-as-a-Service, mobile point of sale and independent software vendor platforms.

1.9   IoT STACK

Layer 7 ⇒	Application Layer
Layer 6 ⇒	User Experience Layer
Layer 5 ⇒	Session/Message Layer
Layer 4 ⇒	RF Layer
Layer 3 ⇒	Hardware Interface Layer
Layer 2 ⇒	Processing and Control Action Layer
Layer 1 ⇒	Physical or Sensor Layer

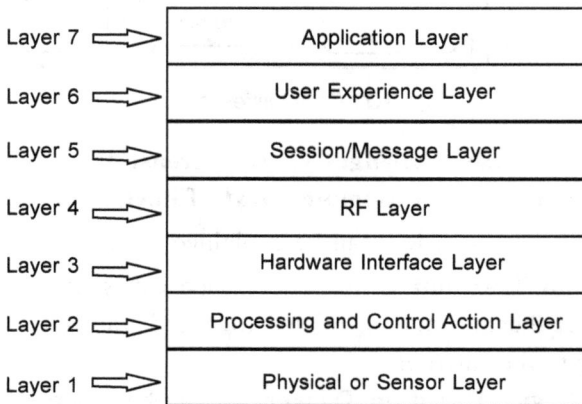

IoT Protocol Stack Layers

Fig. 1.8: IoT Layers

Before we discuss about the IoT stack, let us first of all recall that the ISO/OSI Model which defines a networking framework has seven layers. Each of this layer uses one or more protocols. Similarly, in IoT also we have found seven layers of IoT stack. It is shown in Fig. 1.8.

They are discussed below:

Layer 1: Physical/Sensor Layer - This layer concerns about the physical components i.e., sensors. Sensors are the core components at this layer. Other physical layer components can be temperature-sensor, pressure-sensor, humidity-sensor etc. as far as industrial automation is concerned, PLC, actuator etc are all regarded as the physical layer components. **Please note that this layer is responsible for data collection** i.e., data is sensed here. Sensors of different types and different costs are available in market, so correct selection of sensors is also very vital.

Layer 2: Processing and Control Action Layer - This layer consists of the core components of IoT. Microcontrollers / processors are all at this layer-2. Data is received by these microcontrollers from the sensors. Many development kits are available in market like Arduino, PIC, ARM development boards. OS like Android, IOS, Linux can very well execute the task. **Note that the data collected from the sensors is processed at this layer.** And to find out if the data is meaningful, a microcontroller should be present.

Layer 3: Hardware Interface Layer - This is the next layer that has hardware components and communication standards like RS-232, CAN, SCI, routers, USB etc. occupy this layer. All these components ensure errorless communications.

Layer 4: RF Layer - The protocols used for communication and transport of data based on RF are listed in this layer. Some examples of the protocols are WIFI, RFID, Bluetooth, Li-Fi etc. RF play a major role in the communication channel. It may be **short range (low bandwidth, high Bandwidth) or long range (low bandwidth, high bandwidth).**

Layer 5: Session or Message Layer - analogous to OSI model of networking, session management is equally important in IoT as well. Protocols exist that see how messages/ data are broadcasted to the cloud. It is this layer that has messaging protocols like CoAP, HTTP, FTP, SSH etc.

Layer 6: User Experience Layer - This layer is related to the GUI that the user uses. Graphical user Interfaces (GUI) should be such that it is user pleasing and is rich UI. So, object-oriented programming languages, scripted languages, analytics tools etc. should be included in this layer.

Layer 7: Application Layer - This layer talks about the possible applications that can be built with the help of the other layers present here. It can range from a simple automation application to smart city applications like smart home, smart parking, smart farming etc.

Conclusions: It starts with the sensor layer, where temperature, humidity etc. are measured. Then the data goes to the microcontroller. From there it goes to the cloud and here the messaging protocols take effect. RF protocols like WIFI are used for transport and communication. User's experience is taken care with the Android application designed.

1.10   IoT LEVELS

Just as we have 5 levels of CMM – Capability Maturity Model in software engineering which talks about the level of maturity of a process in an organization, similarly we have 5 levels of IoT applications based on the architectural approach. Let us discuss these levels of IoT now.

Level 1: We say that an application is a Level-1 IoT application if it has minimum complexity and is quite easier to build. Such applications have one sensor. It could be a temperature sensor; pressure sensor etc. **Please note that the data that is sensed or collected is stored locally and data analysis is also done locally.** Monitoring or control is done through an application i.e., webapp or .apk. this is used for simple applications that have lesser or no complexity at all. Data generated at this level is not big data. Everything happens through Internet only. **For instance,** consider your Air Conditioner (AC). The temperature sensor senses the room temperature. Data is stored and analysed locally. Then, based on the analysis, the control action is triggered through mobile application.

Level 2: This level is a bit more complicated than level-1. Because the data is huge here, so cloud storage is done. The frequency of sensing is more here. Analysis is done locally only while cloud is meant for data storages only. **Please note that based on this data analysis, the control action can be triggered through the web application or a mobile application. For example,** farming applications, room fresheners etc. **For instance,** consider your Air Conditioner (AC) again. The temperature sensor senses the room temperature at a faster rate now. Data is big now(huge) so it is stored on cloud but analysed locally only. Then, based on the analysis, the control action is triggered through mobile application.

Level 3: At this level-3, again data is 'big data' **(voluminous)** and sensing is also done at a faster rate but the data is stored on cloud only. **But please note that the data analysis is done on the cloud now,** which was not the case earlier. **Also note that based on this data analysis, the control action can be triggered through the web application or a mobile application. For example,** farming applications, room fresheners etc. where data analysis takes place in the cloud only.

Level 4: Please note that as the volume of data increases, the rate at which it is sensed also increases. At level-4, **multiple nodes** are present that are independent of each other. These nodes have to **upload data to the**

cloud. So, multiple sensors of these multiple devices upload their data onto the cloud. Again, analysis is also done on the cloud and based on the data analysis done, the control action must be triggered through a web app or a mobile application.

Level 5: At this level also, data is large, multiple nodes are involved in the applications and the nodes are not dependent on each other. Data sensing is at a faster rate and cloud storage is done. **But please note that when an application is completely cloud oriented, it is computationally intensive in real-time.** Based on the data analysis done, the control action must be triggered through a web app or a mobile application. So, there may be a coordinator node to handle big data.

In summary, we can say that in IoT the steps followed are:

Sense data ⟶ Transport it ⟶ store it ⟶ analyse it ⟶ control it ⟶ share it.

1.11 IoT APPLICATIONS

The following are the applications of IoT:

1. **Smart Home:** It is a critical application of IoT system. It directly reflects the living standard of the people. A smart home is the one in which all appliances are connected to the IoT platform with the help of different types of sensors. In smart home, IoT technologies are applicable at doors, walls, air conditioners, security cameras etc. all these appliances are controlled by remote control.

2. **Health Care:** These systems can be made intelligent and smart using IoT platforms only. IoT health care systems can sense various conditions of the patients on regular basis. **For example,** short-term or long-term monitoring of pressures in the brain. **Please note that these sensors read this data** (when pressure is increased or decreased in brain) **and then transfer it either to monitors, or mobile or directly to the doctors.** With the help of IoT technologies many intelligent and smart health care systems are already implemented and that they are working perfectly too.

3. **Smart Cities:** Smart cities means smartness in various areas like in traffic management, water distributions, waste management, security etc. in a way, smart city solutions promise its people an intelligent living system by providing all of these features implemented.

4. **Smart Agriculture:** Based on the same lines, the use of IoT in the filed of agriculture (farming) can make an **intelligent agriculture environment.** For farmers and their farming, sensors are installed, say, for weather conditions, earth conditions, irrigation monitoring etc. **For example,** the required temperature by farms, required amount of water etc., an IoT system will automatically take a suitable action.

5. **Smart Transportation:** In a smart transportation IoT-system, a network of sensors is embedded in the vehicle to interact with its surroundings to provide valuable feedback on the roads like weather and traffic condition to the car driver. **For example,** automatic activation and application of brakes for speed control, giving warnings for emergency situations, sensors to monitor the driver's mood and so on.

6. **Military Applications:** Troop monitoring, threat analysis etc. are some of the areas where military is benefitted from IoT.

7. **Smart Parking:** It gives the status of space available for parking in the parking area.

8. **Smart Retail:** Stock administration, instalments etc. are some applications areas of IoT now. IoT provides a chance to retailers to get connected with the customers to enhance the in-store experience. Smart phones will be an easy way for retailers to be connected with their customers, even out of store.

9. **Energy Management:** Power grids of the future will not only be smart but also highly reliable too. Smart grid concept is very popular today. **The basic idea is to collect data in an automated manner and analyse the behaviour of electricity consumers and suppliers for improving efficiency as well as economics of electricity usage. Also note that these smart grids will be able to detect sources of power outages more quickly and at individual household levels like nearby solar panels, making the possible distributed energy system.**

10. **Smart Dust:** It consists of sensors at **the nanotechnology level** that can be deployed in the millions to billions, with a myriad of applications. **They are the computers smaller than the grain of sand** and can be sprayed or injected almost anywhere to measure chemicals in the soil or to diagnose problems in the human body. These devices are the wave of the future for anything from global weather management and smart city monitoring to war theatre mapping and internal medicine. They are a single package with sensing, computation, communication and power to collect data and report it back to home base.

11. **IoT Biometrics** play a greater role in workplaces.

12. **Industrial IoT Powers Distributed Work** during novel COVID-19.

13. **Better Improved Productivity:** Productivity is the topmost priority among the companies worldwide today. It is the deployment of IoT-enabled technologies that addresses these challenges of enhancing productivity. Thus, the projects can be managed efficiently and at the same time at reduced operational costs.

14. **Better Construction Industry:** According to the report by Research and Markets (Jan. 2021), the construction industry will grow 4.2% by the year 2023. IoT solutions in conjunction with 5G can give companies the advantage of higher speeds, lower latencies to create more bandwidths for the plethora of tools and resources. **For example,** Bouygues Construction Material, company in France, has implemented an **asset-tracking product to ensure that the construction sites have compliant equipment or not.** This company has deployed sensors on more than 20000 pieces of equipment across construction sites. Each site looks into the productivity **by tracking geolocation to minimize the equipment use.** Hence, IoT benefits construction in three ways-

    (a) **Productivity: Project delays** need to be avoided. Today, industry is guided by **deadlines.** So, they must remain on **target because delays also increase the budget. IoT-enabled sensors** can keep companies on track and minimize daily tasks like scheduling, inspections and deliveries. Currently, **Digital Management Platforms** (DMP) are used to monitor both **equipment and employees.** Today, managers can view, analyse and navigate **a virtual map in real-time** to access the location and configuration of equipment and also the **links to Quality Control Sheets** (QCS).

    (b) **Security:** At construction sites also, safety and security are very important. The need is of healthy employees and conducive environment because without this the **productivity is bound to fail. IoT-enabled tags are also helpful to reduce theft on sites.**

    (c) **Site Operations:** Power and fuel consumed are the expenses associated with any construction site. IoT devices like fuel sensors or load sensors can help companies now to manage expenses. It does this through real-time monitoring and management of assets. This helps managers to schedule the usage of these devices.

1.12   SENSING

A sensor converts **a physical quantity into a corresponding voltage.** It is a device that when exposed to a physical phenomenon (temperature, displacement, force etc) produces a proportional output signal (electrical, mechanical, magnetic etc). The term **transducer** is often used synonymously with **sensors. Sensor is a device that responds to a change in the physical phenomenon.** On the other hand, a **transducer is a device that converts one form of energy into another form of energy. Please note that the sensors are transducers when they sense one form of energy input and output in a different form of energy.**

Sensors can also be classified as **passive or active. In passive sensors,** the power required to produce the output is provided by the sensed physical phenomenon itself whereas the **active sensors require** external power source. In **embedded systems,** sensors and actuators are used for controlling the system. **Sensors are connected to the input port. Actuators are connected to the output port. Sensors** capture the changes in the environmental variables. Middle systems process the information. **Actuators** are changed according to the input variable. It displays the output. **For example,** an example of control is the air conditioner system. It controls the room temperature to a specified limit.

Specifications of Sensors

Some specifications of sensors are as follows:

1. **Accuracy:** Error between the result of a measurement and the true value being measured.

2. **Resolution:** The smallest increment of measure that a device can make.

3. **Sensitivity:** The ratio between the change in the output signal to a small change in the input physical signal. Slope of the input-output fit line.

4. **Repeatability/Precision:** The ability of the sensor to output the same value for the same input over a number of trials.

5. **Bandwidth:** The frequency range between the lower and upper cut-off frequencies within which the sensor transfer function is constant gain or linear.

Now-a-days, sensors help in developments in construction stemming from long range, low power technologies to make smart construction sites by deploying these sensors only. They keep track of key performance parameters, equipment turnover and utilization rates and inventory.

Types of Sensors

1. **Active Sensors:** They are the sensors that require **an external source of power** (excitation voltage) that provides the majority of the output power of the signal.

2. **Passive Sensors:** These are the sensors in which the output power is almost entirely provided by **the measured signal without an excitation voltage.**

3. **Digital Sensors:** The signal produced or reflected by the sensor is **binary.**

4. **Analog Sensors:** The signal produced by the sensor is continuous and proportional to the measurand.

5. **Mechanical Sensors:** Any suitable mechanical/ electrical switch may be adopted but because **a certain amount of force is required** to operate a mechanical switch, so it is common to use **micro-switches.**

6. **Pneumatic Sensors:** These proximity sensors operate by breaking or disturbing an air flow. The pneumatic proximity sensor is an example of a contact type of sensor. These cannot be used where light components may be blown away.

7. **Optical Sensors:** Optical proximity sensors operate by breaking a light beam that falls on a light sensitive device such as a photocell. These are the examples of non-contact sensors. Please be careful with the lighting environment of these sensors. For example, optical sensors can be blinded by flashes from arc welding processes, airborne dust and smoke clouds may impede light transmission.

8. **Electrical Sensors:** Electrical proximity sensors may be contact or non-contact. Simple contact sensors operate by making the sensor and the component completes an electrical circuit. On the other hand, non-contact electrical proximity sensors rely on the electrical principles of either induction for detecting metals or capacitance for detecting non-metals as well.

9. **Range Sensing:** It is defined as detection of how near or far a component is from the sensing position, although they can also be used as proximity sensors. Distance or range sensors use non-contact analog techniques. Please note that short-range sensing between a few millimetres and a few hundred millimetres is carried out using electrical capacitance, inductance and magnetic technique. Also note that long-range sensing is carried out using transmitted energy waves of various types like radio waves, sound waves and laser.

Deflection and Null Methods

1. **Deflection Method:** The signal produces some **physical (deflection) effect** closely related to the measured quantity and transuded to be observable.

2. **Null Methods:** The signal produced by the sensor is counteracted to minimize the deflection. **Also note that the opposing effect necessary to maintain a zero deflection should be proportional to the signal of the measurand.**

Note: Here, the output is usually an 'electrical quantity' while measurand is a 'physical quantity', property or condition which is to be measured.

Hence, *sensor is a device that responds to a physical stimulus, measures the physical stimulus quantity and converts it into a signal, usually electrical, which can be read by an observer or by an instrument.* A sensor can be very small and itself can be a trackable device. The sensor itself, if not connected, is not part of **IoT or WSN value chain.**

Transducer/Sensor System

It is defined as an element when subjected to some physical change experiences a related change or an element which converts a specified measurand into a usable output by using a transduction principle. Hence, we can say that it is a device that converts a signal from one form of energy to another form.

Transducers/ sensors are not very perfect systems. But based on the sensor parameters or sensor specifications, we can measure its performance as follows:

1. **Range:** The range of sensor indicates **the limits between which the input can vary. For example,** a thermocouple for the measurement temperature might have a range of 25-225° C.

2. **Span:** The span is the **difference between the maximum and minimum values of the input.**

3. **Error:** It is the **difference between the result of the measurement and the true value of the quantity being measured.** A sensor might give a displacement reading of 29.8mm, when the actual displacement had been 30mm, **then the error is (29.8 – 30) mm = -0.2mm.**

4. **Accuracy:** The accuracy defines **the closeness of the agreement between the actual measurement result and a true value of the measurand.** It is often expressed as a percentage of the full range output or full-scale deflection.

5. **Sensitivity: It is defined as the ratio of change in the output value of a sensor to the per unit change in input value that causes the output change.**

6. **Non-linearity: It indicates the maximum deviation of the actual measured curve of a sensor from the ideal curve.**

7. **Hysteresis:** It is an error of a sensor that is defined as the maximum difference in output at any measurement value within the sensor's specified range when approaching the point first with increasing and then with decreasing the input parameter. The hysteresis error value is normally specified as a positive or negative percentage of the specified input range.

8. **Resolution:** It is the smallest detectable incremental change of input parameter that can be detected in the output signal. It can be expressed either as a proportion of the full-scale reading or in absolute terms.

9. **Stability: It is the ability of a sensor device to give same output when used to measure a constant input over a period of time.** The term **"drift"** is used to indicate the change in output that occurs over a period of time. It is expressed as **the percentage of full range output.**

10. **Dead Band/Time: The dead band or dead space of a transducer is the range of input values for which there is no output.** So, the dead time of a sensor device **is the time duration from the application of an input until the output begins to respond or change.**

11. **Response Time: It describes the speed of change in the output on a step-wise change of the measurand.** It is always specified with an indication of input step and the output range for which the response time is defined.

Participatory Sensing

It is the process whereby individuals and communities use even more capable mobile phones and cloud services to collect and analyse systematic data for use in discovery. Participatory sensing is data collection and interpretation. It emphasizes the involvement of citizens and community groups in the process of sensing and documenting where they live, work and play. Participatory sensing can draw on a variety of data collection devices, such as home weather stations and water quality tests but several features of mobile phones make them a special and unprecedented tool for engaging participants in sensing their local environments.

Vehicle Tracking Applications: A number of real-time automotive tracking applications determine the important points of congestion in the city by pooling GPS data from the vehicles in the city. This can be used by other drivers in order to avoid points of congestion in the city. In many applications, such objects may have implicit links among them.

For Example, in a military application, different vehicles may have links depending on their unit membership or other related data. Two classic examples of vehicular applications in the context of participatory sensing are the car phone and Green-GPS systems.

Example 2: Biosensors are the analytical devices combined with biological selective elements like enzymes, antibodies, microorganisms, cells etc. They are made in combination with transducer elements to measure the resultant change in any of optical, electrochemical, thermal, pH, mass, piezoelectric or magnetic properties that occurred by binding of cognate analyte from a complex mixture with biosensors. They differ with **physiochemical-based sensors** only in application of biologically derived substances. Just like **chemical sensors,** any specific alteration in these properties that arouse due to enzyme-substrate, antigen-antibody or cell-microbial surface epitope ligands interactions get transduced to generate measurable data. This data is very much useful in the fields of medicine, healthcare, veterinary sciences, food technology, environmental monitoring, biohazard and bio-warfare agent detection. Biosensors based monitoring of crop diseases, soil health etc. in the field of agriculture need a mention. **A potentiometric biosensor** using bIoTin and fluorescein-labelled antibodies was developed for Salmonella detection in poultry. **Nanotechnology + biosensor applications → will be used for resolving the current problems of medicine and healthcare.** Viral outbreaks are rapid and rampant. Wearable biosensors and body bionics will be advanced next-generation biosensors that will create real-time data feed. If it is integrated with IoT then it will generate big data.

Example 3: Currently, an efficient design of a **Wireless Sensor Network** has become a leading area of research. *A sensor is a device that responds and detects some type of input from both the physical or environmental conditions like pressure, heat light etc. the output of the sensor is generally an electrical signal that is transmitted to a controller for future processing.*

The point is that these sensors need to be interfaced using software and then uploaded onto the cloud. You need to install **Arduino IDE** (Integrated Development Environment) as it supports most of the available embedded boards in the market. **Many sensors like heartbeat sensor, ultrasonic sound sensor, gyro sensor, obstacle sensor, colour sensor pH sensor also can be interfaced.**

It is also possible to **control LEDs, motor or even a fan through a web page.** We need to create a web page that is used remotely to control an LED. It can also be any other sensor or actuator, other than LED.

Another example of simpler sensors could be **pushbuttons and switches** that allow some user input. Light-dependent-resistors (LDRs) help us to measure ambient light levels. Thermistors are the temperature sensors to measure warmness and sensors for humidity-level measurement are very common now a days. Even your microphones allow you to monitor sounds and audio.

Another type of sensor used in our mobiles ts **accelerometer that measures the acceleration that our mobile experiences relative to the freefall. This sensor is used to find out a device's orientation along its three-axes. Now, apps use this data to tell if a phone is in portrait or landscape orientation and whether its screen is facing upward or downward.**

Another type of sensor is **magnetometer that measures the strength amd the direction of the magnetic field.** It is used in compass apps and metal detections apps.

The proximity sensor works by shining a beam of infrared light that is reflected from the object and is picked up by the detector.

Phones too have light sensors, inbuilt barometer etc.

Another sensor: **Pedometer is used to count the number of steps** the user has taken. **Google Nexus 5 is a mobile that has a true pedometer** inbuilt into it. Some mobiles like **Galaxy X5 also have a heart-rate monitor.**

Now a days almost all phones have **fingerprint sensors** also to lock and unlock the phones.

Yest another type of sensor is **a radiation sensor. For e.g., The Sharp Pantone 5 has an app to measure the current radiation level in the area** Cameras, microphones are some more sensors on every mobile.

1.13   ACTUATION

A device or mechanism capable of performing a physical action. Actuators interact with the world. Sensors capture information from the world. The interface between the microcontroller and the sensors or the actuators is either analog or digital. An actuator requires **a control signal and a source of energy.** An actuator is a mechanism by which a control system acts upon an environment. The control system can be simple, software-based, a human or any other input. When the actuation is a motion, then motor have to be used for rotational or linear motion. **Please note that the selection of proper actuator is more complicated than selection of the sensors, primarily due to their effect on the dynamic behaviour of the overall system.** Furthermore, the selection of the actuator dominates the power needs and the coupling mechanisms of the entire system.

For example,

Temperature **sensor** detects heat →sends this detect signal to control centre → control centre sends command to sprinkler → sprinkler turns on and puts out flame (actuator).

In a typical IoT system, a sensor may collect information and route to a control centre where a decision is made and a corresponding command is sent back to an actuator in response to that sensed input.

Light happens to be the one of the most beneficial actuators. RGB LEDs allow us to mix the levels of red, green and blue colours to make whatever colour we want. Several complex visual outputs are also available like LED screens to display text as well as graphics.

Piezo Buzzers can be created that can give simple sounds and music. Piezo elements are used in certain types of microphones that can also respond to vibrations.

An actuator is something that **actuates or moves something. It is a device that converts energy into motion or mechanical energy.** *That is why we say that an actuator is a special type of transducer only.*

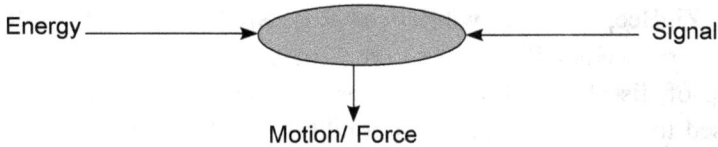

Energy ⟶ ◯ ⟵ Signal

Motion/ Force

Fig. 1.9: An Actuator

From Fig. 1.9, we can say that an actuator is a sort of engine that moves instruments. They have a lot many applications like in buildings, electronic designing, hardware like printers etc. these devices deliver either direct/ straight line, revolving/round or oscillatory movements. There are **thermal actuators, electric actuators and mechanical actuators.** An example of thermal actuator can be a **bimetallic strip**, an **electric motor** will be an electric actuator while a **screw jack** is a mechanical actuator.

Let us now differentiate between the transducers, sensors and actuators in a tabular format.

Table 1.2: Differences Between a Transducer, A Sensor and An Actuator

Transducers	Sensors	Actuators
It converts one form of energy to another form.	It converts different forms of energy into electrical signals.	It converts electrical signals into mechanical energy.
It includes both sensor and actuators.	It is a type of input transducer only.	It is a type of output transducer only.
Either it can work as a sensor or as an actuator, not both.	It converts environment stimulus into signals.	It converts signals into proper mechanical or electrical outputs.
Examples: any sensor or actuator.	Examples: Humidity sensors, temperature sensors, accelerometers, gas sensors etc.	Examples: Motors, pumps etc.

1.14 BASICS OF NETWORKING

Both wired and wireless communication models have been further extended so that every device connected on Internet is able to send and receive information. This has actually given rise to the need of miniature devices like sensors to collect information. Even clod-based services are helping here. These sensors are embedded in smart items for this purpose. As far as IoT sensors are concerned, we have newer technologies today like RFID, WIFI,

Bluetooth, ZigBee, Z-Wave, wireless-M-Bus, SIGFOX, GSM, GPRS, 3G, 4G, 5G, Ethernet, HomePlug and so on. Wireless Sensor Networks (WSNs) consists up of distributed devices network that are connected with sensors and are used to monitor the physical conditions. WSNs also have end hubs that use some sensors in them.

According to the latest report, **"Data Diodes"** bolster IoT security with **one-way traffic only.** Data diodes allow only the data to flow in one direction, effectively shielding the sending devices from an outside attack. As we know that **a diode is a device through which current can pass freely only in one direction. Data diodes apply this technology to the network infrastructure also to allow data to flow in one direction and to stop data from traveling in the other directions in its tracks.** These diodes cannot be compromised by **malicious incoming traffic.** Actually, data diodes provide **hardware-based security to IoT environments. Please note that these IoT environments have become more vulnerable to attacks because the as the volume of connected devices grows and as the networks become wider and to more remote geographies, vulnerabilities increase as the complexity increases.** As usual, security is one of the major challenges of IoT today.

According to the Nokia reports, **"IoT devices now make up** 32.72% **of the infected devices observed".** The threat to IoT is so critical that *Nokia claims that cybercriminals are focusing their effort on IoT and mobile devices.*

In another report by Siemens, **"The growth digitalization of critical infrastructure with an increasing number of IoT devices is raising bar for network security".**

Data diodes work analogous to other hardware-based network flow controllers. For example, this has been applied to the cable connections of RS-232 connector by altering its cable connections like removing pins. Many network gateways can also stop certain data streams through a network. But one of the advantages of **diodes is that you need not patch them, according to** 451 **Research company.** According to Romansky, data diodes concept emerged from the work of DRDO, for secure data transfers. According to another Department of Homeland Security, **"if one-way communication can achieve a task then it is better to use data diodes."**

For better IoT security, we need a multi-layered approach using software and hardware security products. An IoT environment will consist of smart and not-so-smart devices to collect and analyse data. **These smart devices may have more vulnerabilities but they are needed as they have the computing power to run complex security software also as compared to less intelligent devices in an IoT ecosystem.** Former devices and techniques, may be used in IoT security also but they also have vulnerable gaps. **Please note that the more data traffic that's encrypted the better, but encrypting and decrypting data can introduce latency into the network and cause problems for systems that need to respond in real-time to data from sensors.** According to Siemens, **"Considering the ever-increasing connectivity and rapidly increasing cyberattacks, firewalls are no longer the only go-to cybersecurity option.** IoT security technology field involves the use of hardware secure modules (HSM) that includes both data diodes and also endpoint devices with chips to increase security features.

Some places where data diodes can help are:

(a) Repositories of backup and disaster recovery.

(b) Replication of database and other application data.

(c) Traffic flowing to/from remote sensors and other facilities.

Data receive acknowledgement is one of the primary concern for IoT implementors. If this acknowledgement mechanism is not there then data needs to be retransmitted and this needs additional bandwidth. **Also note that, however, data diodes are have some inbuilt understanding of certain communication protocols, diodes can provide the necessary acknowledgement without exposing data.** *When we make a connection to a data diode, we are actually connecting to an application that we have developed, that is aware of the protocol that you are trying to send out.* It has been observed that the proper placement of the data diodes will ensure that the security apps get what they need. According to Siemens report, **"Data diode is secure by default and no misconfiguration or software vulnerability can make it insecure."**

Data diodes cost a few thousand dollars. As data diodes have to work in highly secure and sensitive systems, so life long support is a must for them. Security ratings of these data diodes may also be considered for selection. For example, EAL1 through EAL7 is one of the rating scales for these diodes. EAL7 indicates that the product has undergone formal design verification and has been tested also.

The challenge is the growing range of IoT networks having support of thousands of endpoints. Network security is becoming impossible, so **data diode manufacturers will have to bring security to the edge i.e., to the device itself.**

1.15 M2M COMMUNICATION

M2M communication is the communication among the physical things which do not need human intervention. It is a form of communication that involves one or more entities that do not require any intervention (human) in the process of communication. **M2M is also known as Machine Type Communication (MTC) in** 3**GPP.** M2M communication can be carried over mobile networks also like GSM-GPRS, CDMA networks. In M2M communications, the role of mobile network is largely confined to serve as a transport network. **Please note here that M2M is a subset of IoT as IoT also includes Human-to-Machine (H2M) communications. For example,** RFID, Location-based services (LBS), Lab-0n-Chip (LOC), sensors, augmented reality (AR), Robotics and vehicle telematics are some of the technologies that use both M2M and H2M communications.

Reasons for M2M

1. It supports **multiple application with multiple devices.**
2. It is **information and service centric.**
3. It supports **open-market place.**
4. IoT uses **horizontal enabler approach.**
5. It requires **generic commodity devices.**
6. It is used in **B2B and B2C** also.
7. A **networked machine** is more valuable than an **isolated machine.**
8. When **multiple machines are interconnected, more autonomous applications** can be achieved.
9. **Smart and ubiquitous services** can be enabled by **machine-type devices intelligently communicating with other devices** at any time and at any place.

Key Features of M2M

The following are some of the key features of M2M:

1. **Low Mobility:** M2M devices do not move and if moves only within a certain area.

2. **Time Controlled:** Data can be sent or received only at certain predefined time periods.

3. **Time Tolerant:** Sometimes data transfer can be delayed.

4. **Packet Switched:** Network operator to provide packet-switched service.

5. **Online Small Data Transmissions:** Devices frequently send or receive small amount of data.

6. **Low Power Consumption:** To improve the ability of the system to efficiently service M2M applications.

7. **Location Specific Trigger:** Intending to trigger M2M device in a particular area. For e.g., wake up device.

8. Large number of nodes or devices can be involved in M2M communication.

9. It sends/receive small traffic per machines or device.

10. Large quantity of collective data is generated which can be stored and queried later at any time.

11. There is improved device connectivity because of the cloud data model.

12. The cloud data model optimizes the device data communication aspect thereby reducing the protocol overhead and easing device management.

13. They are free from human interventions. Human intervention is required for operational stability and sustainability.

14. In some situations, the device itself performs data analysis and correlation to trigger business decisions, with no programming skills required.

M2M AND IoT VALUE CHAIN

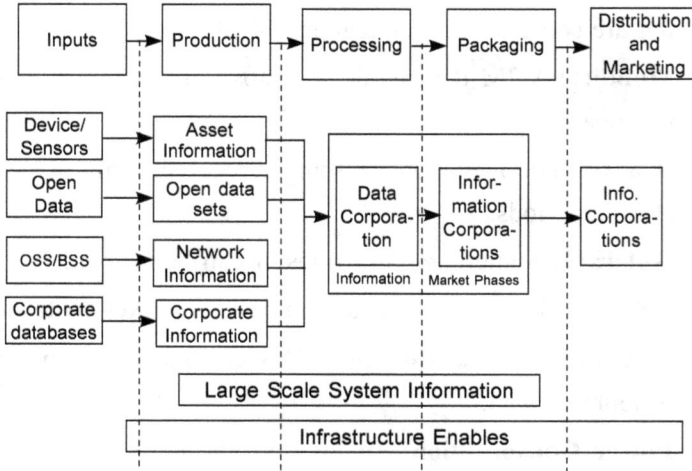

Fig. 1.10: Information-driven Value Chain for IoT

IoT value chains based on data are to some extent enabled by open APIs and the other open web-based technologies. The required data is collected from publicly available resources and taken from other company data. An information market place is available in world for getting data. **Please note that such a market place could still be internal to a company or strictly protected between the value chains of several companies. Also note that open APIs allow for the knowledge contained within different technical systems to become unembedded, creating the possibility for many different economic entities to combine and share their data as long as they have a well-defined interface and description of how the data is formatted.**

Table 1.3: Below Shows M2M Value Chain and IoT Value Chain

M2M Value Chain	IoT Value Chain	Explanation
Input	• Sensors	• Similar to M2M device solution.
	• Open data	• Provided by govt. organization.
	• Operational support systems/ Business support systems	• Used increasingly in tightly-closed information market places.
	• Corporate database	• Contains various databases like SCM, payroll, accounting etc.

Contd../(Table 1.3)

M2M Value Chain	IoT Value Chain	Explanation
Production	• Asset information	• It stores information like temperature over time of container during transit or air quality during a particular month.
	• Open datasets	• It may include maps, rail timetables or demographics about a certain area.
	• Network information	• Contains GPS data, services accessed via mobile network.
	• Corporate information	• Current state of demand for a particular product in the supply chain at a particular moment in time.
Processing	Data combination	Data is mixed together from various sources.
Packaging	Information components	Packaging section of the information value chain creates information components.
Distribution and Marketing	Information product	Company may have market information about a certain area of town.

Let us now study **M2M Value Creation Chain:**

"The value chain" has been a basic business concept for several years now. **Each link in the chain "adds value" in a linear progression from raw materials to finished products or services.** It is a useful concept for identifying key elements in the route to market for new product ideas and for highlighting where new profits can be made. M2M value creation chain is shown in Fig. 1.11.

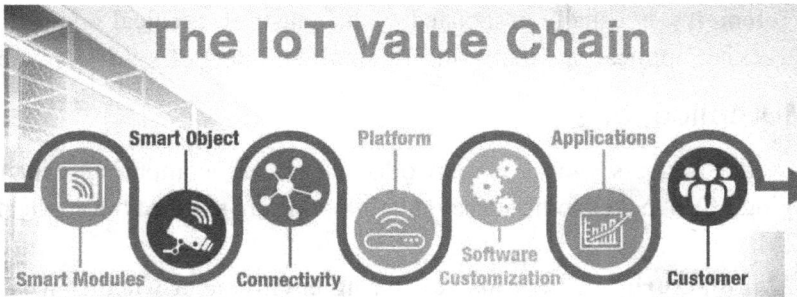

Fig. 1.11: The IoT Value Chain

1. **Inputs:** It is the raw material that converts into product. **For example,** information is converted into data, coal is mined for making domestic steel.

2. **Production (Manufacture):** It processes the raw inputs which become a part of value chain. Data from an M2M solution, meanwhile, needs to be verified and tagged for provenance.

3. **Processing:** Product is prepared for sale.

4. **Packaging: It refers to the process whereby a product can be branded as would be recognizable to end-user consumers.**

5. **Distribution and Marketing:** It refers o the channels-to-market for products.

The 6 Pillars of M2M

The six pillars of M2M are as follows:

1. **Remote Monitoring** is a generic term most often representing supervisory control, data acquisition and automation of industrial assets.

2. **RFID is a data collection method that uses electronic tags for storing data.**

3. **A sensor network** monitors physical or environmental conditions with sensor nodes acting cooperatively to form and maintain the network.

4. **The term smart service refers to the process of networking equipment and monitoring it at a customer's site so that it can be maintained and serviced more effectively.**

5. **Telematics** to the integration of telecommunication and informatics, but most often it refers to tracking, navigation and entertainment applications in vehicles.

6. **Telemetry** is usually associated with industrial, medical and wildlife-tracking applications that transmit small amounts of vehicle's data.

M2M Applications

With better sensors, wireless networks, increased computing capability, deploying M2M makes some sense. The following are some of the applications of M2M:

1. **Manufacturing:** Every manufacturing environment whether it is food processing or general product manufacturing relies on technology, to ensure costs are managed properly and processes are executed efficiently. **Automating manufacturing processes** within such a fast-paced environment is expected to improve processes even more. In manufacturing world, this could highly involve automated equipment

maintenance and safety procedures. **For example,** M2M tools allow business owners to be alerted on their smart phones when an important piece of equipment needs servicing, so they can address issues as quickly as they arise. Sophisticated networks of sensors connected to the Internet could even order replacement parts automatically.

2. **Home Appliances:** IoT already affects home appliance connectivity through platforms like Nest. However, M2M is expected to take home-based IoT to the next level. Manufacturers like LG and Samsung are already slowly unveiling smart home appliances to help ensure a higher quantity of life for occupants. **For example,** an **M2M-capable washing machine** could send alerts to the owner's smart devices once washing is over and a **smart refrigerator** could automatically order groceries from Amazon once its inventory is finished. Many more examples do exist that show that Home Automation can improve the life of residents like systems that allow members of household to remotely control Heating Ventilation and air conditioning systems using their mobile devices.

3. **Healthcare Device Management:** With M2M technology, hospitals can automate processes to ensure the highest level of treatment. Using devices that can react faster than a human healthcare professional in an emergency situation makes this possible. **For example,** when a patient's vital sign drop below normal, then an M2M-connected life support device could automatically administer oxygen and additional care until a healthcare professional arrives on the scene. M2M also allows the patients to be monitored in their own homes instead of in hospitals or care centres. **For example,** devices that track an elderly person's normal movements can detect when he or she has fallen and alerts a healthcare worker to the situation. **Telemedicine** offers another use. **for instance,** some heart patients wear special monitors that gather information about the way their heart is working. The data is sent to implanted devices that deliver a shock to correct an errant rhythm.

4. **Smart Utility Management:** In the new age of **energy efficiency,** automation will quickly become the new normal. As **energy companies** look for new ways to automate the metering process, M2M comes to the rescue, thereby helping energy companies automatically gather energy consumption data, so they can accurately bill customers. **Smart meters** can track how much energy a household or business uses and automatically alerts the energy company, which supplants sending out

an employee to read the meter or requiring the customer to provide a reading. This is even more important as utilities move toward more **dynamic pricing models,** charging the customers for more energy usage during peak times.

5. **Traffic Control:** Traffic control is another **dynamic environment** that can benefit from M2M communications. In a typical system, **sensors monitor variables** like traffic volume and speed. The sensors send this information to computers using specialized software that controls traffic-control devices like lights and variable informational signs. Using the incoming data, **the software manipulates the traffic control devices** to maximize traffic control. **Researchers are studying the ways to create M2M networks that monitor the status of infrastructure such as bridges and highways.** M2M communication appears to have a bright future. It's flexible technology that uses common equipment in new ways. Every day, businesses, engineers, scientists, doctors and many others are finding new ways to use this **new communication tool.**

Types of Nodes in M2M

M2M has three types of sensor nodes and are as follows:

1. **Low-end Sensor Nodes:** These nodes are cheaper and have low capabilities. They are static, energy efficient and simple. The deployment has high density in order to increase network lifetime. These **nodes are resource constrained with no IP support.** These nodes perform **basic functionalities** such as data aggregation, auto configuration and power saving. They are generally used for environment monitoring applications.

2. **Mid-end Sensor Nodes:** These nodes are more expensive than the low-end sensor nodes. These nodes may have **mobility.** They have fewer constraints with respect to **complexity and energy efficiency.** They perform functionalities such as localization, Quality-of-Service (QOS) support, TCP/IP support, power control or traffic control and intelligence. These nodes are used in applications like home networks, Supply Chain Management (SCM), asset management and industrial automation.

3. **High-end Sensor Nodes:** These nodes are deployed in a **low-density manner.** They are able to handle multimedia data (video) with QOS

requirements. An essential feature of these nodes is **mobility. Example** for these types of nodes are smart phones. These nodes are applied in military or bio-medical applications.

M2M Ecosystem

M2M ecosystem consists of device providers, Internet Service Providers (ISPs), platform providers, service providers and service users. It can be divided into four parts:

(a) M2M Area Networks.

(b) Core Networks.

(c) M2M Service Platform.

(d) Stakeholders.

M2M Area Networks form the base of M2M ecosystem. It comprises of multiple M2M devices, either communicating with one another or to a connected platform that is situated remotely (far). We can say that **the local communication between the M2M devices till the M2M gateway forms a M2M area network** (or device domain). M2M Gateway is responsible for enabling **connectivity and communication** between the **M2M devices and Internet. Gateway** is responsible for demarcating between data and control signals on M2M platform. It should also ensure that the M2M devices can access an outside network and vice versa. **For example,** PANs (Personal Area Network) and local nodes in a Wireless Sensor Network (WSN) forms the M2M area network. **M2M communication network/domain** consists of the communication technologies and paradigms for enabling connectivity and communication between M2M gateways and various applications. **For example,** WLAN, WiMAX, LTE and others.

Core Network are the networks that form the core of the communication infrastructure of the M2M ecosystem to carry the heavy load of traffic across the M2M network. This network may be:

Wired.

Wireless.

or   both.

For example, WLAN, GSM, DSL etc. are all related to the core networks only.

The data from M2M area network will be sent via a gateway to the Internet which is managed by ISP. **The RESTful architecture acts as an** interface between the device providers and ISP. RESTful architecture is used in low resource environments. From the ISP, the data reaches the platform provider. The platform provider takes care of device management, user management, data analytics and user access. The data is then through a RESTful architecture which takes care of the business model to the service providers and users (see Fig. 1.12).

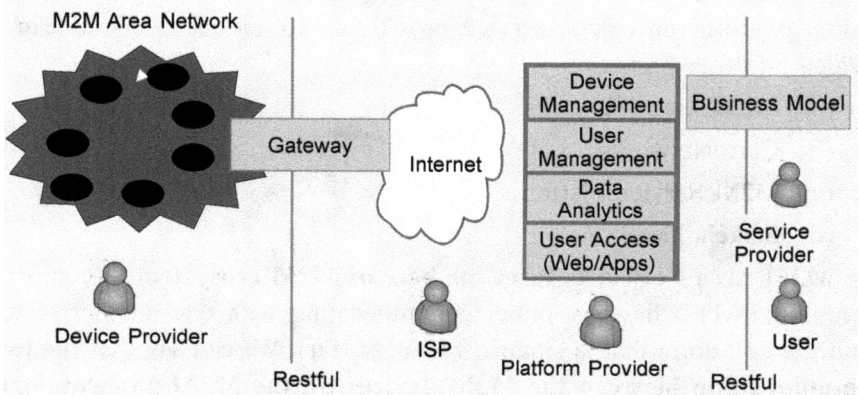

Fig. 1.12: M2M Ecosystem

M2M Service Platform: It includes several functionalities for devices, users, applications and access. The data from these devices, users, applications and access passes through an access network like ZigBee, WIFI etc. and are sent to M2M area network. Similarly, the data from several M2M networks passes through the access network to the core network that supports all platforms like devices, users, applications and access. It is shown in Fig. 1.13.

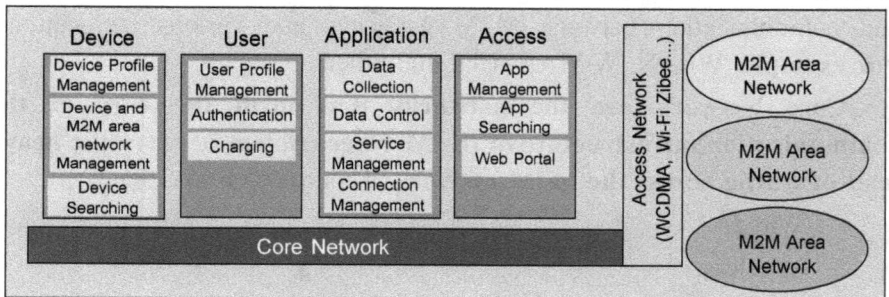

Fig. 1.13: M2M Service Platform

M2M Device Platform: This platform enables access to objects or devices connected to the Internet anywhere at any time. **Registered devices create a database of objects from which managers, users and services**

can easily access information. This platform manages **device profiles** such as location of devices, device type, address and description. M2M device platform provides **authentication and authorization** key management functionalities. It also monitors the status of devices and M2M area networks and controls them based on their status.

M2M User Platform: This platform manages M2M **service user profiles and provides functionalities** such as user registration, modification, charging and inquiry. **Please note that M2M user platform interoperates with the M2M device platform and manages user access restrictions to devices, object networks or services. Also note that service providers and device managers have administrative privileges on their devices or networks.** Administrators can manage the devices through device monitoring and control.

M2M Application Platform: It provides **integrated services based on datasets collected by devices. Heterogeneous data merged** from various devices are used for **creating new devices.** This platform collects **control processing log data** for management of devices by working with the device platform. This platform provides **connection management** with the appropriate network for seamless service.

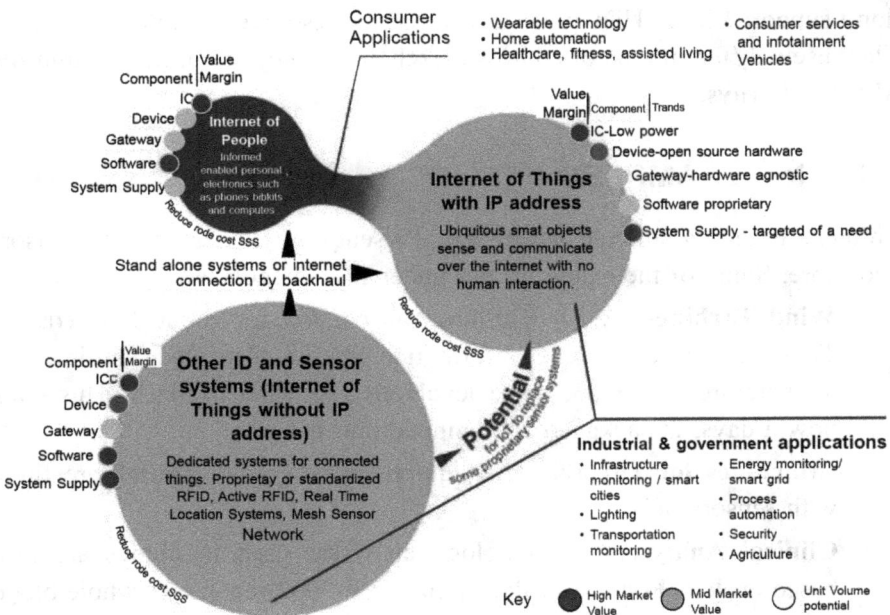

Fig. 1.14: IP-based and non-IP based M2M Network.

M2M Access Platform: This platform provides **app or web access environment to the users. Apps and links redirect to service providers.** Services are usually provided through this platform to M2M devices. This platform provides **app management for smart device apps. App management manages app registration by developers and provides a mapping relationship between apps and devices. Mapping function** provides an app list for suitable devices.

These M2M Networks May be:

(a) IP-based.

(b) Non-IP-based.

In both the networks, *the communications layers are same. M2M area network management provides various features like fault-tolerance, scalability, low cost, low complexity, energy efficient, dynamic configuration capabilities, minimized management traffic and application dependence which includes data-centric application, emergency application and real-time applications.* **Both M2M network and IP Network follow the same stack structures, hence the communication is possible and direct between them.** Also, there is no need of adaptors or protocol tunnels. On the other hand, **non-IP-based networks** scheme is used with low-end and mid-end M2M devices as they don't support TCP or UDP protocols. These are resource-constrained devices. They use a different type of addressing schemes. They are limited within **the M2M gateways.**

1.16 IoT EXAMPLES

Things are getting smarter day by day. Present day phones have 14 sensors and more. Some of the examples put under IoT category are as follows:

1. **Wind Turbines:** A wind turbine can contain for about **400 sensors.** These sensors can deliver information like wind's speed, its direction, temperature, vibration, noise levels etc., to wind turbines. This data, now a days, is packaged and shipped into the cloud.

2. **Machines for Farming:** All equipment related to farming are fitted with sensors only.

3. **Clinical Analysers:** Hematology analysers used in clinics are also based on IoT. **For Example,** Sysmex XE-5000 reports 31 whole blood parameters at a rate of 150 samples per hour.

4. **Alarm:** As the alarm rings, you get up and see that you still have 5 mins. For train to leave and this is checked by the clock with the train timings online.

5. **Medicine Time:** A blinking light might alarm you about your medicine time.

6. **Smart Cities:** IoT has made remarkable changes in the smart cities by providing smart buildings, smart power, smart water, better air quality, noise control and monitoring, traffic congestion control, smart streetlights, smart parking and smart communications are some of the IoT examples only.

7. Safe Home Security System, water-level monitoring, digital clock, street light control, motor speed control, home automations etc are some of the areas where IoT has helped a lot.

8. ML tools are basically data-driven. AI/ML/DL has been used to extract data using sensors. Present day AI (= ML + DL) applications along with IoT has proved to be very useful.

9. Present day need is that these IoT devices must be used with cloud/fog/edge computing.

10. Researchers have found 5G as a driving force for IoT.

1.17 SENSOR AS A SERVICE (SE-AAS)/XAAS

Today, everything is being offered as services on the cloud platform like SAAS, PAAS, TAAS and so on. All these services can be put under "Any-Thing-as-a-Service" (XAAS). In the field of IoT, even sensors are at our service. So, it is called as Sensor-as-a Service (Se-AAS) in a sensor-cloud architecture. **Please note that as virtualization of resources is the core concept of cloud computing, similarly, in sensor-cloud, virtualization of sensors is done so as to provide services to multiple users. Also note that just as cloud computing follows "Pay-per" use model, so does this sensor-cloud architecture.**

In sensor cloud architecture, a user application is served by a set of homogeneous or heterogeneous sensor nodes. There is a pool of sensor nodes from where these nodes are selected as per the user requirements.

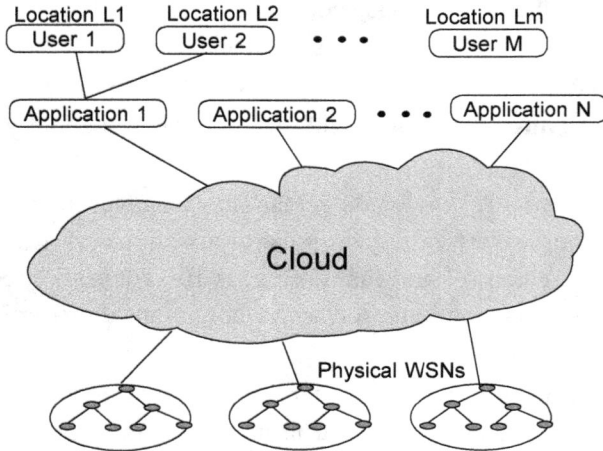

Fig. 1.15: Sensor-cloud Environment

The sensed data is brought to **heterogeneous pool** of physical sensors wherein physical to logical sensor mapping is done. Also, the **virtualization logic** works here. Now the information flows from this virtual group (say, VG_1, VG_2,....VG_n) to different applications where different users are working, when the user sends the request for sensed data.

Actors

In a sensor-cloud architecture, three types of actors are present

   (a) End-users.   (b) Sensor Owner.

   (c) Sensor-cloud Service Provider (SCSP).

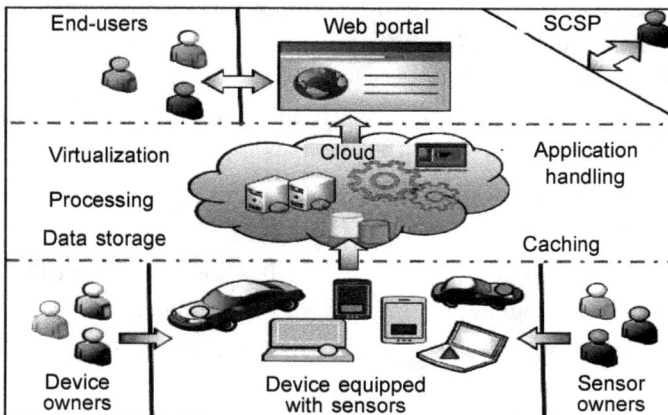

Fig. 1.16: Sensor-cloud Architecture

1. **End-user:** They are also known as the **customers of sensor-cloud services.** This is shown in Fig. 1.16. End-users register with the infrastructure through a **web portal** (a portal is a small web app designed for some specific purpose/task). Then, the user selects the template of services available in this set-up. Then through the web portal, the end-user receives the services. **Please note here that depending on the type and duration of the service, the end-user pays the charges to SCSP.**

2. **Sensor Owner:** As studied earlier that this sensor-cloud architecture is based on Se-AAS i.e., Sensor-as-a-Service. Hence, the deployment of sensors is mandatory so as to provide services to the end-users. These sensors are owned by the sensor owners. **Please note that a particular sensor owner can own multiple homogeneous or heterogeneous sensor nodes. Also note that based on the user's requirements, these sensor nodes are virtualized and then assigned to serving multiple applications at the same time.** A sensor owner receives rent on "pay-per-use" basis of the sensor nodes.

3. **Sensor-Cloud Service Provider (SCSP):** It performs several functions like management of sensor owners, end-users handling, resource handling, database management, cloud handling etc. **Note that SCSP receives rent from end-users with the help of a pre-defined pricing model (pay-per-use).** this pricing actually includes infrastructure cost, sensor owner's rent and the revenue of the SCSP. Different algorithms are working here. SCSP shares this rent (from end-users) and shares some amount with the sensor owners too.

As shown in Fig. 1.16, a sensor -cloud architecture can be viewed from 2 view-points:

1. **User's View** wherein the end-user interacts with a web interface for selecting the templates of the services. So, the user is not knowing about the complicated processes that are running at the back-end.

2. **Real View** is wherein the complicated processing of sensor-cloud architecture is involved. It includes many tasks like sensor allocation, data extraction from sensors, virtualization of sensor nodes, maintenance activity, data caching etc. using some particular algorithm.

1.18 ROLE OF CLOUD IN IoT

First of all, let us see what a cloud is?

According to the University of Emory, **"Cloud computing is a computing paradigm where the boundaries of computing will be determined by economic rationale rather than technical limits."** The proper selection of the cloud service is the challenge today. The role of cloud in IoT is to be understood as storage for lots of the IoT applications takes place in cloud. A common platform is made available on the cloud and whosoever uses it will have to pay-on-use basis. This makes it more cost feasible and hence more economical. Cloud is given more weightage here as it is more effective, economical and efficient technology for data storage. We already know about cloud services like SaaS, PaaS, IaaS, SeAAS and so on. Even TAAS (Testing-as-a-Service) is being used today. Also we know some of its service providers/ vendors like AMAZON WEB SERVCES, MS-AZURE, ADAFRUIT etc.

Challenges of IoT with Cloud

1. **Security Issues:** Security has been always a challenge for any application, till date. So, security and privacy are the major concern in the area of IoT also. Data is voluminous but at the same time as it crosses the firewall, it becomes easy to hack it. So, some of the activities to be performed for better security are:

   (a) Do periodic monitoring of the network activities like try to monitor unusual events in the network. You can even choose private cloud if your data is confidential. Use authentic anti-virus solutions.

   (b) Read the letter of contract that is being signed between you and the cloud service provider.

   (c) Because the data is received from multiple sensor nodes. **Please note here that it is equally important to interpret this data in the correct sequence.** This makes data more secure.

2. **Cost of Bandwidth:** Cloud computing is preferred for storage because there is no need to invest on hardware and to maintain it as this is the job of cloud service provider and not the end-user. Also, the customer service and related technical support is available for (24*7). **Please note that if the IoT application is on a small-scale** (demanding lesser resources) **then requirement for investment in bandwidth would not**

be much. On the other hand, **also note here that if the application is data-intensive, then the investment would be large.** But IoT is all about big data only (through sensors, mainly). So, there is the need for huge investment.

3. **Portability of Data:** When data is to be moved to the cloud, we must take care of how safe it is to move the data, how much easy it is to move data, what downtime is needed and what technology is being used to migrate data to the cloud? **Note that it is important to answer for these queries for secure data migration from the cloud. Also note that all these challenges are doubled when combined with IoT.** This is so because the data that is received from sensors is at a very fast speed.

4. **Reliability and Robustness: Reliability** refers to the failure-free operation. In IoT field, also better reliability is needed as the data is very fast. Just storage of data is not sufficient but its reliability is equally important. **Robustness in IoT refers to the deluge (flood) of data that could be fast or slow also, needs to be maintained properly.**

5. **Cost Factors:** One of the features of cloud computing is that it can scale well depending on the demand. So, costing can be controlled and optimized if proper planning of IoT and cloud is done.

6. **Owner of Data:** Who is the owner of data? Is it the users who generates data or is it the cloud service provider? In IoT, the ownership-related issue is multiplied and hence is a very big challenge.

7. **Experience Required:** The combination of (IoT + Cloud Computing), requires a lot of expertise and skills too. Now, IoT uses sensor-based cloud architecture, so complete understanding of sensors is needed. Regular upgradation of knowledge of experts of both the fields is also mandatory.

1.19 SECURITY ASPECTS IN IoT

For security of IoT, following principles of IoT can be established:

1. **Identity:** Trust is always tied to an identity. Hence, every device needs a unique identity that can't be changed. The device must also be able to prove its identity at all times.

2. **Positive Intention:** The device and linked service have positive intentions.

3. **Predictability and Transparency:** The functional scope of the service provided by devices is known to its full extent. There are no undocumented/secret functions. The behaviour of the system can be checked at any time by independent third parties.

4. **Reputation:** An increasing number of positive interactions between the things gradually form a **reputation-based intelligent network.**

Security Challenges

1. **Devices NOT Reachable:** Most of the time a device is not connected.

2. **Devices Can be Lost and Stolen:** It makes security difficult when the device is not connected.

3. **Devices are Not Crypto-engines:** Strong security is difficult without processing power.

4. **Devices have Finite Life:** Credentials need to be tied to lifetime.

5. **Devices are Transportable:** They will cross borders.

Vulnerabilities of IoT

1. Today, cars that come with high-end technologies like Bluetooth capability, GPS mounted dashboards, automatic transmission and remote start by smart phones and many other different apps [re-installed in the car's dashboard monitor. All these technological advancements can cause fatal vulnerabilities.

2. Medical devices are in no way an exception from vulnerabilities with IoT as well. Some students of University of Alabama, were able to hack into the WIFI system of a pacemaker implanted inside an iStan (i.e., a dummy robotic patient used to train medical students).

3. Two nuclear power plants monitoring systems were infected by virus. It is called as **Slammer Worm. It is a SQL worm if injected then it would cause a Denial-of-Service (DoS) attack.**

4. Household appliances are also vulnerable from different types of external attacks. Security breach on these IoT objects can take place in two ways. Either the system will be physically compromised or the central server monitoring the devices could be compromised.

5. One of the humongous applications of cloud computing and IoT is in the area of personal fitness tracking through smart phones and smart watches. The three biggest smart device Oss like Apple iOS, Google

Android and MS Phone have their own apps connecting to a central cloud network so as to track a user's daily fitness goals and the progress update. Tis service requires a user account in the device but if the app on the phone and watch are identical, these devices can be sync automatically if either one had a pre-existing account. **Please note that here the vulnerable point is if the smart watch is stolen or lost, there lies a possibility of the consumer's data retrieval even if the data is residing within the phone.**

The Key Elements of IoT Security

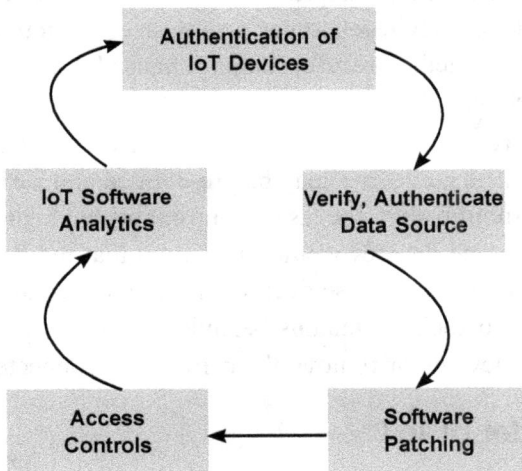

Fig.1.17: Elements of IoT Security

1. **Authenticate IoT Devices:** This is to be done before they integrate with the centralized network. This step avoids the risk of spoofing attacks on the IoT device which appears as a legitimate device on your network. Attacked devices collect data from other networked devices or transmit malicious data to remaining devices on the network.

2. **Authentication:** It is important to authenticate and verify software source running on your IoT device. Software not authenticated faces the risk of being compromised and the device cannot detect such tampering issues unless software is supported with a digital signature of the vendor.

3. **Software Patching:** Avoids the IoT device from being compromised. However, software updates from authenticated sources must be accepted

only. Software patches minimize risks of data loss or interference with business operations. **For example,** a device is put for updating, all local data is written on a central network, other devices know when the updating device goes offline and the update is performed, verified before returning back to the operational mode.

4. **Access Controls:** They secure IoT devices as well as the enterprise. Users are assigned roles to perform specific operations. Roles include querying current state of the IoT devices, software updates on these devices and change device configurations. Other systems present on the network work on the principle of least privilege that allows users only a minimal set of privileges to perform business functions and technical processes. This method restricts damage caused due to a security breach of user's personal data.

5. **IoT Software Analytics** must be designed on the basis of **anomaly detection.** Basic guidelines may be pre-defined and variation from these guidelines should alert the user. **For example,** higher-than-expected traffic from some devices would alert users that the devices have been compromised and are in use even after a malicious attack. Considering the response to such anomalous behaviour, you can perhaps switch off the affected devices or remove them from the connected network.

Security Model of IoT

Table 1.4 shows security model for IoT:

Table 1.4: Security Model for IoT

Application Layer	IoT Application.
	Application support layer (Middleware Technology Security).
Transportation Layer	Local Area Network
	Core Network (Internet Security)
	Access Network (Ad hoc Security, GPRS Security, WIFI Security)
Perception Layer	Perception Network (RFID Security) (WSN Security)
	Perception Node (RSN Security)

The following are the main features of IoT security model:

1. **Data and Privacy Protection** is one of the application challenges of IoT. In IoT, RFID systems, WSNs sensors perceive for the end of the

information technology, which protect the integrity and confidentiality of information by the **password encryption technology.**

2. There are many ways to **encrypt data and information like random hash lock protocol** (hash function), **hash chain protocol, extract key from an infinite channel, Encrypted identifier** and so on.

3. **Identity Authentication and Access Control** can determine the communication between both sides and confirm each other's true identity, prevent disguised attacks to ensure the authenticity, validity of the information and so on.

4. IoT must ensure the **security of all layers.** In addition, IoT security should also include the security of whole system crossing the perception layer, transportation layer and application layer.

5. **Perception Layer** includes RFID security, WSNs security, RSN security and many others.

6. **Transportation layer includes access network security, core network security and local network security.** These are 3G access network security, ad-hoc network security, WIFI security etc for these sub-layers.

7. Different network transmission has different technology. **Application layer includes application support layer and specific IoT applications.** The security in support layer includes middleware technology security, cloud computing platform security etc.

8. IoT applications in different industries have different application requirements. Thus, networking security is a **large multi-layered security system.** In addition, considering security of each layer also considers **cross-layer integration of heterogeneous network security issues.**

9. **Perception Layer** is mainly about **information collection, object perception and object control.** Perception layer can be divided into two parts: perception node (sensors or controllers); perception network that communicates with transportation network.

10. **Transportation Layer** mainly provides ubiquitous access environment for perception layer, perception of information transmission and storage and application layer load, other related businesses. This layer can be divided into three layers by function: the access network, the core network and local area. It is the combination of a variety of heterogeneous networks.

11. **Application Layer** is an advanced layer above the transportation layer, supports all sorts of business services and realizes intelligent computation and resource allocation in screening, selecting, producing and processing data. During the whole process, the application support layer can recognize valid data, spam data and even malicious data and filter them in time.

12. **Application Support Layer** can be organized in different ways according to different services. Usually, it includes middleware, M2M, cloud computing platform and service support platform.

It is not good to neglect the security aspect of IoT. IoT security is a nightmare. Actually, IoT is a concatenation of 3 technologies as follows:

- Information Technology.
- Operations Technology.
- Consumer Technology.

IoT is a network of electronics, home appliances, vehicles, software, sensors, actuators, internet, which enables these objects to connect and exchange data. **Please note here that each thing is uniquely identified by its in-built address and inter-operability is also possible within Internet.** Hackers, in fact crackers, can attack everything in IoT too. So, technology should be such that it is able to provide best access control, secure booting process, updates and patches. When we talk of IoT security, we mean protection of connected devices and network. **Also note that as the number of IoT devices will increase, hackers will be able to break into our lives through multiple doors.** Sensitive data like passwords, location of device are transferred wirelessly from sensors to devices like Arduino, Raspberry Pi etc. and thus are more vulnerable to attacks. So, they need more of security.

According to the latest Gartner's report, by 2050, 2000 billion devices will be connected by IoT.

Although newer encryption and authentication standards are appearing every day, yet another type of attack **"Side-Channel-Attack"** may occur. Its focus is not on **data transfer** rather this attack collects *operational features, execution time, power customers, magnetism estimation of the design to retrieve keys.* Even penetration testing may be done on these devices. Thus, **security-related information** should be monitored, controlled and be further used for threat predictions. In nutshell, we can say that IoT security needs to face the following challenges:

- Access control.
- Authentications.
- Privacy.
- Trust.
- Confidentiality.
- Securing middleware.
- Mobile security.
- Policy enforcement.
- Flexible infrastructure as environment is dynamic.
- Each device or system security.
- Security for all processes at each level.
- Secure movement between each level.

An IoT application is vulnerable to many types of attacks and thus security feature of these devices must not be ignored.

In next chapter, we will study about the IoT models, its security models and so on.

SUMMARY

In this chapter, we have studied about what is an IoT, its characteristics and its challenges as well as its area of domain. Also, we have seen its conceptual framework, architectural view, physical design, logical design and applications of IoT. Even the security aspect of IoT has been explained. IoT and robotics are the captivating technologies today for commercial purposes. IoT gives connectivity from the physical environment to the embedded objects. M2M connectivity needs networking intelligence also. It is predicted that the combination of IoT and Robotics will give enormous applications in future technological trends.

When we say Internet of Everything (IoE), It Means:

$$IoE = IoT + Intelligence \text{ (In The Network)}$$

The term "intelligence" here means that a network of different things must possess visibility across earlier different systems along with the orchestration and convergence properties. Major components of IoE are people, process, data and things. Therefore, IoT consists of the following:

$$IoE = IoT + IoH + IoD$$

Where,   IoE: Internet of Everything;
          IoT: Internet of Things;
          IoH: Internet of Humans;
          IoD: Internet of Digital.

In IoT, 'T' stands for physical or virtual things that have the capability to send the data or information without human intervention. On the other hand, IoE includes accepting communications started by the users. As per the CISCO reports, IoE is a communication and connection among data, things, process and people but in an intelligent way. Interactions are among IoT, machines and M2M. IoE theory includes not only M2M communications but also machine-to-people (M2P) and technology-assisted people-to-people (P2P) communications. And sensors happen to be the essential part of any IoT and IoE-based devices and applications. Also, we have seen in this chapter, that the fusion of sensors with embedded connectivity and processing enables awareness. Now-a days people talk of Medical IoT for healthcare using cloud services. Doing this has many benefits like reduced cost, better results of treatment, timely intervention, enhanced disease management, regular patient monitoring, reporting, error reductions, better diagnosis, better drug management and many more. Also, we have studied that using sensors and Arduino board we can assist farmers to get data about temperature, rainfall, pest control and soli moisture so as to enable smart farming. Today there is an increase in the demand for IoT semiconductors too. IoT microcontrollers, IoT connectivity chipsets, IoT AI Chipsets, IoT Security chipsets are some of the demands today and many have been achieved too. The number of active IoT device connections are estimated to have grown from 3.6 billion in 205 to 11.7 billion in 2020. By the end of 2025, a total of 30 billion IoT connections is being forecast. Smart watches, small wireless accessories have prompted many more industries to jump into this field of IoT ecosystem.

MULTIPLE CHOICE QUESTIONS [MCQS] WITH ANSWERS

1. The network of physical objects embedded with electronics, software, sensors and network connectivity that enables these objects to collect and exchange data is called as:
   (a) IoE.
   (b) IoT.
   (c) IIoT.
   (d) None of the above.

2. A system that can automatically modify itself in the face of a changing context to best answer a set of requirements is known as:

(a) Self-adapting system.   (b) Self-replicating system.

(c) Self-configuration system.   (d) None of the above.

3. The main goal of IoT is:

(a) To make things move.

(b) To connect things anytime, anyplace.

(c) To study things around us.

(d) None of the above.

4. A simple equation that shows what IoT is:

(a) [Physical Object] + [Controllers, Sensors, Actuators] + [Internet] = Internet of Things.

(b) Things + Internet only.

(c) Internet only.

(d) None of the above.

5. "Things" in IoT represented best by the equation:

(a) All things at Home.

(b) All things in Kitchen.

(c) [Hardware] + [Software] + [Service] = [Things]

(d) None of the above.

6. _____ are used during the design and implementation phase of a concrete system architecture:

(a) Services.   (b) Databases.

(c) Views.   (d) All of the above.

7. A useful concept to identify key elements in the route to market for new product ideas is:

(a) Food chain.   (b) Value chain.

(c) Data chain.   (d) None of the above.

8. A data collection technology that uses electronic tags for storing data is:

(a) VD.   (b) ID.

(c) RFID.   (d) None of the above.

9. Which new cloud and IoT based service is added for IoT:
   (a) Sensors.
   (b) Se-AAS.
   (c) Multi-meters.
   (d) None of the above.

10. The term used to describe approaches like software architectural styles and programming patterns that allow real-world objects to be the part of WWW is:
    (a) IIoT.
    (b) IoT.
    (c) IoE.
    (d) WoT.

11. REST stands for:
    (a) Representational State Transfer.
    (b) Reused Software Technology.
    (c) Referred State Technology.
    (d) None of The Above.

12. An open source IoT platform is:
    (a) Python.
    (b) ThingSpeak.
    (c) Alexa.
    (d) None of the above.

13. One of the early prototypes of the Web-of-Things (WOT) is:
    (a) Energie Visible.
    (b) Energetic Visible.
    (c) Virtually Visible.
    (d) None of the above.

14. A characteristic of sensor by which the sensor produces a different set of outputs if the data is recorded in different directions is known as:
    (a) Linearity.
    (b) Calibration.
    (c) Hysteresis.
    (d) None of the above.

15. If a sensor has a digital output, the output is essentially an approximation of the measured property. Such an error is called as the:
    (a) Zero error.
    (b) Quantization error.
    (c) Aliasing error.
    (d) None of the above.

16. If the input variable with some noise changes periodically at a frequency proportional to the multiple of the sampling rate then the error is known as:
    (a) Quantization error.
    (b) Dynamic error.
    (c) Aliasing error.
    (d) None of the above.

17. A wireless technology that uses minimum amount of power is:

    (a) WIFI.   (b) CDMA.

    (c) Bluetooth.   (d) None of the above.

18. As per CISCO survey, how many devices will be connected to IoT by 2020:

    (a) 3 billion.   (b) 20 billion.

    (c) 40 billion.   (d) 50 billion.

19. Many industrial giants like Google, Freescale, Silicon labs. Samsung are developing which protocol for IoT:

    (a) Process protocol.   (b) Thread protocol.

    (c) Thing protocol.   (d) None of the above.

20. 'I' in IIoT stands for:

    (a) Intelligent.   (b) Industry.

    (c) Instagram.   (d) None of the above.

Answers

1. b	2. a	3. b	4. a	5. c	6. c
7. b	8. c	9. b	10. d	11. a	12. b
13. a	14. c	15. b	16. c	17. c	18. d
19. b	20. b				

CONCEPTUAL SHORT QUESTIONS WITH ANSWERS

Q1. Name some baseline technologies that are closely related to IoT. Explain them.

Ans. Three baseline technologies associated with IoT are as follows:

    (a) Machine-to-Machine Communication (M2M).

    (b) Cyber-Physical Systems.

    (c) Web of Things.

M2M Communication: It refers to the communications and interactions between machines and devices. There is no manual assistance. The focus of the telecommunication providers is on machine interactions via 3G, 4G, 5G or satellite or other public networks. **For example,** M2M communication is an important aspect of warehouse management, remote control, robotics, traffic control SCM and tele-medicines. It includes sensors, RFID, WIFI computing software etc. Telemetry is the best-known example of M2M communications. Today researchers have from pure engineering field to everyday products like home heating units, electric meters and other Internet-connected appliances. M2M presently, does not have a standardized connected device platform but it is expected that M2M will become more pervasive and that the vendors will have to accept and agree the standards for device-to-device communication.

Cyber-Physical Systems (CPS): CPS represent the next generation embedded intelligent ICT systems that are **interconnected, interdependent, collaborative, autonomous and provide communication, computing, monitoring of physical components or processes in various applications.** New generation CPS must be **scalable, distributed, decentralized** allowing interactions with humans, environment and machines while being connected to Internet. Such systems have features like **adaptability, reactivity, optimality and security.** We can say that CPS is becoming an **'invisible neural network' of the world.** Actually, CPS integrates computing elements with the physical components and processes so that they can communicate with sensors. **Note that CPS use sensors to connect all distributed intelligence in the environment to gain a deeper knowledge of the environment.** Common applications of CPS fall under **sensor-based communication-enabled autonomous systems. For example,** several WSNs monitor some aspects of the environment. Other types of CPS include smart grid, autonomous automotive systems, medical monitoring, process control systems, distributed robotics and automatic pilot avionics.

Web-of-Things (WOT): It is a term used to explain the **approaches, software architectural styles and programming patterns** that allow **real-world objects** to be the part of WWW. Similarly, what the web (Application Layer) is to the Internet (Network Layer), the Web-of-Things provides an Application Layer that simplifies the creation of IoT applications. **Please note that WOT reuses existing, well-known web standards used in the programmable web** like REST, HTTP, JSON; **semantic web** like Microdata; **real-time web** like WebSocket and the **social web** like social networks.

As far web developers are concerned, WOT enables access and control over IoT resources and applications using mainstream web technologies like HTML, JavaScript, Ajax, PHP etc. **that is why the approach to build WOT is based on REST (Representational State Transfer Protocol) and REST APIs that helps developers and deployers.** Again, security and scalability issues are related to WOT also. **For example, "Energie Visible"** is a project wherein the sensors are capable of monitoring and controlling the energy consumption of household devices. **Also note that they offered their functionality through a RESTful API, then this API is used to create a physical Mashup.**

For Example 2, Nimbits is an open-source data historian server built on cloud computing architecture that provides connectivity among devices using data points.

Example 3, ThingSpeak is an open source IoT platform created by Hans Scharler to collect, analyse and to act on data generated by sensors.

Example 4, EVERYTHING is a platform for making connected and unconnected devices as part of the web based on WOT architecture.

Q2. Define The Following Terms:

    (a) IIoT.

    (b) IoE.

    (c) INDUSTRY 4.0

    (d) Range.

    (e) Drift.

    (f) Sensitivity.

    (g) Selectivity.

    (h) Resolution.

    (i) Response and Recovery Time.

    (j) Linearity.

    (k) Hysteresis.

    (l) Calibration.

    (m) Full-scale Output.

    (n) Precision.

    (o) Accuracy.

    (p) Quantisation Error.

    (q) Dynamic Error.

    (r) Aliasing Error.

Ans. Some common terminologies used in IoT are defined now.

    (a) **IIoT:** It stands for Industrial Internet of Things. The focus is on association among machines along with human interventions.

    (b) **IoE:** It stands for Internet of Everything.

    (c) **Industry** 4.0: It portrays an arrangement of ideas to drive the following modern insurgency that merges availability ideas and mechanical setting. **For example,** 3D-printing advances or the presentation of new enlarged reality equipment.

(d) **Range:** The range of a sensor is defined as the domain in which they work with an acceptable error. If the input is not in the range, then the output is unpredictable.

(e) **Drift: If the output signal slowly changes or varies for the same input over a long period then this is called drift.** The drift will cause an error in the measured value. The drift may result from ageing of the sensor, temperature variance or physical changes in the sensor.

(f) **Sensitivity: It is defined as the change in output per unit change in input of the property being measured.** The sensitivity of the sensor may be **constant or linear** for the entire range of sensor or may vary **exponentially if the sensor is a non-linear sensor.** The sensitivity of a sensor under real conditions may differ from the value specified. **This is known as sensitivity error. If the output signal differs from the correct value by a constant, the sensor is said to have an offset error or bias.**

(g) **Selectivity: It is the ability of the sensor to measure a target property in the presence of other properties.** Note that the sensor should be sensitive only to the measured property and it should be insensitive to any other property likely to be encountered in its application. **For example, if an oxygen sensor does not react to other gases like CO_2 then it has good selectivity.**

(h) **Resolution:** The resolution of a sensor is defined as the smallest change it can detect in the quantity that it is measuring. The resolution of a sensor with a digital output is usually the smallest resolution the digital output it is capable of processing. **Please understand that the more is the resolution of a sensor, the more accurate is its precision.** A sensor's accuracy does not depend on its resolution.

(i) **Response and Recovery Time:** The response time is the time taken by the sensor for its output to reach 95% of its final value when it is exposed to a target material. The Recovery Time is defined conversely.

(j) **Linearity:** If the sensitivity of the sensor is constant for the range, then it is called as linearity of the sensor. Linear sensors are easy to use while non-linear sensors need some complex mathematical equations to measure the physical property. Non-linearity means the deviation of a sensor's transfer function from a straight-line transfer function. It is defined as the amount of time the output differs from an ideal transfer function over the full range of the sensor.

(k) **Hysteresis:** It is the characteristic of a sensor by which the sensor produces a different set of outputs if the data is recorded in different directions i.e., increasing or decreasing inputs. A hysteresis error causes the sensor output value to vary which depends on the sensor's previous input values. The present reading may depend on the past input values. This is observed in magnetic-analog sensors.

(l) **Calibration:** It is defined as the process of tuning the output of the sensor with accurately known input so as to make a meaningful measurement.

(m) **Full-scale Output:** It is defined as the difference between the output for maximum input and the output for minimum input. The full-scale range of a sensor defines the maximum and minimum values of the measured property. Also note that since the range of the output signal is always limited the output signal will eventually reach a minimum or maximum value, when the measured property exceeds the limit.

(n) **Precision:** It is defined as the ability of a sensor to produce the same output when repeatedly measured for the same input. The precision is determined using statistical analysis like standard deviation.

(o) **Accuracy:** The accuracy of a sensor defines how close the output is to the real value. It defines the maximum error the sensor may produce.

(p) **Quantisation Error:** If the sensor has a digital output, the output is essentially an approximation of the measured property. Such an error is called as the **quantisation error.**

(q) **Dynamic Error:** If the signal is monitored digitally, the sampling frequency can cause a **dynamic error.**

(r) **Aliasing Error:** If the input variable or the added noise changes periodically at a frequency proportional to the multiple of the sampling rate, then **aliasing error** may occur.

Q3. Explain the following types of sensors:

    (a) Analog sensors.   (b) Digital sensors.

    (c) Scalar sensors.   (d) Vector sensors.

Ans.(a) Analog Sensors: These sensors produce a **continuous output signal or voltage that is generally proportional to the quantity being measured. For example,** the temperature of a liquid can be measured using a thermometer or thermocouple like geyser, which continuously responds to the temperature changes as the liquid is heated up or cooled down.

(b) **Digital Sensors:** These sensors produce a **discrete digital output signals or voltages that are generally proportional to the digital quantity being measured.** Digital sensors produce a binary output signal in form of a **"logic 1" or "logic 0".** Digital sensors have been developed to overcome the problems that we had in analog sensors. These sensors are used in water, waste water management. They measure parameters like pH, conductivity, dissolved oxygen, ammonium, nitrates, strong acidic presence etc. So, a digital sensor will consist of the sensor itself, a cable and a transmitter.

(c) **Scalar Sensors:** These sensors produce output signal (or voltages) that is generally proportional to the magnitude of the quantity being measured. Some physical quantities like temperature, pressure, strain, color etc are scalar quantities, so their magnitudes only are sufficient to convey the information. **For example,** the temperature of a room can be measured using a thermometer or a thermocouple which responds to temperature changes irrespective of the orientation of the sensor or its direction.

(d) **Vector Sensors:** These sensors produce output signal or voltage which is generally proportional to the magnitude, direction as well as the orientation of the quantity being measured. **Physical quantities like sound, image, velocity, acceleration, orientation etc.** are vector quantities as only their magnitude is not sufficient to convey the complete information. **For example,** the acceleration of a body can be measured using an accelerometer, which gives the component of acceleration of a body with respect to x, y, z coordinates axes.

Q4. Throw some light on the research directions for IoT.

Ans. Some of the research directions for IoT are as follows:

1. The **aim of the IoT Strategic Research Agenda** (IoT-SRA) is to direct the research efforts to focus on the areas of identified **significant value creation.**

2. We are standing on the brink of a new ubiquitous computing and communication era, one that will radically **transform our corporate, community and personal environments.**

3. **Development of new technology like smart phones, embedded systems, cloud computing, sensors, actuators, nano-electronics, network virtualization and software** needs Internet connection all of the time.

4. The **high-level expert group** on key enabling technologies (KETs) presented its final report. Tis expert group was created with the aim to elaborate a European strategy to develop several KETs— nanotechnology, micro-electronics, photonics, bIoTechnology and manufacturing systems and allow them to be exploited by industry, more effectively and efficiently.

5. The **reduction in the critical dimensions while keeping the electrical field constant** and at the same time, a user obtained at **a higher speed with reduction in power consumption** of a digital MOS circuit.

6. **The International Technology Roadmap for Semiconductors** has highlighted in its early editions and its associated benefits in terms of performances, the traditional parameters in **Moore's Law.**

7. **Mobile Data Traffic** will increase rapidly. According to a survey in 2015, it has been observed that the data traffic increased and is increasing till date and the mobile operators are facing problem to provide the required bandwidth to the client and customers.

8. **Extra Frequency Spectrum** is not available in some countries. So, proposed solutions are the seamless integration of existing WIFI networks into the **mobile ecosystem** and also this will have a very big impact on **IoT ecosystems** too.

9. It is mandatory to develop a **"multi-com chip" to integrate all processes. In a single silicon package, it is expected to cover WIFI and baseband communications.** The architecture of mobile devices is likely to change as well as the "**baseband chip**" will be taking the control of the routing process, so the connectivity components are connected to the baseband. Hence, thetre will be a change in the **architectural design.**

10. Now-a-days many **European projects address IoT technologies**, its domain knowledge as well as it has been mentioned that these

fields can be **heterogeneous and specialized.** Also, there is a need for integration of the individual results.

11. That is why, the **integration of knowledge has been conceptualized** as the process through which some specialized cognizance situated in multiple projects across Europe is applied.

12. **The Agenda of Strategic Research and Innovation** has been developed. With proper support of a European-led community of inter-related projects and their stakeholders with dedication to the *innovation, creation, development* and the use of IoT technology.

Q5. **Explain with examples the IoT service that uses WebSocket based communication model.**

Ans. **WebSocket supports full-duplex, two-way communication between client and server. WebSocket APIs** reduce the network traffic and latency as there is no overhead for connection setup and termination requests for each message. The following figure shows the WebSocket model.

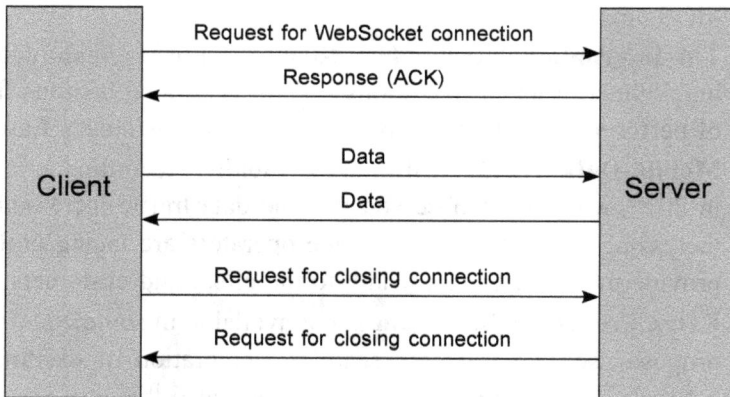

Fig. 1: The WebSocket Model

Please note that WebSocket uses a standard HTTP request-response sequence to establish a connection. When the connection is established, the WebSocket API provides a read and write interface for reading and writing data over the established connection in an asynchronous full-duplex manner. WebSocket also provides an interface for asynchronously closing the connection from either side.

Q6. **Give some architectural constraints of REST.**

Ans. The architectural constraints of REST are as follows:

1. It needs that **a service offers one or more operations** and that the **services wait for clients to request these operations.**
2. It requires communication between **service consumer** (client) **and service provide** (server) **to be stateless.**
3. It requires responses to be clearly labelled as **cacheable or non-cacheable.**
4. It requires all service providers and consumers within a **REST-complaint architecture to share a single common interface** for all operations.
5. It requires the ability to add or remove intermediaries at runtime without disrupting the system.
6. It allows logic within clients (like web browsers) to be **updated independently** from the server-side logic using executable code shipped from service providers to consumers.

Q7. Give some advantages and some disadvantages of IoT.

Ans. Advantages of IoT

1. Better consumer involvement and communication.
2. Supports for **technology optimization.**
3. Supports for **wide range of data collection.**
4. Reduced wastages.

Disadvantages of IoT

1. It reduces the safety and security of devices that are on IoT as they are connected to Internet. Hence, this **information is vulnerable to attacks** by the hackers and crackers.
2. Some issues also arise due to the **flexibility of an IoT system** i.e., these systems integrate easily with other systems.
3. IoT is a diverse and complex network. **Any failure of IoT software or IoT hardware can have serious consequences too. It has been found that even power failures can have a lot of inconvenience.**
4. There is **no international standard of compatibility** for tagging and monitoring equipment.

Q8. How is IoT different from traditional computing paradigm? What is meant by autonomy in IoT?

Ans. IoT differs from the traditional computing paradigm. The data can be small in size and frequent in transmission. **Also note that the number**

of devices or nodes that connect to the network are also greater in IoT than in traditional computing paradigm.

Q9. "Self-adapting and self-configuration are two important characteristics of IoT". Support this statement.

Ans. Self-adaptive is a system that can automatically modify itself in the face of a changing context, to best answer a set of requirements. IoT devices may have the capability to dynamically adapt with the changing contexts and take actions based on their operating conditions.

On the other hand, **self-configuration basically,** consists of the actions of neighbour and service discovery, network organization and resource provisioning. The system is capable to readjust itself. Readjustment of the system is required if its environment changes or to reach an objective set for the system.

Q10. What are the reasons of shifting from M2M to IoT?

Ans. As we know that M2M communication is the communication among the physical devices/ things that do not need human intervention. M2M communication involves one or more entities that do not necessarily require human interaction during communication. **It is also named as Machine Type Communication (MTC) in 3GPP.**

It can be carried over **mobile networks** like GSM, GPRS, CDMA etc). In M2M communication, the role of mobile network is largely confined to serve as a **transport network. Please note that M2M is only a subset of IoT. Also note that IoT is more encompassing phenomenon because it also includes Human-to-Machine communication (H2M). For instance,** Radio Frequency Identification (RFID). Location-based Services (LBS), Lab-on-Chip (LOC), sensors, augmented reality, robotics and vehicle telematics are some of the technology innovations that employ both M2M and H2M communications.

Reasons to Shift FromM2M to IoT are as Follows:

1. **IoT** supports **multiple application with multiple devices.**
2. It is **information and service centric.**
3. It supports **open market place.**
4. **IoT uses horizontal enabler approach.**
5. It requires **generic commodity devices.**
6. It is used in **B2B and B2C communications.**

Q11. What do you mean by data management in IoT? What challenges are faced for data management? Also explain the data collection and analysis (DCA) module.

Ans. **It is defined as the ability to manage data information flow.** If data management is done at the management service-layer then information can be **accessed, integrated and controlled. Please note that higher level applications can be shielded from the need to process unnecessary data and reduce the risk of privacy disclosure of the data source.** As studied, data is received from sensors and actuators. And it is **relayed by the micro-controller** through WIFI, GPRS, RFID, ZigBee and open connectivity to the router. This data has to be refined from the database or repository (storage) using the so-called data-mining algorithms like clustering and classification which analyses **semantically and syntactically.** Some of the challenges of data management are as follows:

- Data Collection and Analysis (DCA).
- Big Data.
- Semantic Sensor Networking.
- Virtual Sensors.
- Complex Event Processing.

Functions of Data Collection and Analysis (DCA) Module:

1. **Data Storage:** It provides storage of the customer's information collected by sensors.
2. **User Data and Operation Modelling:** It allows the customers to create new sensor data models to accommodate collected information and the modelling of the supported operations.
3. **On-Demand Data Access:** It provides APIs to access the collected data.
4. **Customer Rules:** It allows the customer to establish its own filters and rules to correlate events.
5. **Customer Task Automation:** It provides the customer with the ability to manage his automatic processes.
6. **Customer Workflows:** It allows the customers to create his own workflow to process the incoming events from a device.

Q12. Define data acquisition. What does it consist up of?

Ans. Data Acquisition (DAQ) is the process of measuring an electrical or physical phenomenon such as voltage, current, temperature, pressure or sound with a computer. This system consists of sensors, DAQ measurement hardware and a computer with programmable hardware. These DAQ systems use the processing power, productivity, display and connectivity capabilities of industry-standard computers providing a more powerful, flexible and cost-effective measurement solution.

A typical DAQ system consists of:

(a) **Measurement Hardware:** It consists of A/D converter, a digital input card, a counter card.

(b) **Control Hardware:** It consists of D/A converter, a digital output, control switching card, electromechanical switches and transducers.

Benefits of DAQs

1. **Data Redundancy/Duplicate data** is reduced.
2. It reduces updating errors and increased consistency.
3. It provides more data integrity and independence from application programs.
4. Better data security.
5. Reduced data entry, storage and retrieval costs.
6. Facilitated development of new application programs.
7. Better data access to users through SQL.

Q13. Explain IoT data life cycle.

Ans. The following figure shows IoT data life cycle

Note the following points as is shown in figure above:

1. The life cycle starts from data production to aggregation, transfer, filtering and pre-processing. Finally, to storage and archiving.
2. **Querying and analysis** are the end points that initiate and consume data production.
3. **Production, collection,** aggregation, filtering and some fundamental querying are considered as online and communication-intensive operations.
4. **Intensive pre-processing, long-term storage and in-depth analysis** are considered as **offline storage-intensive operations.**

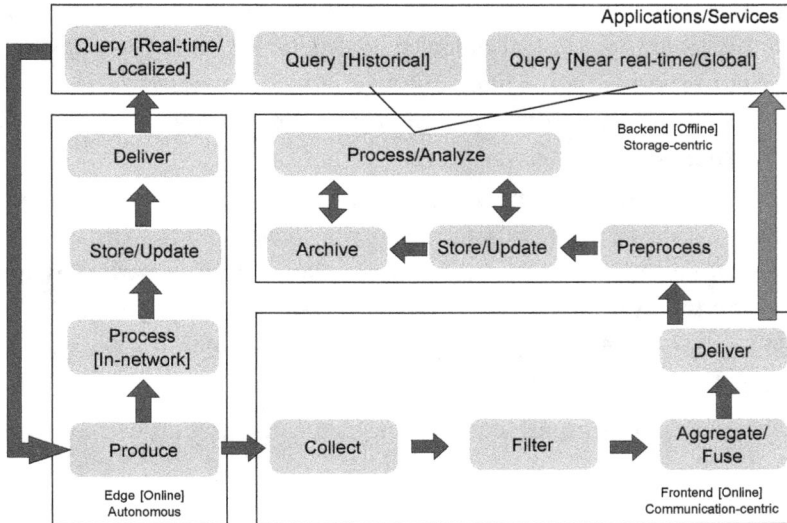

Fig. 2: IoT Data Lifecycle

5. **Storage operations** aim at making data available on **the long-term for constant access or updates whereas archival is related to read-only data.**

6. **Querying: Data-intensive systems** depend on querying as the core process to access and retrieve data. In relation to IoT, a **query can be issued either to request real-time data** to be collected for temporal monitoring purposes **or to retrieve a certain view of the data** stored within the system.

7. **Production:** Data production involves **sensing and transfer of data by the "Things"** within the IoT framework and **reporting this data** to interested parties **periodically.**

8. **Collection:** The **sensors and smart objects** in an IoT system may store the data for a certain time interval or may report it to the governing components. **Also note that wireless technologies like Zigbee, WIFI and cellular communication are used by the objects to send the data to the collection points.**

9. **Aggregation/Fusion:** These techniques deploy **summarization and merging operations in real-time** to **compress the volume of data** to be stored and transmitted.

10. **Delivery: Wired or wireless broadband communications** may be used there to transfer data to **permanent data stores.**

11. **Pre-processing:** IoT data will come from **variety of sources** with different types of formats and structures. *Data may need to be pre-processed to handle missing data, remove redundancies and integrate data from different sources into a unified schema before being committed to storage.*

12. **Storage/ update-archiving:** Efficient storage, organization and the updating of data is handled in this phase. **Archiving means the offline long-term storage of data that is not immediately needed for the system's ongoing operations.**

Q14. What infrastructural challenges are required for data processing in IoT?

Ans. There are four main data processing infrastructural challenges as follows:

1. **Storage:** As we know that the volume of data, its veracity, velocity, its variety and its vulnerability are always a challenge as far as big data is concerned. **Please note that it has been found that the increase in the volume of data, will increase the need for storing the data and processing of data.** More complex storage mediums are needed with higher I/O speeds to meet the big-data issues. **Direct-attached storage (DAS), Network-attached Storage (NAS) and Storage area network (SAN) are some of the enterprise architectures** that are commonly in use.

2. **Transportation: Data is transferred from one place to other place and then the processed data is loaded into the memory for manipulation.** The data is transported between computer and storage layers. *Increase in the bandwidth is NOT the solution to this problem.*

3. **Processing: Data processing needs to combine the logic and mathematical computation in one cycle only.** This processing can be accomplished by CPU, memory and software. **Better CPU speeds, better memory storages and software-based approaches are used to transform and process data.**

4. **Throughput:** One of the major challenges of data processing is **throughput.** Many different architectural layers like hardware, software networking and storage are responsible for storage. Each layer has its own restrictions and constraints that causes limitation in the overall throughput and speed of data processing.

Q15. Distinguish between M2M and IoT in a tabular format.

Ans. The following table gives the differences between the two.

Machine-to-Machine (M2M)	Internet-of-Things (IoT)
It supports single application with a single device.	It supports multiple application with multiple devices.
It is communication and device centric.	It is information and service centric.
It supports closed business operations.	It supports open market place.
It uses vertical system solution approach.	It uses horizontal enabler approach.
It requires specialized device solutions.	It requires generic commodity devices.
It is used in B2B.	It is used in B2B and B2C, both.

Q16. Define the following terms

  (a) Global value chain.   (b) Industrial Internet of Things.

Ans. (a) **Global Value Chain:** A value chain describes the full range of activities that firms and workers perform to bring a product from its conception to end use and beyond including design, production, marketing, distribution and support to the final consumer.

  (b) **Industrial Internet of Things (IIoT):** IIoT is made up of a multitude of devices connected by communication software. The resulting systems and even the individual devices that comprise it, can monitor, collect, exchange, analyse and instantly act on information to intelligently change their behaviour or their environment, all without human-interventions.

Q17. Explain what is SCADA?

Ans. As explained earlier, that IoT has 4 pillars- RFID, WSN, M2M and SCADA. SCADA is an **autonomous system based on the closed-loop theory or a smart system via a network in a facility** like a plant or a building. It is a **supervisory control, a data acquisition specialized software** used in industry but it can be applied to small systems that consists of Human-Machine-Interfaces (HMI). It could be a touch panel for user's GUI. *According to Harbour research, smart systems are a new generation of systems architecture that provides real-time awareness based on inputs from machines, people, video streams, maps, new feeds, sensors and more that integrate people, processes and technology to enable collective awareness and decision making.* People, information and technology are becoming more connected, distributed and pervasive, enabling the convergence of physical and virtual worlds. Network awareness includes knowledge, people and Things. These forces are forming a new trend that we call as "**Smart Business**". **It is a concept in which inputs from machines, people, video streams, maps, new-feeds, sensors and more is digitized and placed onto networks.** These inputs are integrated into the systems that connect people, processes and knowledge to enable collective awareness, creativity and better decision making. **Also note that the foundation of Smart Business is made up of Smart systems only that is based on embedded computing and networking technology to deliver smart, remotely monitored goods that will support entirely new modes of customer-device interaction and service delivery.**

Q18. Compare the four pillars of IoT with their relevance to networks.

Ans. IoT is a glue that fastens the four pillars through a common set of best practices, networking methodology and middleware platform.

The following table compares the 4-pillars of IoT with networks:

Table: Compares 4-pillars of IoT Paradigms and Their Related Networks

4-pillars of IoT / Networks	Short-range wireless	Long-range wireless	Short-ranged wired	Long-range wired
RFID	Yes	Some	No	Some
WSN	Yes	Some	No	Some
M2M	Some	Yes	No	Some
SCADA	Some	Some	Yes	Yes

Q19. Compare Web of Things (WOT) and Internet of Things (IoT).

Ans. The following points compare WOT with IoT.

1. WOT provides an application layer that simplifies the creation of IoT applications.
2. The Web, like email, is one of the services that runs on the Internet.
3. The key components of web are URL, HTML and HTTP.
4. Web is a system of interlinked documents accessed via Internet. The term was coined by Tim Berners-Lee in 1990.
5. Internet is used to identify **the massive interconnection of computer networks around the world.** It refers to the physical connection of paths between two or more computers. WWW is a general name for accessing Internet via HTTP.

6. WOT refers to **reusing the web standards to connect the rapidly expanding eco-system of embedded devices built into everyday smart objects.** Standards like HTTP, REST, RSS etc are used to access the functionality of smart objects.

7. WOT uses HTTP as an **application protocol** rather than as a transport protocol as done in the world of web services. It exposes the synchronous functionality of smart objects through a REST interface, **also known as RESTful API** and more generally respects the blueprints of **Resource-oriented architectures.**

8. It exposes the **asynchronous functionality** (events) **of smart objects** through the use of largely accepted **web syndication standards** like Atom or server-push web mechanism like Comet.

9. WOT is the **next logical step** in this IoT evolution toward **global networks of sensors and actuators** enabling new applications and providing new opportunities.

10. **WOT has a flat-architecture as compared to the traditional client-server architecture. Please note that if we have to integrate Things directly to the web then the Things must be addressable** i.e., all Things must have an IP address and thus should be IP-enabled when connected to Internet. **Also note that WOT also requires connectivity and interoperability at the application layer.**

11. Some WOT applications are Arduino, Japan Geiger Map, Nanode, National Weather Study Project (NWSP) and AgSphere. **Arduino** is an open-source electronics platform based on easy-to-use hardware and software, **Japanese Nuclear Safety Commission's regulations** prescribe some rules and regulations that a monitoring system at a power nuclear plant must follow, **Nanode** is an open-source Arduino-like board that has inbuilt web connectivity and **NWSP is a large-scale environmental study project** that deploys hundreds of **mini weather stations** in schools throughout Singapore.

Q20. What is Cloud-of Things? What are the main features of cloud-based IoT platform?

Ans. We know that cloud computing refers to a new way pf creating, designing, developing, testing, deploying, running and maintaining the applications on the Internet.

Main Features of Cloud-based IoT Platform

1. **CloudThings is an architecture that is an online platform allowing system integrators and solution providers to leverage a complete "Things-based" application infrastructure for** developing, deploying, operating and development of Things applications and services that consist of 3 main modules:

    (a) **CloudThings Service Platform for Things** is a set of cloud services (IaaS) allowing user's to run any application on cloud hardware on "pay-per" basis. **CloudThings service platform** simplifies the application development, eliminates the need for infrastructure development, shortens time to market and mitigates **Things Management and Maintenance Costs (TMMC).**

    (b) **The CloudThings Service Platform** provides unique device management capabilities. It **communicates directly** with devices and provides storage to **collect "Things" data** and transmit **Things events.** Large amount of sensor data can be processed, analysed and stored using the computational and storage resources of the cloud.

    (c) **The CloudThings Service Platform** allows sharing of sensor resources by different users and applications under a **flexible usage mode.**

2. **The CloudThings Developer Suite** for Things is a **set of cloud-service tools** (PaaS) for Things application development. These tools include **Web Service Application Programming Interfaces** (API) that provide complete development and deployment capabilities to "Things" developers.

3. **The CloudThings Operating Portal for Things is a set of cloud services (SaaS) that support deployment and handle or support specialized processing services** including service subscription management, community coordination, "Things" connection, Things discovery, data intelligence and Things composition.

Q21. Explain CoAP protocol.

Ans. The following points are worth noting about CoAP protocol:

1. **CoAP stands for Constrained Application Protocol. It is a web transfer protocol for use with constrained nodes and constrained networks** like lossy, low power networks.

2. **It is a client-server protocol that provides one-to-one "request/**

report" interaction model with accommodations for multi-cast although multi-cast, is still in its infancy stages of IETF standardization.

3. It is designed for **simplicity, low overhead and multicast support** in resource constrained environments.

4. It is a **web protocol that runs over UDP for IoT.** Datagram Transport Layer Security (DTLS) is used to protect **CoAP transmission.**

5. The protocol is designed **for M2M applications like** smart energy and building automation.

6. It provides a **request/response interaction model between application end-points**, supports **in-built discovery of services and resources and includes key concepts of the web** such as URIs and Internet media types.

7. It is designed to easily **interface with HTTP for integration with the web** while meeting specialized requirements like **multicast support**, very low overhead and simplicity for constrained environments.

8. This protocol is designed to **interoperate with HTTP and the RESTful web** through **simple proxies** making it natively compatible to the Internet. CoAP is based on **REST architecture that is a general design for accessing internet services**.

9. The CoAP protocol stack is shown in figure below.

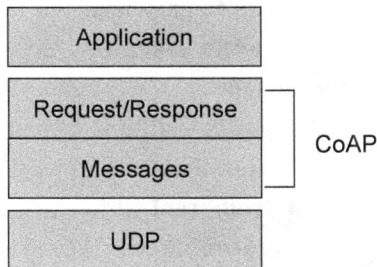

Fig. 3: CoAP Protocol

10. **CoAP** is based on the exchange of **compact messages** that (by default) are transmitted over UDP. CoAP messages use simple **binary format** only.

11. **Message Layer** supports four types of messages: CON (confirmable), NON (non-confirmable) ACK (Acknowledgement), RST (Reset).

12. **Reliable Message Transport:** Keep re-transmission until get ACK

with the same ID. Using default time-out and decreasing counting time exponentially when transmitting CON. **If the recipient fails to process message**, it responses by replacing ACK with RST.

13. **Unreliable Message Transport:** It is transporting with NON type message. It doesn't need to be ACKed but has to contain message ID for supervising in case of retransmission. **If the recipient fails to process message, server replies RST.**

14. **Piggy-backed:** Client sends request using CON type or NON type message and receives response ACK with confirmable message immediately, for successful response, ACK contains response message (identified by using token), for failure response, ACK contains failure response code.

15. **Separate Response:** If a server receives a CON type of message but not able to response this request immediately, it will send an empty ACK in case of client resends this message. When servers ready to response this request, it will send a new CON to client and the client replies a confirmable message with acknowledgement. ACK is just to confirm CON message, no matter CON message carry request or response.

Q22. What do you mean by "Digital Twin"? Explain.

Ans. John Vickers in 2003 at NASA, presented the idea of **"Digital Twin"**. The main objective is to have a computerized duplicate of a physical resource that lives and advances in a virtual world over the physical resource's lifetime. **IBM defines digital twin as follows- "A digital twin is a virtual representation of an object or system that spans its lifecycle, is updated from real-time data and uses simulation, machine learning and reasoning to help decision-making."** It is a tool that helps engineers and operators to understand how products are performing and how they will perform in future. So, it is a **virtual model that is designed to accurately reflect a physical object** being studied. The data that is collected through sensors is then applied to the digital copy. With this data, virtual model can be used to run simulation experiments and the results of this are then applied to the original physical object.

EXERCISE QUESTIONS

1. Why is it that IoT systems must be self-adopting and self-configuring?
2. Differentiate between IoT and M2M.
3. What are the advantages of analog and digital sensors?
4. Explain IoT privacy and security solutions.
5. Write short notes on:
   (a) Actuators.
   (b) IoT Cloud-based Services.
   (c) Applications of IoT.
6. What is IoT? Give an architectural view of IoT.
7. How does the IoT device data organise? What are the uses of data after analysis of acquired data?
8. Explain the major components of IoT in detail.
9. Define wireless sensors and its applications.
10. Define M2M technology. Give some examples and usages of M2M industrial IoT.
11. Explain with the help of a neat diagram the architecture of M2M.
12. Explain how IoT can be used in smart city streetlight control and monitoring?
13. Explain the logical and physical design of IoT.
14. List the challenges while opting for IoT and cloud computing. How can we overcome them?
15. Give an example of an IoT system in which information and knowledge are inferred from data.
16. What do you mean by "THINGS" in IoT?
17. List some main characteristics of IoT.
18. Name some IoT functional blocks.
19. What are the risks related to IoT? How can we solve them?
20. You are the manager of an organisation. You desire to make the best use of IoT for your company. What are the business suggestions that you can give to your company?
21. Explain the IoT Stack in detail with a neat diagram.

22. Explain the 5-layered IoT levels with an example of each.
23. Explain the following with respect to IoT:
    (a) Smart Home.
    (b) Health Care.
    (c) Smart Cities.
    (d) Smart Agriculture.
    (e) Smart Transportation.
24. Explain how IoT and ML, together can boost growth in the field of agriculture, healthcare?
25. Is IoT the future for smart India? Throw some light on the Indian market scenario.

2 IoT AND ITS COMPONENTS

2.0 INTRODUCTION

IoT is beginning to pervade more and better aspects of our life. Today the scenario is, "Everyone, everywhere is using the Internet of Things". So, using Internet, connected things are used to collect information, send information and analyse it. IoT is an architecture that combines available technologies. IoT has four components namely, sensors, IoT gateway, cloud server and mobile apps. The data that is collected by sensors is shared/ passed to the IoT gateway. **This gateway is a mediator between the sensor nodes and WWW.** It processes data that is collected from sensor nodes and then transmits this to **the Internet infrastructure.** After this the data is transmitted through the gateway onto **the cloud server** where it is stored. Then using the **mobile app,** the user can view and access the data processes in the cloud server. This is how IoT and its elements work. Actually, we have two types of IoT protocols:

(a) The IoT Network Protocol.

(b) The IoT Data Protocol.

Interactions between humans and machines are on the verge of a radical shift through IoT. IoT is well-poised to usher in the next technological revolution due to Internet, machine learning and deep learning advancements. As the world is expanding rapidly, so does the global IoT spending. There are, no doubt, some nagging security concerns with IoT and we say IoT security is still in its infancy.

- According to a survey by Cradlepoint, about 70 % organisations have adopted of plan to adopt IoT solutions in next few years to come.
- Gartner also predicts that 20.8 billion devices will be connected by 2020-21.

DOI: 10.1201/9781003728641-2

- Bain predicts that the combined markets of IoT will grow to about US$ 520 billion in 2021 that is more than the double of the US$ 235 billion spent in 2017.
- IoT has the potential to bring the next industrial revolution, transform the society and establish new ecosystem to serve humanity. People are receiving services on demand (cloud-based) and societies will be benefitted from optimal resource use.
- According to Deloitte report, the IoT units in India are expected to see a fast growth of 32 times to reach 1.9 billion units by 2020, from the current of 60 million.
- Also, Deloitte reports that application vendors focus on both horizontal and vertical solutions are expected to get 50% of share of the Indian IoT market.
- Even network operators are increasing their investments in new networks like SigFox to increase connectivity-based ROIs.

2.1 RFID

RFID or Radio Frequency Identification is a simple and cheaper way of a device/object/item identification. It uses the phenomenon of **Electromagnetic Fields only.** It is being used today by industries to automatically identify and track the tags connected to objects. Actually, tags in RFID store data electronically. RFID system consists of two parts- **time and reader.** The **top component** consists of a **microchip** and this chip is used to store and process information. The 2nd part is **antenna** that is also used in the top-right and is needed for receiving and transmitting a signal. In order to read the information encoded on a tag we use a **radio transmitter-receiver** which is called as **interrogator or a reader** and this emits a signal to the tag. Then the time will be spawned with the information from the magnet back, the reader will then transmit the results, read so far, to an RFID computer program.

The following are some of the **salient features of RFID:**

1. RFID systems can be seen as a next generation technology for **bar-codes.**
2. RFID devices are **wireless microchips** used for tagging objects for **automated identification.**
3. RFID tag is a simplified, low cost, disposable **contactless smart card.**

4. RFID tags include a **chip that stores a static number (ID) and attributes of the tagged object and an antenna** that enables the chip to transmit the stored number to a reader.

5. Tags are characterised by a **unique identifier** and are applied to objects. Readers trigger the tag transmission by generating an appropriate signal which represents a query for the possible presence of tags in the surrounding area and for the reception of their IDs.

6. Fig. 2.1 below shows a basic RFID system.

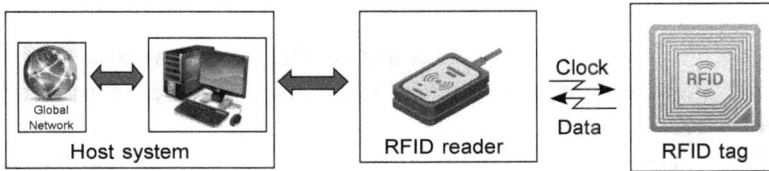

Fig. 2.1: Basic RFID System

7. As shown in figure, RFID systems consist of a reading device called as a **reader, and one or more tags.** The reader is a powerful device with lot of memory and computational resources.

8. **Passive Tags** have limited computational capacity, no ability to sense the channel, detect collisions and communicate with each other. They respond only at the reader commands. They collect energy via radio waves.

9. **Semi-passive Tags** have an on-board power source that can be used to energise their microchip.

10. **Active Tags** sense the channel and detect collisions. They need a battery source to operate at a distance of about 100 meters from the RFID reader.

11. **Please note that accordingly, RFID systems can be used to monitor objects in real-time without the need of being in LOS** (LINE-OF-SIGHT). This allows for mapping the real world into the virtual world.

12. **An RFID system involves hardware known as readers and tags as well as RFID software or RFID middleware.** Readers can also be mobile or hand-held.

13. **RFID systems operate in the Industry, Scientific and Medical (ISM) frequency band that ranges from 100 KHz to 5.8 GHz.**

14. **RFID technology has been deeply embedded to IoT** to identify devices and to link these devices to the internet.

15. RFID **communicates on ISO-EPC global standards and operate at** 120KHz-150KHz or 13.56MHz and 433MHz.

16. **Range** of RFID communication is about 10 to 100m operating at 10-100 Kbps.

17. Basic **Applications** of RFID include toll tax collections, goods tracking, smart dust, airport baggage tracking and so on.

RFID Anti-collision Procedure

Collision due to simultaneous tag responses is one of the key issues in RFID systems. **Tag collision results in wastage of bandwidth, energy and increases identification delays.** RFID readers must use an **anti-collision protocol** to reduce collisions and hence help reduce the identification delays. Tag collision happens **when two or more tags reflects-back their individual identification radio signals to the reader** at the same time thus confusing the reader identification process.

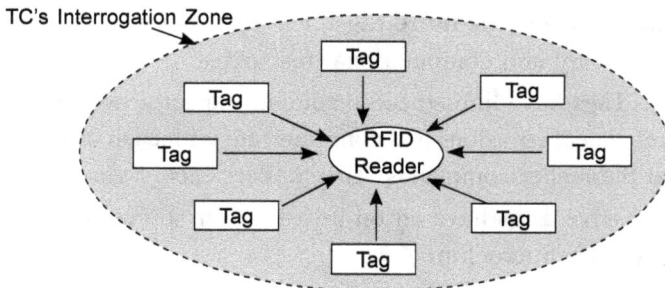

Fig. 2.2: RFID Anti-collision Procedure.

RFID **anti-collision protocols** are often categorized as ALOHA -based protocols and tree-based protocols. In **pure ALOHA-based RFID systems,** a tag responds with its ID randomly after being energized by a reader. On the other hand, **in slotted ALOHA-based RFID systems,** tags transmit their id in synchronous time slots. The collision occurs at **slots boundary** only. Hence, there are **no partial collisions.**

RFID Middleware and Its Benefits

1. RFID middleware needs to allow users to configure, deploy and issue commands directly to readers through a common interface. **For instance,** users should be able to tell a reader when to **"turn-off"** if needed.

2. The following Fig. 2.3 shows **RFID Middleware:**

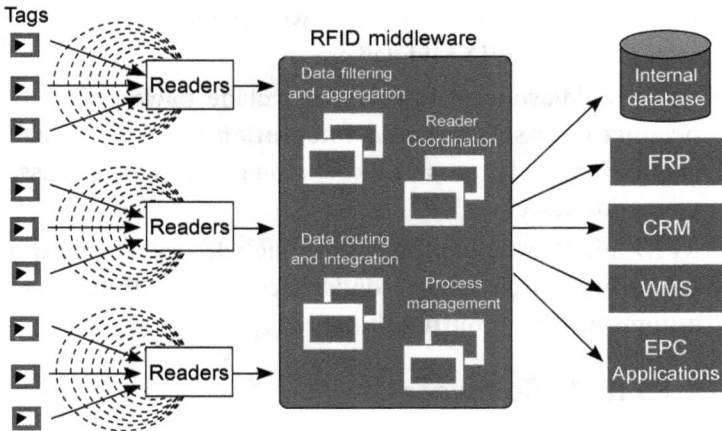

Fig. 2.3: RFID Middleware

3. After RFID middleware **captures EPC data from the readers,** it must be able to **intelligently filter and route the data** to a suitable destination.

4. Look for middleware that includes both **low-level logic and more complex algorithms. Comprehensive solutions** also offer tools for **aggregating and managing EPC data in either a federated or central data source.**

5. **RFID middleware solutions** need to provide the **messaging, routing and connectivity features** required to reliably integrate RFID data into existing SCM, ERP, WMS or CRM systems, ideally through a **service-oriented architecture (SOA).**

6. SOA is essentially **a collection of services.** These services communicate with each other. The communication can involve either simple data exchange or two or more services coordinating some activity such as order placement or inventory control.

7. Middleware needs to provide **a library of adapters** to popular WMS and SCM applications like SAP or Oracle E -Business Suite. Application Programming Interfaces (APIs) and adapters for using standard technologies like XML, SOAP etc. to integrate with other 3rd party applications.

8. RFID middleware should provide the following:
   • B2B integration features like **partner profile management.**
   • Support for **B2B transport protocols.**

- **Integration with a partner's data over communications** like EDI, web-based systems like AS2 or a well engineered system specifically for EPC data RFID Middleware.
- RFID middleware platforms that include **packaged routing logic, product data schemes and integration** with typical RFID-related applications and processes like shipping, receiving and asset tracking are major assets.
- RFID middleware platforms must include features for **dynamically balancing processing loads** across **multiple servers** and **automatically rerouting data.**

Uses of RFID Middleware

The following are some of the benefits of RFID middleware:

- **Minimized network traffic** through **intelligent filtering.**
- **Lower reader management costs** through centrally coordinated readers.
- Immediate visibility to pertinent RFID data through **routing, filtering and track-and-trace tools.**
- **Minimized on-going integration costs** through standard APIs and **pre-packaged application integration tools.**
- **Well-architected RFID middleware** can enable more strategic opportunities that go way beyond these initial rather obvious benefits.

Drawbacks of RFID Middleware

The following are some of the drawbacks of RFID middleware:

- RFID needs **costly batteries** use.
- They can be easily **intercepted** (tapped).
- It needs **time and cost.**
- It should be **programmed.**
- **Loss of jobs** if labour is unskilled.
- Its coverage **range is limited** to 3m.

Applications of RFID Systems

RFID applications fall under two main categories

(a) **Short Range Applications:** Here, the reader and the tag are in close proximity like in access control.

(b) **Medium to Long Applications:** where the distance may be greater.

Some of the applications of RFID are as follows:

1. **Asset Tracking:** This system can **read multiple tags at once.** So, it is possible to easily locate the assets.

2. **Supply Chain Management (SCM):** (RFID + SCM), together has **improved the impact of SCM further, total inventory cost has been reduced and it has even increased customer satisfaction.**

3. **Manufacturing Industries** have also been benefitted as they can now **monitor their process of production and improve it** further and thus gain more efficiencies with access to **real-time data.**

4. **Contactless Payments** are also possible because of RFID systems only.

5. **Retailers** are using this technology in order **to improve supply chain visibility and also to reduce the chances of out-of-stock of items.**

6. **Better Security:** RFID systems are secure to use. this is because of contactless access. Also, it provides time and attendance information for better security purposes.

Case Study of RFID Usage

1. The US military and commercial industry use RFID technology to streamline and increase business practices.

2. Pacific Northwest National Lab. (PNNL) is using this technology for different types of markets.

3. In Europe, Munich City Library has the largest RFID -based library.

4. Electronic labelling (e-labelling) are RFID tags that appear on shipping boxes, for instance. E-label is made from polyethylene media and PCB driven by a copper coil antenna. **Please note that the tag has no power supply attached to itself. Also note that the tag is energized by signal waves that are broadcast from the reader antenna.**

2.2 WIRELESS SENSOR NETWORKS (WSNS)

Some important points regarding WSNs are as follows:

1. WSN is concerned more with **sensing and information collection.** Other networks include *Body Sensor Network (BSN), Visual Sensor Network (VSN), Vehicular Sensor Networks, underwater/ acoustic sensor networks, interplanetary sensor networks, fieldbus networks* etc.

2. The **extended scope of WSN** is the **Ubiquitous Sensor Network** (USN) i.e., **a network of intelligent sensors** that could one day become ubiquitous.

3. **A WSN is defined as a network formed by a large number of sensor nodes where each node is equipped with some sensors to detect physical phenomena.** In IoT, the sensor nodes and devices are interconnected to transmit useful measurement information via **distributed sensor networks.**

4. VSN devices come with **image sensors, adequate processing power and memory. They use wireless communication interfaces** to collaborate and jointly solve tasks like tracking persons within the network. In all applications, VSNs monitor a potentially large group of people and record sensitive image data which might contain identities of persons, their behaviour, interaction patterns or personal preferences.

5. Please understand that the central idea of VSNs is to keep data processing local to reduce the amount of transmitted data.

6. The following Fig. 2.4 shows a VSN network.

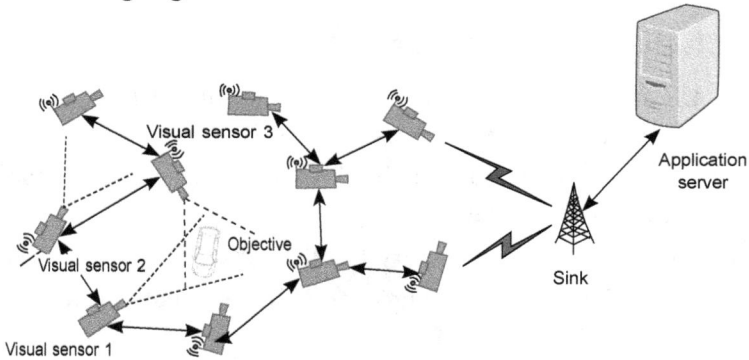

Fig. 2.4: VSN Network

7. **Explanation:** A single VSN device has only a limited field of view but VSNs are typically designed to cover larger areas. Hence, **multiple spatially distributed nodes are needed. Also note that to avoid centralized control and data processing, VSN's use peer to peer communication for coordination, configuration, data exchange, handover of tracked objects or data fusion.**

8. To simplify deployment of spatially distributed VSNs, they rely not only on dedicated communication networks but also make use of existing infrastructure which is not under full control of the VSN operators.

9. The term **"context" is defined as any information that can be used to characterize the situation of an entity.** This definition is traditionally associated with the **design of context-aware applications** where contexts are information that describes the situation of any entity relevant to the application.

10. The entities can be **people, places or things. The applications are context consumers that receive information from the context producers** and may also produce their own context that they provide to other context consumers e.g., other applications. **Please note that by exchanging context, the applications can adapt their behaviours according to the shared contexts and as a result, the overall performance can be optimized.**

11. **Also note that context can be shared between the context producers and consumers in the network. Context for the IoT system is any shareable knowledge** to represent situations or conditions from different parts of the system. The **range of contexts** can include device context, network contexts, system contexts and environment contexts.

12. The **device context provides knowledge about local device conditions,** such as the energy state, storage level and services provided by a node.

13. **The network context represents network wide situations and states** like network topology, overall transmission capacity or path qualities in the network.

14. **The system context represents the status of IoT system like** the current executing tasks of an application or the state of the IoT system performance which can be shared with the underlying network.

15. **The environment context provides knowledge for a network to understand the changes of its environmental properties or attributes like** the occurrence of a fire incident or detection of hazardous objects.

16. **Mobile Sensor Networks (MSNs)** are the examples of WSNs in which **nodes can move under their own control.**

17. **Mobile Networked Systems** combine the most advanced concepts in **perception, communication and control to create computational systems capable of interacting in a meaningful way with the physical environment**, thereby extending the individual capabilities of each network component and network user to encompass a much wider area and range of data.

18. WSN is *a network of devices that can communicate the information gathered from a monitored field through wireless links.*

19. The data is forwarded through **multiple nodes and with a gateway**, the data is connected to other networks like **wireless Ethernet.**

20. WSN is **a wireless network that consists of base stations, number of nodes of wireless sensors.**

21. For **radio communications network**, WSN uses different topologies like star, tree, and mesh.

22. Depending of the environment, **the types of networks are decided so that those can be deployed underwater, underground, on land etc.** Various types of WSNs include terrestrial WSNs, underground WSNs, underwater WSNs, multimedia WSNs and mobile WSNs.

23. These are **similar to wireless ad hoc networks** in the sense that they rely on **wireless connectivity.** Networks are also formed spontaneously so that sensor data can be transported wirelessly.

24. A WSN is built of **nodes from a few to several hundreds or even thousands, where each node is connected to one or more sensors.**

25. The sensor nodes in WSN have short radio transmission range **and hence intermediate nodes act as relay nodes to transmit data towards the destination/ sink node using multi-hop path.** It is shown in Fig. 2.5 below.

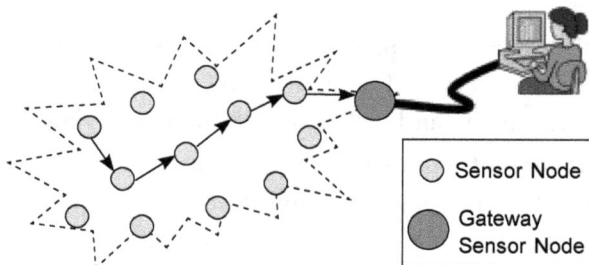

Fig. 2.5: Sensor Nodes in WSN

26. It uses either routing or flooding propagation techniques between the hops of the network.

27. **Note that it is the size and cost constraints on sensor nodes that result in the corresponding constraints on resources like energy, memory, speed and communication bandwidth.**

28. Each sensor node has a certain **area of coverage** for which it can reliably report the particular quantity that it is observing.

29. Many **sources of power consumption in sensors** are like signal sampling, conversion of physical signals to electrical signals, signal conditioning and analog-to-digital conversion.

30. **Spatial density of the sensor nodes** in the field may be as high as 19-20 nodes per cubic meter.

31. Location finding unit consists up of a transceiver which transmits or receives data. Transceivers lack unique identifiers. There operation states are – **transmit, receive, idle and sleep. Present day transceivers have inbuilt state machines that perform some operations automatically. Also note that most transceivers operating in idle mode have a power consumption that is almost equal to the power consumed in receive mode.** Hence, it is better to completely shut down the transceiver rather than to leave it in the idle mode when it is not transmitting or receiving. **Note that a significant amount of power is consumed when switching from sleep mode to transmit mode in order to transmit a packet.**

32. Sensor nodes often make use of ISM band that gives free radio, spectrum allocation and global availability.

33. The possible choices of wireless transmission media are radio frequency (RF), optical communication (laser) and infrared.

34. **Also note that lasers require less energy but need line-of-sight for communication, are sensitive to atmospheric conditions. Infrared, like lasers needs no antenna but it is limited in its broadcasting capacity.**

35. **Radio frequency communication is the most relevant that fits most of the WSN applications.**

36. WSNs tend to use **licence-free communication frequencies** like 173, 433, 868 and 915 MHz and 2.4 GHz.

37. The **processor** processes data and controls the functionality of other components in the sensor node. For example, microcontroller, microprocessor, digital signal processors etc.

38. A microcontroller is many a times found in embedded devices like sensors nodes because its cost is less, more flexibility to connect to other devices, easier programming and low power consumption.

39. **Please note that the general-purpose microprocessor generally has higher power consumption than a microcontroller and hence is not considered to a good choice for sensor nodes.** Digital signal processors may be used for broadband wireless communication applications.

However, in WSNs the wireless communication is a good choice. Hence, we say that the advantages of DSPs are not usually of much importance to WSNs.

40. WSNs may be placed at remote areas and changing battery there may be costly. **Please note that more energy is needed for data communication than any other process.** Current sensors are able to **renew their energy** from solar sources, temperature differences or vibrations. There are two power saving policies used namely, **Dynamic Power Management (DPM) and Dynamic Voltage Scaling (DVS). DPM** conserves power by shutting down parts of the sensor node which are not currently used or active. While DVS system varies the power levels within the sensor node depending on the non-deterministic workload. **Also note that by varying the voltage along with the frequency, it is also possible to obtain quadratic reduction in power consumption.**

41. There are four (4) modes by which **sensors detect the objects or sense the data** and are as follows:

   (a) Single Source, Single Object Detection **(SSSO).**

   (b) Single Source, Multiple Object Detection **(SSMO).**

   (c) Multiple Source, Single Object Detection **(MSSO).**

   (d) Multiple Source, Multiple Object Detection **(MSMO).**

In **Single Source, Single Object detection, a single object will be detected by a single sensor node.** The detected data will be sent to the sink node via the intermediate sensors. This is shown in Fig. 2.6(a).

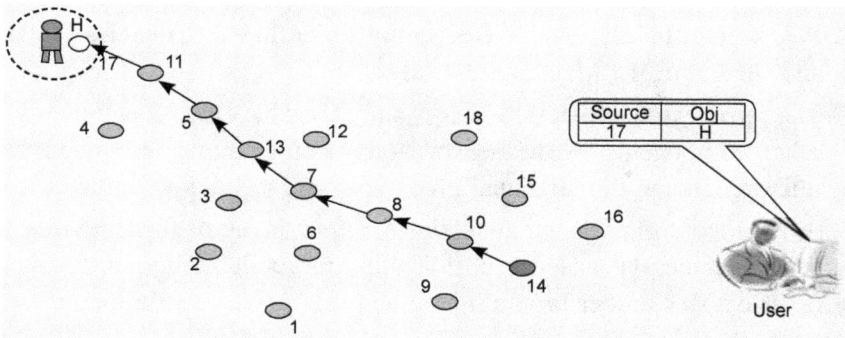

Fig. 2.6(a): Single Source, Single Object Detection (SSSO).

In **Single Source, Multiple Object detection, a single source will detect multiple objects.** The detected data on reaching the sink node will identify various objects. Fig. 2.6(b) shows SSMO detection.

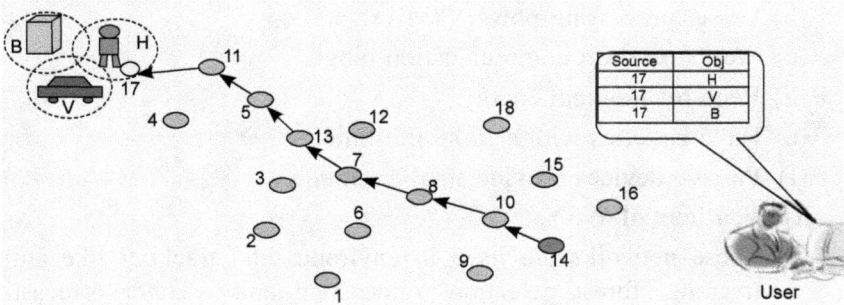

Source	Obj
17	H
17	V
17	B

Fig. 2.6(b): Single Source, Multiple Object Detection (SSMO).

In **Multiple Source, Single Object detection, same object will be detected by multiple sensor nodes.**

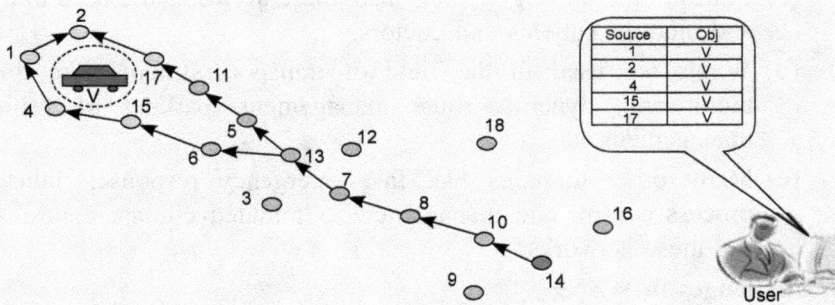

Source	Obj
1	V
2	V
4	V
15	V
17	V

Fig. 2.6(c): Multiple Source, Single Object Detection (MSSO).

In **Multiple Source, Multiple Object detection, more than one object will be detected by more than one sensor node.** This is expensive and can be applied for security critical applications. It is shown in Fig. 2.6(d).

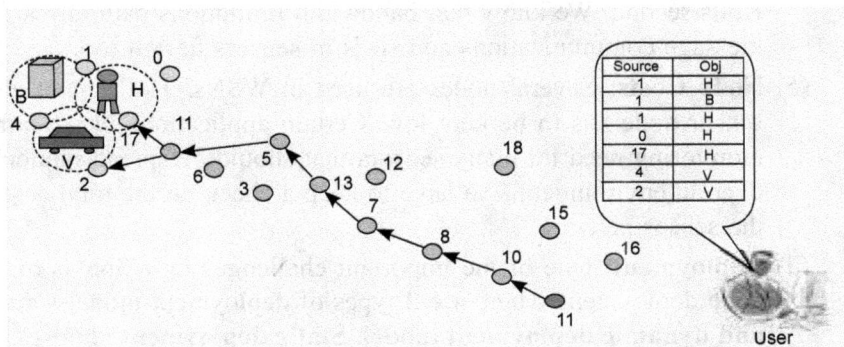

Source	Obj
1	H
1	B
1	H
0	H
17	H
4	V
2	V

Fig. 2.6(d): Multiple Source, Multiple Object Detection (MSMO).

42. **Limitations of WSNs:**

(a) They have small storage capacity (a few KB).

(b) Lesser processing power (8MHz).

(c) Works on short communication range.

(d) Requires minimal energy.

(e) Have batteries with a finite life time.

(f) Passive devices provide smaller energy.

43. **Applications of WSNs**

(a) These networks are used in environmental tracking like animal tracking, forest detection, forecasting and weather forecasting, seismic activities identifications.

(b) Military applications use these networks to track enemy, security threats etc.

(c) In health monitoring systems also, these networks are used to track and monitor patients and doctors.

(d) WSNs are used in the field of transport systems like traffic monitoring, dynamic route management, parking of vehicles management etc.

(e) Many other domains like fast emergency response, industrial process control and management, automated climate control etc. use these networks.

44. **Challenges in WSNs**

Some of the challenges faced by WSNs are as follows:

(a) **Energy Efficiency:** Sensor nodes operate with limited energy budgets.

(b) **Limited Bandwidth:** Lesser power is used in data processing rather than transmitting it. Wireless communications are limited to 10-100 Kbits/second. We know that bandwidth limitations naturally affect message communications and so is in sensors design too.

(c) **Node Costs:** Several nodes are used in WSNs. The cost of each sensor node has to be kept low. Certain applications like weather monitoring need lot many sensors that should be spread randomly over an environment. We have to keep a check on the total cost of the sensor network.

(d) **Deployment:** One of the important challenges in WSNs is of the node deployment. There are 2 types of deployment models- **static and dynamic deployment model. Static deployment chooses the best location according to the optimization strategy and the location of the sensor nodes has no change in the lifetime of the WSN.** On the other hand, **dynamic deployment throws the nodes randomly for optimization.**

(e) **Design Constraints:** As we have studied that **the main objective of WSN is to create smaller, cheaper and more efficient devices.** WSN hardware as well as software design have many challenges with some restricted constraints.

(f) **Security and Privacy:** As far as the security and privacy of WSNs is concerned, we need to consider two things- **node authentication and data confidentiality.**

45. **Sensor Web:** Sensor web is a combination of **Service Oriented Architecture (SOA) + grid computing + sensor networks.** Many sensor nodes form a **web view. Sensor web brings the heterogeneous sensors into an integrated and uniform platform** supporting dynamic discovery and access. The **main goal of a sensor web** is to offer reliable and connectionless services to its end users. **Please note that this means that it provides the middleware infrastructure and the programming environment for creating, accessing and utilizing sensor services through the web.** Its architecture is shown in Fig. 2.7.

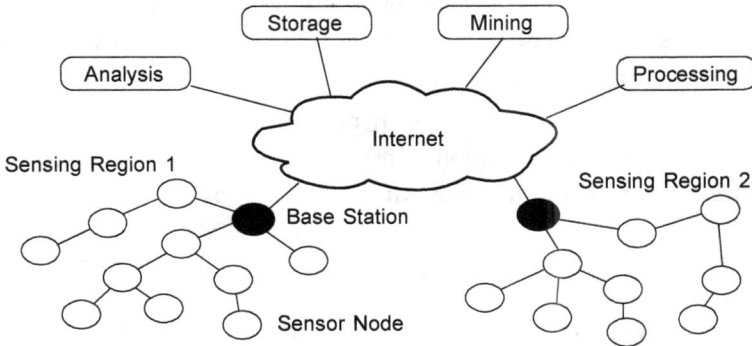

Fig. 2.7: Sensor Web

46. **Sensor Web Enablement (SWE):** It is a standard developed by Open Geospatial Consortium (OGC) that encompasses specifications for interfaces, protocols and encoding that enable discovering, accessing, obtaining sensor data and sensor processing services.

47. **Cooperation and Its Types: WSN nodes communicate with each other with the help of intermediate nodes. These intermediate nodes are called as relays.** Energy considerations of WSNs can also not be ignored. Wireless nodes are energy bound. Nodes may or may not cooperate during WSN communications. Cooperation is of two types:

(a) **Total Cooperation:** From the successor nodes if **all relay requests are accepted** then it is called as **total cooperation.** Here, the nodes will rapidly exhaust limited energy.

(b) **Total Non-cooperation:** Herein, **no relay requests are accepted from the successor nodes. Energy is conserved** but the **network throughput** will go down rapidly.

48. Many **Security Challenges** are found in cooperation also. Some are as follows:

    (a) It is an open, shared medium and dynamically changing I terms of position system. So, putting security into work here is open to challenge.

    (b) No certification authority to implement security in WSNs.

    (c) Malicious code presence is also an open challenge.

    (d) Nodes are vulnerable to attacks, hacking and can be easily captured and compromised by the attacker.

49. Nodes in WSN may be **normal nodes or may be misbehaving nodes.** Misbehaving may be **intentional or unintentional. Intentional behaviour** may be due to **selfish nodes or malicious nodes, unintentional nodes** may be due to **failed nodes or badly failed nodes.**

50. Some nodes in WSNs may misbehave temporarily. Detection of such nodes is needed for smooth functioning of the network. **This temporary misbehaviour is known as dumb behaviour.**

2.3 PARTICIPATORY SENSING TECHNOLOGY

It is the process whereby individuals and communities use even more capable mobile phones and cloud services to collect and analyse systematic data for use in discovery. Participatory sensing is data collection and interpretation. It emphasizes the involvement of citizens and community groups in the process of sensing and documenting where they live, work and play. Participatory sensing can draw on a variety of data collection devices, such as home weather stations and water quality tests but several features of mobile phones make them a special and unprecedented tool for engaging participants in sensing their local environments.

Vehicle Tracking Applications: A number of real-time automotive tracking applications determine the important points of congestion in the city by pooling GPS data from the vehicles in the city. This can be used by other drivers in order to avoid points of congestion in the city. In many applications, such objects may have implicit links among them.

For example, in a military application, different vehicles may have links depending on their unit membership or other related data. Two classic examples of vehicular applications in the context of participatory sensing are the car phone and Green-GPS systems.

Example 2: Biosensors are the analytical devices combined with biological selective elements like enzymes, antibodies, microorganisms, cells etc. They are made in combination with transducer elements to measure the resultant change in any of optical, electrochemical, thermal, pH, mass, piezoelectric or magnetic properties that occurred by binding of cognate analyte from a complex mixture with biosensors. They differ with **physiochemical-based sensors** only in application of biologically derived substances. Just like **chemical sensors,** any specific alteration in these properties that arouse due to enzyme-substrate, antigen-antibody or cell-microbial surface epitope ligands interactions get transduced to generate measurable data. This data is very much useful in the fields of medicine, healthcare, veterinary sciences, food technology, environmental monitoring, biohazard and bio-warfare agent detection. Biosensors based monitoring of crop diseases, soil health etc. in the field of agriculture need a mention. **A potentiometric biosensor** using bIoTin and fluorescein-labelled antibodies was developed for Salmonella detection in poultry. **Nanotechnology + biosensor applications will be used for resolving the current problems of medicine and healthcare.** Viral outbreaks are rapid and rampant. Wearable biosensors and body bionics will be advanced next-generation biosensors that will create real-time data feed. If it is integrated with IoT then it will generate big data.

Example 3: Currently, an efficient design of a **Wireless Sensor Network** has become a leading area of research. *A sensor is a device that responds and detects some type of input from both the physical or environmental conditions like pressure, heat light etc. the output of the sensor is generally an electrical signal that is transmitted to a controller for future processing.*

The point is that these sensors need to be interfaced using software and then uploaded onto the cloud. You need to install **Arduino IDE** (Integrated Development Environment) as it supports most of the available embedded boards in the market. **Many sensors like heartbeat sensor, ultrasonic sound sensor, gyro sensor, obstacle sensor, colour sensor pH sensor also can be interfaced.**

It is also possible to **control LEDs, motor or even a fan through a web page.** We need to create a web page that is used remotely to control an LED. It can also be any other sensor or actuator, other than LED.

Another example of simpler sensors could be **pushbuttons and switches** that allow some user input. Light-dependent-resistors (LDRs) help us to measure ambient light levels. Thermistors are the temperature sensors to measure warmness and sensors for humidity-level measurement are very common now a days. Even your microphones allow you to monitor sounds and audio.

Another type of sensor used in our mobiles is **accelerometer that measures the acceleration that our mobile experiences relative to the freefall. This sensor is used to find out a device's orientation along its three-axes. Now, apps use this data to tell if a phone is in portrait or landscape orientation and whether its screen is facing upward or downward.**

Another type of sensor is **magnetometer that measures the strength amd the direction of the magnetic field.** It is used in compass apps and metal detections apps.

The proximity sensor works by shining a beam of infrared light that is reflected from the object and is picked up by the detector.

Phones too have light sensors, inbuilt barometer etc.

Another sensor: **Pedometer is used to count the number of steps** the user has taken. **Google Nexus** 5 **is a mobile that has a true pedometer** inbuilt into it. Some mobiles like **Galaxy X**5 **also have a heart-rate monitor.** Now a days almost all phones have **fingerprint sensors** also to lock and unlock the phones.

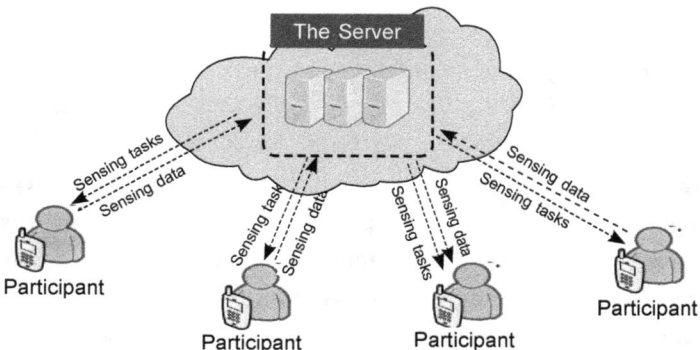

Fig. 2.8: Participatory Sensing Model

Yest another type of sensor is **a radiation sensor. For e.g., The Sharp Pantone 5 has an app to measure the current radiation level in the area.** Cameras, microphones are some more sensors on every mobile.

2.4   EMBEDDED PLATFORMS FOR IoT– EMBEDDED COMPUTING BASICS

To make IoT design possible and easy, an embedded computing board has been developed. Many students do their projects based on these boards. Some of the **commonly available boards in market that are driven by microcontrollers or processors** are as follows:

- Raspberry Pi.
- Arduino.
- NodeMCU.
- Intel Edison.
- Intel UP Squared Grove IoT Development Kit.

Note that all these boards are small but smart. Also note that the cost involved is minimal i.e., they are cheaper and are easily available.

Before discussing their interfacing, let us first of all discuss about Arduino.

Arduino: is a tiny computer that can be connected by the user to the electrical circuits. The brain of this board is Arduino Uno, that is a ATmega328p chip where you can store your programs that will tell Arduino, what to do. Some of the salient features of Arduino are:

1. Arduino is **open-source product, software or hardware** that is accessible and flexible to users. It is flexible as it offers many digital and analog pins.
2. Communication is using a **serial protocol.**
3. Arduino is **cross-platform that can work on Windows, Mac or LINUX platforms too.**
4. You can **install the Arduino IDE** that supports most of the available **embedded boards** in the market. **Arduino is an open-source electronics platform** based on easy-to-use hardware and software. Arduino boards are able to **read inputs** like light on a sensor, a finger on a button or a Twitter message and turn it into an **output** like activating a motor,

turning on an LED, publishing something online. The **Arduino Uno** can be powered via the USB Connection or with an external power supply. The power source is selected automatically. In has 14 digital input/output pins, of which 6 can be used as PWM outputs, 6 analog inputs, a 16 MHz crystal oscillator, a USB connection, a power jack an ICSP header and a rest button. **The board can operate on external voltage supply of 6 to 20 volts. If supplied with less than** 7V then the 5V pin may supply less than 5V and the board may be unstable. On the other hand, **if using more than** 12V, then the voltage regulator may overheat and damage the board. The recommended range is 7 to 12 volts.

5. Some of the boards from Arduino family group are- Arduino Mega, Arduino Micro, Arduino MKR1000 and Flora.

6. Arduino has many applications like LED controlling, LCD displays, servo motors, motion detection, water-level indicator and many more sensors are controlled by Arduino.

7. **Shields are the boards that will expand the functionalities of your** Arduino. **Shields are the boards that will expand the functionalities of your** Arduino. You can just plug them over the top of the Arduino.

Interfacing a Gas Sensor to Arduino

What is this gas sensor? MQ-02/05 is a gas sensor that is being used here. This sensor is capable of detecting H_2 (Hydrogen gas), LPG, CH_4 (methane gas), alcohol and smoke. It is used in malls today to detect smoke/fire so that water can be then sprinkled to control it. Its working is very fast. **Please note that whenever any flammable gas flows through this sensor, the coil inside burns and its resistance decreases. Also note that that is why the output voltage starts increasing, that can be detected using a microcontroller.**

Notes:

1. Greater the gas concentration, greater is the output voltage.

2. Lower the gas concentration, lower is the output voltage.

Interfacing Sensors to a Web Page

The objective is to create a web page that is used to remotely control the LED with the help of NodeMCU. You can even apply the same steps to simulate the working of a motor or a fan through a web page.

The following steps may be followed to connect the LED to NodeMCU:

Step 1: Connect the LED on any preferred pin (any sensor would have the following pins- analog pin, digital pin, GND and VCC (+5V) and change the number in the code i.e., D0, D1, D2,....,Dn has to be properly updated.

Step 2: Feed the SSID and password of the your WIFI network.

Step 3: Now use Arduino IDE - goto Tools - Boards. Select NodeMCU 1.0. then upload the code.

Step 4: Open the serial monitor in the Arduino IDE and then press the RST button in the NodeMCU. An IP is assigned and displayed. It is the IP assigned for NodeMCU.

Step 5: Any browser can be opened from your computer and type URL.

Step 6: You will see ON/OFF buttons on the screen. When you press them, you will observe that LEDs are glowing or turning off.

This is shown in the pin diagram below.

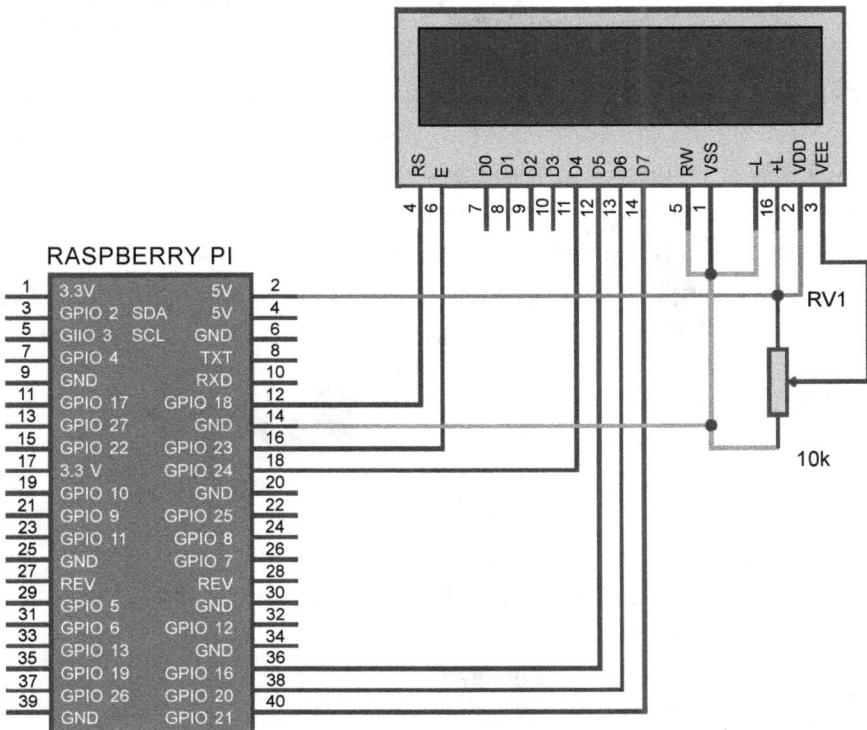

Fig. 2.9: Connection of LED to NODEMCU

Raspberry Pi

A **Raspberry Pi is a credit card-sized computer basically designed for education.** It was inspired by BBC Micro in 1981. Creator Eben Upton's goal was to create a low-cost device that would improve programming skills and hardware understanding at the pre-university level. **Please note that Raspberry Pi is slower than a modern laptop but is still a complete LINUX computer and can provide all expected abilities that implies, at a low-power consumption level.** Various versions of Raspberry Pi are as follows:

Versions	Remarks
Raspberry Pi 1	The original Raspberry Pi had 256MB of RAM which increased to 512 MB in a later version. It has a 26-way GPIO connector.
Pi 0	It includes the GPIO connector but the header pins are not soldered.
Raspberry Pi 2	It swapped the single core processor for a much faster quad-core processor and increased the memory to 1GB RAM.
Raspberry Pi 3	It changes the processor to a more powerful 64-bit processor. It also adds WIFI and Bluetooth which previously needed to be added as a USB device. Another Raspberry Pi 3 model was also launched in 2016.

To get this Raspberry Pi working an SD card needs to be prepared with LINUX OS installed on it. Raspberry Pi users have made many creative projects using this device. It can also be programmed to assist in **housekeeping your network** by functioning as LDAP server, web server, DNS server etc.

The Raspberry Pi foundation recommends Python language. Any language which will compile for ARMv6 can be used. By default, it is installed on C, C++, Java, Scratch and Ruby.

Windows 10 IoT core—a no cost edition of Windows 10 offered by Micrsoft that runs natively on the Raspberry Pi 2.

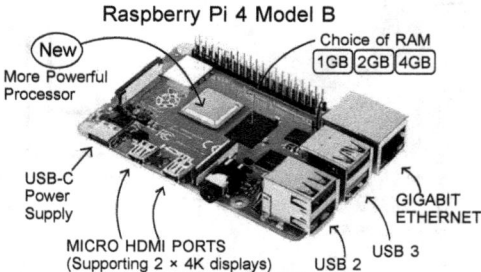

Fig. 2.10: Raspberry Pi Block Diagram

Let us now see the block diagram of a Raspberry Pi.

From the Fig. 2.10, it is seen that **Raspberry Pi does not have a separate CPU, RAM or GPU.** Instead, they are all squeezed into one component called as a **System on Chip or SoC unit.** Raspberry Pi is an **open hardware with the exception of its primary chip,** the Broad-comm SoC which runs the main components of the board—CPU, graphics, memory, USB controller etc. All Raspberry Pi models share the following features:

1. **Operating Systems:** Raspian RaspBMC, Arch LINUX, Rise OS, OpenELEC Pidora. Various OS can be installed on Raspberry Pi through SD cards. Most use a MicroSD slot located on the bottom of the board. The Raspberry Pi primarily uses Raspbian, a Debian-based Linux OS. Many other OS can also run-on Raspberry Pi.

2. **Video Output:** HDMI Composite RCA.

3. **Power Source:** Micro USB.

4. **The Components of** Raspberry Pi are given in a tabular format:

Components	Description
Processor	Raspberry Pi uses an ARM processor which is also installed in a wide variety of mobile phones. This CPU is single core, however, it does not have a co-processor to perform floating point calculations.
Memory	Model B Raspberry Pi has 512MB SDRAM (Synchronous Dynamic RAM). It stores programs that are currently being run in the CPU.
USB Ports	Board has two USB ports. USB port can provide a current up to 100 mA. Using powered hub, it is possible to connect more devices.
HDMI Output	High-Definition Multimedia Interface (HDMI) supports high-quality digital video and audio through a single cable. It is also possible to connect a computer monitor with a DVI connection to HDMI using a converter.
Composite Video Output	It supports composite video output with RCA jack and also support PAL and NTSC. TVDAC pin can be used to output composite video.
Audio Output	Audio output jack is 3.5mm. This jack is used for providing audio output to old TV along with the RCA jack for video.

Components	Description
GPIO Pins	Both models have a total of 26 GPIO pins, organized into one pin header, named the P1 header.
	The newer Raspberry Pi adds 8 more GPIO pins in a new pin header called P5.
	Not all GPIO pins are programmable. Some of them are 5.0 VDC or 3.3 VDC positive power pins, some of them are negative ground pins and a few of them are marked DNC (do not connect).
	The P1 header has 17 programmable pins and the P5 header adds 4 more.
	Reading from various environmental sensors. Writing output to dc monitors, LEDs for status.
Power Input	Micro-USB connector is used for power input.
Status LED	It has 5 status LED.
CSI	Camera Serial Interface (CSI) can be used to connect a camera module to Raspberry Pi.
SD Card slot	This card is used for loading operating system.

Now The Question is What are GPIO Pins?

1. The Raspberry Pi comes with a set of 26 **exposed vertical pins** on the board. These pins are a **General-Purpose Input/Output** interface (GPIO) that is deliberately not linked to any specific native function on the Raspberry Pi board.

2. These GPIO pins are **explicitly for the end users** to have low-level hardware access directly to the board for purpose of attaching other hardware boards, peripherals, LCD display screen and other hardware devices to the Pi.

3. The Raspberry Pi draws its power from a micro-USB port and requires a micro- USB-to-AC adapter. **Please note that because Pi is a microcomputer and not simply a cellular phone getting a battery topped off, you need to use a high-quality charger with stable power delivery that provides a consistent 5V with at least 700 mA minimum output for older model units and 2.5A for Pi 3.**

Is Raspberry Pi Same as a PC?

Let Us Compare These Two Now.

1. In Raspberry Pi, OS is installed on **SD card.** On the other hand, in a PC OS is installed in **hard disk.**

2. Raspberry Pi does not have their own CPU and RAM.

3. **Processing power of Raspberry Pi is less** as compared to PCs.

4. Raspberry Pi uses **less power** than PCs.

Serial, SPI and I2C Interfaces on Raspberry Pi

I. Serial Interface:

1. It uses peripherals for serial communication.

2. Transmit (T_x) and Receive (R_x) pin is used for serial communications.

II. Serial Peripheral Interface (SPI)

1. It is a **communication protocol used to transfer data between micro-computers like Raspberry Pi and peripheral devices.** These peripheral devices may be either **sensors or actuators.**

2. SPI uses 4 **separate connections** to communicate with the target device. These connections are the serial clock (CLK), Master Input Slave Output (MISO), Master Output slave Input (MOSI) and Chip Select (CS).

3. The clock pin sense pulses at a regular frequency, the speed at which Raspberry Pi and SPI device agree to transfer data to each other.

4. For ADC, clock pulses are sampled on their **rising edge, on the transition from low to high.**

5. The MISO pin is a data pin used for the master to receive data from the ADC. Data is read from the bus after **every clock pulse.**

6. The MOSI pin sends data from the Raspberry Pi to the ADC. The ADC will take the value of the bus on the **rising edge** of the clock. **This means that the value must be set before the clock is pulsed.**

7. **The Chip Select (CS)** line chooses which particular SPI device is in use. **If there are multiple SPI devices** then they can all share the same CLK, MOSI and MISO.

III. I2C

1. I2C is a communication protocol that the Raspberry Pi can use **to speak to other embedded devices** like temperature sensors, displays, accelerometers etc.

2. It is s useful bus that allows **data exchange between microcontrollers and peripherals with a minimum of wiring.**

3. **I2C is a two-wire bus,** the connections are called **SDA (Serial Data) and SCL (Serial Clock).** Each I2C bus has one or more masters (Raspberry Pi) and one or more slave devices like the I/O Expander.

4. **As the same data and clock lines are shared between multiple slaves,** we need some way to choose which device to communicate with.

How Raspberry Pi Controls LED?

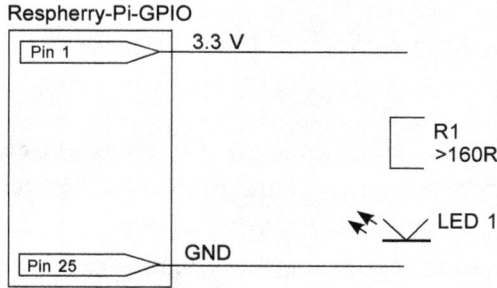

Respherry-Pi-GPIO

Pin 1   3.3 V

R1
>160R

LED 1

Pin 25   GND

But if **multiple LEDs** are to be interfaced then it can be done as follows:

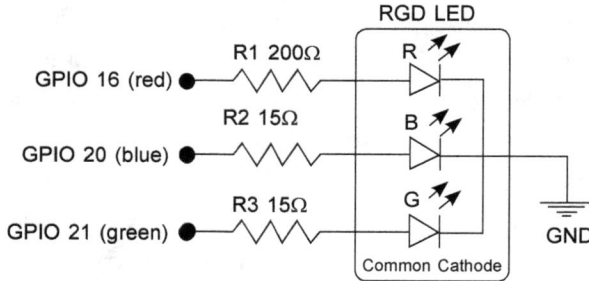

RGD LED

R1 200Ω   R

GPIO 16 (red)

R2 15Ω   B

GPIO 20 (blue)

R3 15Ω   G

GPIO 21 (green)   GND

Common Cathode

In this case LED will initially be OFF as the GPIO pins are initialized as inputs on power ON. The following steps are followed:

1. Install Python 2 library Rpi.GPIO. a library that will let us control the **GPIO pins. Installation Commands are:**
   - sudo apt? get update
   - sudo apt? get install python?dev
   - sudo apt? get install python? rpi.gpio

   As shown in figure that the current flows from anode (+) to cathode (−). **Also note that the anode is longer pin and cathode is shorter pin.**

2. Open up IDLE, the Python programming software and create a New File. Save it as led.py (say) and input the code from the code listing.

Please note that this code tells Python to use the GPIO module, so we can connect to the GPIO pins, by importing the module.

3. Next, **import the time module.** So, we can create a delay between commands. Then we tell the code to treat the GPIO pins as the number, they are on the board and to turn the 7th pin into an output.

4. We alternate between TRUE and FALSE so that it turns the pin ON and OFF. **Once it is cycled a few times,** it will print the message 'Done' into IDLE and finally turn OFF the GPIO pins.

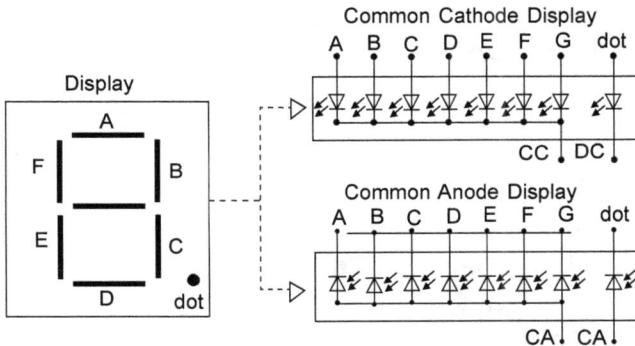

Turn LED ON for 2 seconds and off for 1 sec, loop forever. In this example, we use control LED by controlling the voltage at the anode (+). But it can also be done with cathode (-).

Source code:

```
import RPi.GPIO as GPIO
import time
def main( ):
GPIO.cleanup( )
GPIO.setmode(GPIO.BOARD)        # to use Raspberry Pi board pin nos.
GPIO.setup(11, GPIO.OUT)        # set up GPIO output channel
while True:
GPIO.output(11, GPIO.LOW)       #set RPi board pin 11 low. Turn off
LED.
 time.sleep(1)
GPIO.output(11, GPIO.HIGH)      # set RPi board pin 11 HIGH. Turn
ON LED.
time.sleep(2)
main( )
```

For Example: Display digit on 7-segment LED. It is the most direct way to control display.

S1: Connect pin 3/8 of 7-seg-LED to V_{cc}.

S2: Connect the other 8 pins to 8 GPIO pins.

S3: Configure the 8 GPIO pins as OUT.

For instance, display "2". Turn ON segments A, B, D, E, G and turn off segments C, F, DP. Set A, B, D, E, G to LOW and set C, F, DP to HIGH. Set pin 7, 6, 2, 1, 10 LOW and set pin 4, 9, 5 HIGH.

2.5 COMMUNICATIONS

Let us first of all study sensor data communication protocols.

1. **Direct Transmission Protocols:** The following are the main features of this protocol-
   - In direct communication protocol, **each sensor sends its data directly to the base station. If the base system is far off from the node** then direct communication will require a large amount of transmit power from each node.
   - This will quickly **train the battery of the nodes and reduce the system lifetime.** However, the only receptions in this protocol occurs at the base station, so if either the base station is close to the nodes or the energy required receiving data is large, this may be an acceptable method of communication.

2. **Minimum Transfer Energy (MTE) Protocol:** The following are the main features of this protocol-
   - In these protocols, **nodes act as routers for other nodes** data in addition to sensing the environment. These protocols differ in the way the routes are chosen.
   - Some of these protocols only consider **the energy of the transmitter and neglect the energy dissipation of the receivers** in determining the routes.
   - Depending on the **real-time costs of the transmit amplifier** and the **radio electronics, the total energy expended in the system might actually be greater** using MTE routing than direct transmission to the base station.
   - **Please note that in MTE routing, the nodes closest to the base station will be used to route a larger number of data messages**

to the base station. Also note that that is why these nodes will die out quickly causing the energy required to get the remaining data to the base station to increase and more nodes to die.

(i) Communication Models in IoT

Device-to-Device Communications: This communication is between two or more end devices through an intermediate server via different networks like Internet and to establish communication using protocols like Bluetooth, Zigbee etc. **Note that this model can be used to transfer data packets within devices which operate at small data rate.**

Device-to-Cloud Communications: An **edge device connects directly to an Internet service through wired network or wireless connections** to exchange data to establish a connection between an edge device and an IP network that connects to service provider namely a **cloud.**

Device-to-Gateway Model: The edge device is connected to an intermediate server. **For example,** an application in a smart phone to communicate with device and exchange data with device to cloud service.

Back-end Data Sharing Model: This model analyses **data from cloud along with data from other service providers.** Here, a device is connected directly to a one service provider and meanwhile that service provider also gets the input data from other sources in the background.

Which model to select?

If you have to build a small application like switching ON/OFF the lights, we can use **a simple model** network device to device communication model. Other models focus on cloud services more.

(ii) Communication Protocols in IoT

IoT covers a colossal scope of ventures. It utilizes cases that scale from a solitary compelled device up to enormous **cross-platform arrangements of embedded technologies and cloud frameworks** that are improving every day. Entwinning everything are various heritage and developing protocols for communication that enable devices and servers to communicate with each other in better ways. Next, we provide an outline rundown of mainstream conventions that help IoT in terms of power. This technology is based on **ad-hoc technology/ad-hoc piconets that is a local area network with a very limited coverage. Bluetooth finds its applications** in audio players, home automation, smart phones, toys, hands free headphones and sensor networks.

1. Bluetooth

- A **short distance communication** development.
- A new **Bluetooth Low-Energy (BLE)/Bluetooth Smart** show a rapid growth.
- This Smart/BLE is **not basically for document exchange.** It is better for smaller information.
- Devices that use **Bluetooth Smart port-ins** combine the **Bluetooth Core Specification ver.** 4.**0 or higher,** with a joined vital **information rate and a centre arrangement for a RF handset, baseband and a custom stack.**
- Bluetooth offers a **uniform structure** for a wide range of devices to connect and communicate with each other.
- Bluetooth technology has achieved a **global acceptance** that any Bluetooth enabled device across the worlds can be connected with Bluetooth enabled devices.
- **Low power consumption** of Bluetooth technology.
- **Range of up to** 10 **meters** have paved the way for several usage models.
- It offers **interactive conference** by establishing an **ad-hoc network of laptops.**
- **Bluetooth usage** model includes cordless computer, intercom, cordless phone and mobile phones.
- Bluetooth technology operates in unlicensed industrial, scientific and medical ISM band at 2.4 to 2.48 GHz.
- It uses spread spectrum hopping, full-duplex signal at a nominal rate of 1600 hops/sec.
- It supports 1Mbps data rate for ver. 1.2 and 3 Mbps data rate for ver. 2.0 combined with error data rate.
- Bluetooth operating range depends on the device.
- **Note that the transmit power and therefore the range of a Bluetooth module is defined by its power class.** There are 3 defined classes of power as follows:

Class Number	Max. Output Power (dBm)	Max. Output Power (mW)	Max. Range
Class 1	20 dBm	100 mW	100m
Class 2	4 dBm	2.5 mW	10m
Class 3	0 dBm	1mW	100 cm

Here, class 3 radios have a range of up to 1 meter or 3 feet.

Class 2 radios are mostly found in mobile devices having a range of 10m or 30 feet.

Class 1 radios are basically in industrial use cases having a range of 100 meters or 300 feet.

- Every single Bluetooth device has a unique 48-bit address (called as BD_ ADDR). This will usually be presented in form of a 12-digit HEX value. The **most significant half** (24 bits) of the address is an organization unique identifier (OUI), which identifies the manufacturer. The **lower 24-bits** are the more unique part of the address. This address should be visible on most Bluetooth devices

- To create Bluetooth devices between two devices we follow the following steps

- **Inquiry:** If two Bluetooth devices know nothing about each other, then one must run an inquiry to try to discover the other. One device sends out the inquiry request and any device listening for such a request will respond with its address and its name and other information.

- **Paging/Connecting: Paging is defined as the process of forming a connection between two Bluetooth devices.** Before this connection can be initiated, each device needs to know the address of the other, that is found in the inquiry process.

- **Connection:** After a device has completed the paging process, it enters the connection state. While connected, a device can either be **actively participating** or it can be put into **a low power sleep mode.**

Please note that when two Bluetooth devices share a special affinity for each other, they can be bonded together. Also note that bonded devices can automatically establish a connection whenever they are close enough. These bonds are nothing else but pairing that occurs between the connecting Bluetooth devices only. It is seen that when these devices pair, then they share their addresses, names and profiles and store them in memory. **Also, they share a common secret key that allows them to bond**

whenever they are together in future also. This **pairing process needs an authentication** wherein a user must validate the connection between devices. The **flow of the authentication process varies and depends on the interface capabilities** of one device or another.

2. Zigbee

Zigbee is an IEEE 802.15.4 based specification for a suite of high-level communication protocols used to create PANs i.e., Personal Area Networks with small, low-digital radios like for home automation, medical device data collection etc. It is designed for small scale projects that need wireless connection. Hence, **Zigbee is a low-power, low data rate and close proximity** (personal area) **wireless ad-hoc network.** Some of its features are:

- **It's** low power consumption limits transmission distances to 10-100 meters LOS (line-of-sight). It depends on the power output and environmental conditions.
- **Zigbee devices can transmit data over long distances through a mesh network of intermediate devices to reach more remote ones.**
- **Zigbee** is used in low data rate applications that require long battery life and secure networking.
- **Zigbee Networks** are secured are secured by 128-**bit symmetric encryption keys.**
- **Zigbee has a defined rate of** 250 **Kbits/s,** that is best option for intermittent data transmissions from a sensor or input device.
- **Zigbee** that is IEEE 802.15.4 standard, offers star, tree and mesh topologies.

Star Topology: The star topology consists of a **coordinator** (c) and several end devices/ nodes (E).

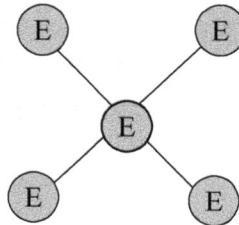

Fig. 2.11: Star Topology in Zigbee

Where, C = Coordinator

E = End device.

In this topology, the end device communicates only with the coordinator. Any packet exchange between end devices must go through the coordinator.

Advantages: It is a simple topology and packets go through at most two hops to reach their destination.

Disadvantages: The **operation of the network depends on the coordinator** of the network. Because **all packets between devices must go through coordinator, the coordinator may become bottleneck.** Also, there is no alternative path from the source to the destination.

Tree Topology: Here, the network consists of a **central node/root tree which is a coordinator, several routers and end devices.** The **function of the router** is to extend the network coverage. The **end nodes** that are connected to the coordinator or the routers are known as **children. Please note that only routers and the coordinator can have children.** Each end device is only able to communicate with its **parent** (router or coordinator). The **coordinator and routers can have children** and thus are the only devices that can be parents. An **end device cannot have children** and hence may not be parent. A special case of tree topology is known as **cluster tree topology.** The tree topology is shown in Fig. 2.12.

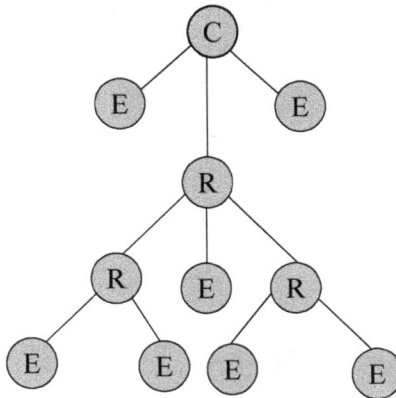

Fig. 2.12: Tree Topology in Zigbee

Where E = End Device

C = Coordinator

R = Router.

Disadvantages of Tree Topology

1. If one of the parents become disabled, then the children of the disabled parent cannot communicate with other devices in the network.

2. Even if the two nodes are geographically close to each other, they cannot communicate directly.

Note: Cluster-tree topology is a special case of tree topology only in which a parent with its children is called as a cluster. Each cluster is identified by a cluster ID. Zigbee does not support cluster tree topology. But IEEE STANDARD 802.15.4 does support it.

Mesh Topology: It is also known as a peer-to-peer network. It consists of one coordinator, several routers and end devices and is shown in Fig. 2.13 below-

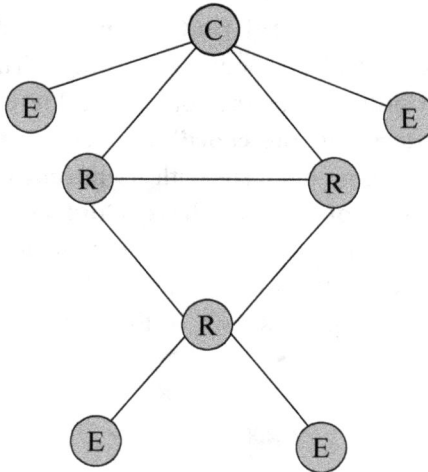

Fig. 2.13: Mesh Topology in Zigbee

Where E = End device
      C = Coordinator
      R = Router.

Characteristics of Mesh Topology

1. A mesh topology is a **multi-hop network. Packets pass through multiple hops to reach their destination.**
2. **The range of network** can be increased by adding more devices to the network.
3. It can eliminate **dead zones.**
4. A mesh topology is **self-healing. It means that during transmission, if a path fails, the node will find an alternate path to the destination node.**

5. Devices can be close to each other so that they can use less power.

6. Adding or removing a device is easy.

7. Any source device can communicate with any destination device in the network.

Disadvantages of Mesh Topology

1. It requires greater overhead.

2. It uses a complicated routing protocol than a star topology.

3-types of ZigBee Devices are Found:

(a) **ZigBee Coordinator (ZC):** ZC forms the **root** of the ZigBee network tree and may act as **a bridge between networks.** There is a single ZigBee coordinator in each network that initially initiates the network. It stores information about the network under it and outside it. **Please note that it acts as a trust centre and repository for security keys.**

(b) **ZigBee Router (ZR): ZigBee Routers** are capable of running applications as well as relaying information between nodes connected to it. **Also note that routers can act as an intermediate router, passing on data from other devices.**

(c) **ZigBee End Device (ZED):** It contains just enough **functionality** to talk to the parent node, either the coordinator or a router. It **cannot relay data** from other devices. This relationship allows the node to be asleep a significant amount of time thereby giving **long battery life.** A ZED requires **least amount of memory** and therefore can be less expensive to manufacture than a ZR or ZC.

Applications of ZigBee

Some applications of ZigBee are as follows:

1. Building **automation.**

2. Remote control (RF4CE or RF for consumer electronics).

3. **Smart energy** for home energy monitoring.

4. **Healthcare** for medical and fitness monitoring.

5. **Home automation** for control of smart homes.

6. **Light link** for control of LED lighting.

7. **Telecom** services.

2.6 6LoWPAN

6LoWPAN is an abbreviation of **IPv6 over Low-Power Wireless Personal Area Networks.** The concept originated from the idea that- **"the Internet Protocol could and should be applied even to the smallest devices and that low-power devices with limited processing capabilities should be able to participate in IoT."** It allows **low power devices** to connect to the Internet. 6LoWPAN was created by Internet Engineering Task Force (IETF). 6LoWPAN protocol is based on IPv6. It operates in a **fully asynchronous way.** It uses a **mesh topology.** It uses a **routing algorithm** which does not take care of the **sleeping node.** So, it needs approaches like **low power listening for energy saving purpose.**

Features of 6LoWPAN

1. It allows IEEE 802.15.4 radios to carry 128-bit addresses of Internet Protocol Version 6 (IPv6).
2. Header compression and address translation techniques allow the IEEE 802.15.4 802.15.4 radios to access the Internet.
3. IPv6 packets are compressed and reformatted to fit the IEEE 802.15.4 packet format.
4. Requires low bandwidth.
5. Consumes low power and are battery operated only.
6. It supports star and mesh topologies.
7. Relatively low cost with other technologies.
8. The 128-bits of IPv6 are divided into 2 parts- The network prefix (64-bits) and the host address (64-bits).
9. The 6LoWPAN header compression mechanism omits the 64 most significant bits (network prefix) because they are fixed for a given 6LoWPAN.
10. The least significant 64-bits can address a very large address space, up to (1.84467441 * 1019).
11. Hence, 6LoWPAN provides options for compressing the host address, the common usage is 16 bits.
12. **Note that a 128-bit IPv6 address can be compressed down to** 16 **bits using 6LoWPAN.**

13. 6LoWPAN has 3 types of headers- dispatch header, mesh addressing header and fragmentation header.

14. **Dispatch Header is a 32-bit Header.** 0, 1 is the identifier for **dispatch type. Dispatch** actually initiates communication and is 6-bit and it identifies the next header type. The **Type Specific Header** is determined by the Dispatch header. (see figure).

15. **Mesh Addressing Header is a 32-bit Header.** 0, 1 is the **identifier** for mesh addressing header. V has 2 values 0 and 1. **The value of V is 0,** if the originator is 64-bit extended address and 1 if 16-bit address. Also, F has 2 values—0 and 1. **The value of F is 0** if destination is 64-bit address and 1 if 16-bit address. **Hops left** is decremented by each node before sending to the next hop. **Originator address** is the source address and **Final address** is the destination address. (see figure).

16. **Fragmentation Header:** In fragmentation header, the first fragment is 32-bits. And the subsequent fragment is also 32-bits. Two cases arise here:

   (a) **If The Datagram Fits Within a Single 802.15.4 frame,** then it is unfragmented and the 6LoWPAN encapsulation should not contain a fragmentation header.

   (b) **If The Datagram Does Not Fit Within a Single IEEE 802.15.4 frame, then** it shall be broken into link fragments.

   Please note that as the fragment offsets can only express multiples of 8-bytes, all link fragments for a datagram except the last one must be multiples of 8-bytes in length. Also note that the first link fragment shall contain the first fragment header and the second and subsequent link fragments shall contain a fragmentation header.

   The Fig. 2.5 below show the packet format of 6LoWPAN, its headers, fragmentation headers.

   Version: 4-bit Internet Protocol version number = 6.

   Traffic Class: 8-bit traffic class field.

   Flow Label: 20-bit flow label.

   Payload Length: 6-bit unsigned integer. Length of the IPv6 header is in octets.

   Next Header: 8-bit selector. Identifies header type immediately following the IPv6 header. Uses the same values as the IPv4 protocol field.

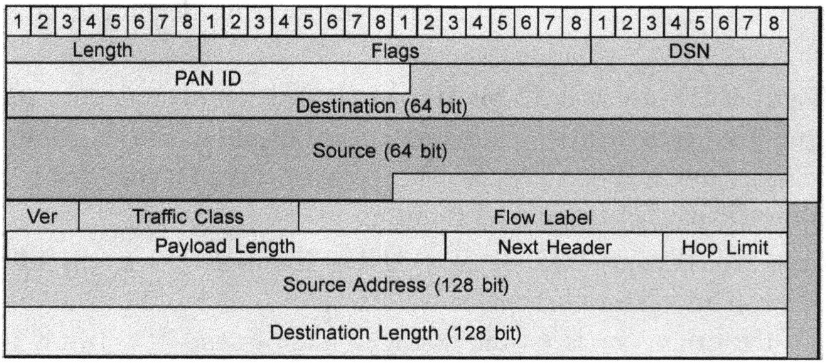
1 2 3 4 5 6 7 8 1 2 3 4 5 6 7 8 1 2 3 4 5 6 7 8 1 2 3 4 5 6 7 8
Length
Flags
DSN
PAN ID
Destination (64 bit)
Source (64 bit)
Ver
Traffic Class
Flow Label
Payload Length
Next Header
Hop Limit
Source Address (128 bit)
Destination Length (128 bit)

Hop Limit: *8-bit unsigned integer. Decremented by 1 by each node that forwards the packet. The packet is discarded if the hop limit is decremented to zero.*

Source Address: *128-bit address of the originator of the packet.*

Destination Address: *128-bit address of the intended recipients of the packet.*

There are 3-types of 6LoWPAN Headers and are shown below.

01	000001	IPv6 Uncompressed		
01	000010	PPv6 HCL Compressed Encoding		
01	111111	Additional Dispatch byte		
Dispatch Header				
10	O	P	Hops Left	Orig. Address, Final Address
Mesh Header				
11	100	Datagram Size		Datagram Tag
First Fragment Heade				
11	100	Datagram Size		Datagram Tag
Datagram Offset				
Subsequent Fragment Header				

We have already discussed about the dispatch and mesh headers. Let us see the parts of fragmentation header now.

(a) **Datagram Size: It is a 11-bit field that encodes the size of the entire IP packet before link layer fragmentation but after IP layer fragmentation.** The value of Datagram size shall be the same for all link-layer fragments of an IP packet. For IPv6, this shall be 40 octets (i.e., the size of uncompressed IPv6 header) more than the value Payload Length in the IPv6 header of the packet. **Also note that this packet may already be fragmented by hosts involved in the communication i.e.,** this field needs to encode a maximum length of 1280 octets.

(b) **Datagram Tag: The value of the datagram tag shall be the same for all link-fragments of a payload (like IPv6) datagram.** The **sender** shall increment **Datagram Tag** for successive and fragmented datagrams. The incremented value of Datagram Tag shall **wrap from 65,535 back to zero.** This field is 16 bits long and its **initial value is not defined.**

(c) **Datagram Offset:** This field is present only in the second and subsequent link fragments. It shall specify the **offset in increments of 8 octets,** of the fragment from the beginning of the payload datagram. The first octet of the datagram like the start of IPv6 header, has an **offset of zero, the implicit value of Datagram Offset in the first link fragment is zero.** This field is 8-bits long.

Routing in 6LoWPAN

- Routing per se is a two phased problem that is being considered for 6LoWPAN
  1. **Mesh Routing** in the PAN Space
  2. Routability of packets **to/from the IPV6 domain from/to the PAN domain**.
- Some of the routing protocols currently being developed by 6LoPAN Community those are **Load, Dymo-Low, Hi-Low**.

There are many types of protocols but the common ones are LOADng and RPL. Figure below shows nodes in a mesh network and a gateway node to IPv6 domain.

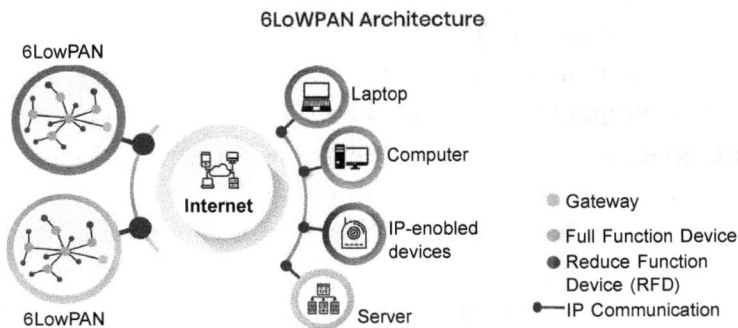

6LoWPAN Architecture

6LowPAN

Laptop

Computer

Internet

IP-enabled devices

Server

6LowPAN

Gateway
Full Function Device
Reduce Function Device (RFD)
IP Communication

Fig. 2.14: Routing in 6LoWPAN

For Instance,

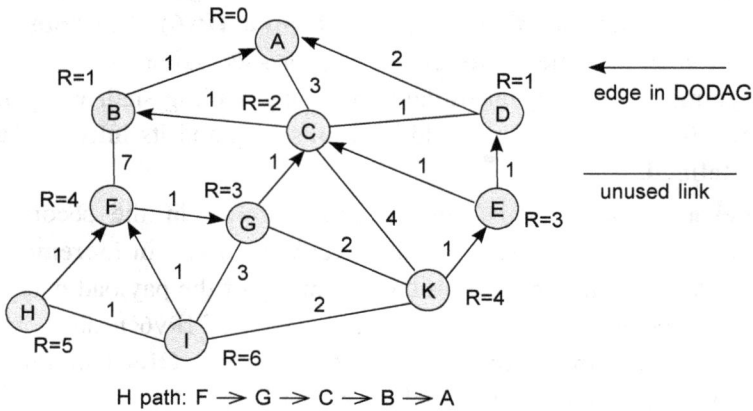

H path: F → G → C → B → A

Let us discuss these two routings now.

1. **LOADng Routing:** From Ad-hoc-Demand Distance Vector (AODV), a routing protocol designed for wireless and mobile ad-hoc networks, LOADng protocol has been derived. AODV protocol establishes routes to destinations on demand, however, LOADng routing is **extended for use in IoT.** Some tasks of LOADng includes generation of Route Requests (RREQs) by a LOADng router (originator) for discovering a route to a destination, forwarding of such RREQs until they reach the destination LOADng router, generation of Route Replies (RREPs), if a route is detected to be broken then a Route Error (RERR) message is returned to the **originator** of that data packet to inform the originator about the route breakage, optimized flooding is supported, reducing the overhead incurred by RREQ generation and flooding. Only the destination is permitted to respond to an RREQ. **Also note that the RREQ/RREP messages generated by a given LOADng router share a single unique monotonically increasing sequence number.**

2. **RPL Routing: RPL is an abbreviation for IPv6 Routing Protocol for Low-Power and Lossy Networks.** This routing maintains routing topology using **low-rate beaconing. Please note that beaconing rate increases on detecting inconsistencies like** node/link in a route is down. Herein, the routing information is included in the datagram itself. It follows either **proactive routing** that maintains a routing topology or a **reactive routing** which resolves routing inconsistencies. RPL separates **packet processing and forwarding from the routing optimization**

objectives (like energy minimization, latency minimization, constraints satisfaction of node power bandwidth etc.) which helps **low-power lossy networks** (LLN). Also, RPL supports **message confidentiality and integrity.** It supports **data path validation and loop detection.** RPL operations require **bidirectional links.** In some LLNs, those links may exhibit **asymmetric properties. Also note that the reachability of a router should be verified before the router can be used as a parent.**

4. RFID (RADIO-FREQUENCY IDENTIFICATION)

RFID or Radio Frequency Identification is a simple and cheaper way of a device/object/item identification. It uses the phenomenon of **Electromagnetic Fields only.** It is being used today by industries to automatically identify and track the tags connected to objects. Actually, tags in RFID store data electronically. RFID system consists of two parts- **time and reader.** The **top component** consists of a **microchip** and this chip is used to store and process information. The 2nd part is **antenna** that is also used in the top-right and is needed for receiving and transmitting a signal. In order to read the information encoded on a tag we use a **radio transmitter-receiver** which is called as **interrogator or a reader** and this emits a signal to the tag. Then the time will be spawned with the information from the magnet back, the reader will then transmit the results, read so far, to an RFID computer program.

The following are some of the **salient features of RFID:**

1. RFID systems can be seen as a next generation technology for **bar-codes.**

2. RFID devices are **wireless microchips** used for tagging objects for **automated identification.**

3. RFID tag is a simplified, low cost, disposable **contactless smart card.**

4. RFID tags include a **chip that stores a static number (ID) and attributes of the tagged object and an antenna** that enables the chip to transmit the stored number to a reader.

5. Tags are characterised by a **unique identifier** and are applied to objects. Readers trigger the tag transmission by generating an appropriate signal which represents a query for the possible presence of tags in the surrounding area and for the reception of their IDs.

6. Figure 2.15 below shows a basic RFID system.

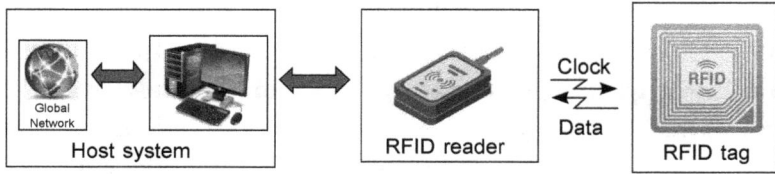

Fig. 2.15: RFID System

7. As shown in figure, RFID systems consist of a reading device called as a **reader, and one or more tags.** The reader is a powerful device with lot of memory and computational resources.

8. **Passive Tags** have limited computational capacity, no ability to sense the channel, detect collisions and communicate with each other. They respond only at the reader commands. They collect energy via radio waves.

9. **Semi-passive Tags** have an on-board power source that can be used to energise their microchip.

10. **Active Tags** sense the channel and detect collisions. They need a battery source to operate at a distance of about 100 meters from the RFID reader.

11. **Please note that accordingly, RFID systems can be used to monitor objects in real-time without the need of being in LOS** (LINE-OF-SIGHT). This allows for mapping the real world into the virtual world.

12. **An RFID system involves hardware known as readers and tags as well as RFID software or RFID middleware.** Readers can also be mobile or hand-held.

13. **RFID systems operate in the industry, Scientific and Medical (ISM) frequency band that ranges from 100 KHz to 5.8 GHz.**

14. **RFID technology has been deeply embedded to IoT** to identify devices and to link these devices to the internet.

15. RFID **communicates on ISO-EPC global standards and operate at** 120KHz-150KHz or 13.56MHz and 433MHz.

16. **Range** of RFID communication is about 10 to 100m operating at 10-100 Kbps.

17. Basic **applications** of RFID include toll tax collections, goods tracking, smart dust, airport baggage tracking and so on.

RFID Anti-collision Procedure

Collision due to simultaneous tag responses is one of the key issues in RFID systems. **Tag collision results in wastage of bandwidth, energy and increases identification delays.** RFID readers must use an **anti-collision protocol** to reduce collisions and hence help reduce the identification delays. Tag collision happens **when two or more tags reflects-back their individual identification radio signals to the reader** at the same time thus confusing the reader identification process.

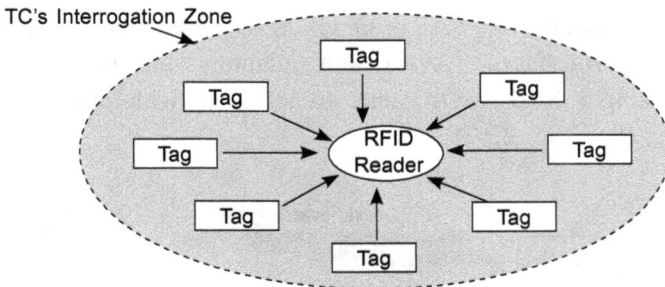

Fig. 2.16: RFID Anti-collision Procedure

RFID **anti-collision protocols** are often categorized as ALOHA -based protocols and tree-based protocols. In **pure ALOHA-based RFID systems,** a tag responds with its ID randomly after being energized by a reader. On the other hand, **in slotted ALOHA-based RFID systems,** tags transmit their id in synchronous time slots. The collision occurs at **slots boundary** only. Hence, there are **no partial collisions.**

RFID Middleware and Its Benefits

1. RFID middleware needs to allow users to configure, deploy and issue commands directly to readers through a common interface. **For instance,** users should be able to tell a reader when to **"turn-off"** if needed.
2. The following figure shows **RFID middleware**
3. After RFID middleware **captures EPC data from the readers,** it must be able to **intelligently filter and route the data** to a suitable destination.
4. Look for middleware that includes both **low-level logic and more complex algorithms. Comprehensive solutions** also offer tools for **aggregating and managing EPC data in either a federated or central data source.**

5. **RFID middleware solutions** need to provide the **messaging, routing and connectivity features** required to reliably integrate RFID data into existing SCM, ERP, WMS or CRM systems, ideally through a **service-oriented architecture (SOA).**

6. SOA is essentially **a collection of services.** These services communicate with each other. The communication can involve either simple data exchange or two or more services coordinating some activity such as order placement or inventory control.

7. Middleware needs to provide **a library of adapters** to popular WMS and SCM applications like SAP or Oracle E -Business Suite. Application Programming Interfaces (APIs) and adapters for using standard technologies like XML, SOAP etc. to integrate with other 3rd party applications (See Fig. 2.17).

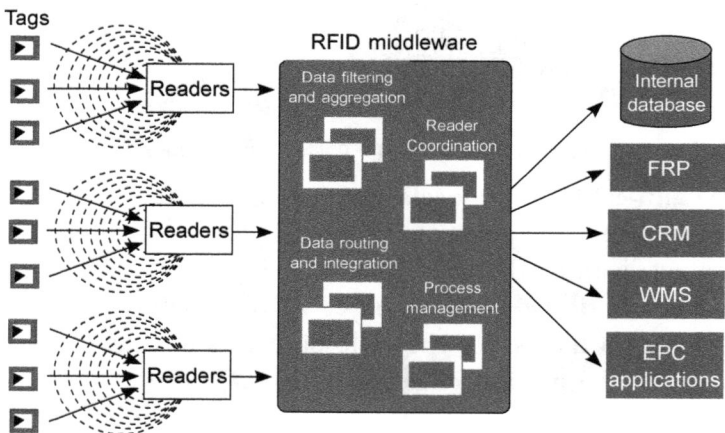

Fig. 2.17: RFID Middleware

8. RFID Middleware Should Provide The Following:

• B2B integration features like **partner profile management.**

• Support for **B2B transport protocols.**

• **Integration with a partner's data over communications** like EDI, web-based systems like AS2 or a well engineered system specifically for EPC data RFID Middleware.

• RFID middleware platforms that include **packaged routing logic, product data schemes and integration** with typical RFID-related applications and processes like shipping, receiving and asset tracking are major assets.

- RFID middleware platforms must include features for **dynamically balancing processing loads** across **multiple servers** and **automatically rerouting data.**

Uses of RFID Middleware

The following are some benefits of RFID middleware:

- **Minimized network traffic** through **intelligent filtering.**
- **Lower reader management costs** through centrally coordinated readers.
- Immediate visibility to pertinent RFID data through **routing, filtering and track-and-trace tools.**
- **Minimized on-going integration costs** through standard APIs and **pre-packaged application integration tools.**
- **Well-architected RFID middleware** can enable more strategic opportunities that go way beyond these initial rather obvious benefits.

Drawbacks of RFID Middleware

The following are some drawbacks of RFID middleware:

- RFID needs **costly batteries** use.
- They can be easily **intercepted** (tapped).
- It needs **time and cost.**
- It should be **programmed.**
- **Loss of jobs** if labour is unskilled.
- Its coverage **range is limited** to 3m.

Applications of RFID Systems

RFID applications fall under two main categories:

(a) **Short Range Applications:** Here, the reader and the tag are in close proximity like in access control.

(b) **Medium to Long Applications:** where the distance may be greater.

Some of the applications of RFID are as follows:

1. **Asset Tracking:** This system can **read multiple tags at once.** So, it is possible to easily locate the assets.

2. **Supply Chain Management (SCM):** (RFID + SCM), together has **improved the impact of SCM further, total inventory cost has been reduced and it has even increased customer satisfaction.**

3. **Manufacturing Industries** have also been benefitted as they can now **monitor their process of production and improve it** further and thus gain more efficiencies with access to **real-time data.**

4. **Contactless Payments** are also possible because of RFID systems only.

5. **Retailers** are using this technology in order **to improve supply chain visibility and also to reduce the chances of out-of-stock of items.**

6. **Better Security:** RFID systems are secure to use. this is because of contactless access. Also, it provides time and attendance information for better security purposes.

Case Study of RFID Usage

1. The US military and commercial industry use RFID technology to streamline and increase business practices.

2. Pacific Northwest National Lab. (PNNL) is using this technology for different types of markets.

3. In Europe, Munich City Library has the largest RFID -based library.

4. Electronic labelling (e-labelling) are RFID tags that appear on shipping boxes, for instance. E-label is made from polyethylene media and PCB driven by a copper coil antenna. **Please note that the tag has no power supply attached to itself. Also note that the tag is energized by signal waves that are broadcast from the reader antenna.**

2.7 HART AND WIRELESS HART

Some of the main features of HART and wireless HART are as follows:

1. It is an acronym for **Highway Addressable Remote Transducer Protocol.**

2. **Wireless HART is the current release of HART.**

3. HART standard was developed for **networked smart field devices.**

4. The wireless protocol makes the implementation of HART **cheaper and easier.**

5. HART covers, the greatest number of **field devices** available in any field network.

6. Wireless HART enables **device placements more accessible and cheaper** like the top of a reaction tank, inside a pipe or at widely separated warehouses.

7. HART includes 5 layers of the OSI model: physical layer, data link layer, network layer, transport layer and application layer.

8. The main difference between the wired and unwired versions is in the physical layer, data link layer and network layer. **Also note that the wired HART does not have a network layer.**

At this junction, we should compare wireless HART and ZigBee.

Wireless HART	ZigBee
A wireless HART node hops after every message changing channels every time it sends a packet.	It does not feature hopping at all and hops only when the entire network hops.
At the MAC layer, wireless HART utilizes Time Division Multiple Access (TDMA) allotting individual time slots for each transmission.	It applies Carrier Sense Multiple Access with Collision Detection (CSMA/CD).
It represents a true mesh network where each node is capable of serving as a router so that if one node goes down, another can replace it ensuring packet delivery.	It utilizes a tree topology that makes nodes along the trunk critical.
Wireless HART devices are all backward compatible allowing for the integration of legacy devices as well as new ones.	It shares the same basis for their physical layers but ZigBee, ZigBee Pro, ZigBee IP are otherwise incompatible with each other.

2.8 NEAR FIELD COMMUNICATION (NFC)

Some of The **Main Features** of NFC are as Follows:

1. It is a form of **contactless communication** between devices like smart phones or tabs.

2. It allows a **user to wave the smart phone** over a NFC compatible device to send information without needing to touch the devices together or go through multiple steps setting up a connection.

3. It maintains **interoperability between different wireless communication methods** like Bluetooth and other NFC standards like FeliCa, that is popular in Japan.

4. It is a **fast and easier technology** and is very popular in USA, EUROPE and some parts of Asia too.

5. The NFC Forum enforces **strict standards that manufacturers** must meet when designing NFC compatible devices.

6. NFC's **data transmission frequency** is 13.56 MHz.

7. NFC can transmit **data at a rate** of either 106, 212 or 424 Kbps. **Tags** store between 96 and 512 bytes of data.

8. **Communication Range** is less than 20 cm.

9. NFC has many **applications** like smart phone-based payments, parcel tracking, information tags in posters, computer games, toys, low power home automation systems etc.

10. It is a **wireless connection** and is similar to the connection of other technologies like WIFI or Bluetooth but with a shorter range, generally between 10 and 20 cm. its short range allows for avoiding possible security problems like reading of our transmission.

11. It has almost immediate connection with a **transfer rate** that can reach 424 Kbit/s.

12. The chips included in NFC technology do not need to be connected to a main battery. This is its **autonomy.**

Working of NFC

Principle: "It works on the principle of magnetic induction. A reader emits a small electric current which creates a magnetic field that in turn bridges the physical space between the devices. The generated field is received by a similar coil in the client device where it is turned back into electrical impulses to communicate data like id number, status information or any other information." It is shown in figure below. **Passive NFC tags use the energy from the reader to encode their response while active or peer-to-peer tags have their own power source.**

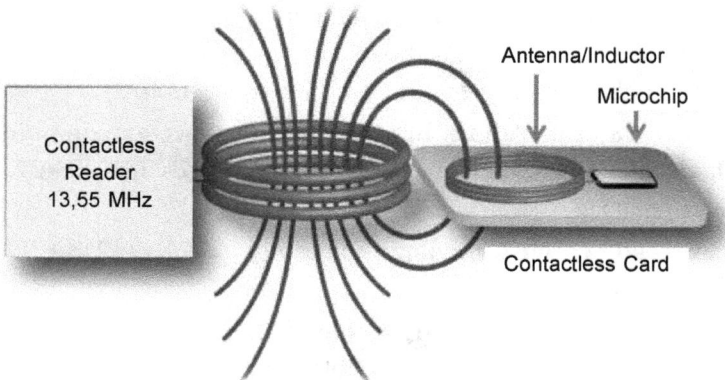

Fig. 2.18: NFC Working

Types of NFCs

NFC Devices are of Two Types:

(a) Passive Devices.

(b) Active Devices.

Passive devices are those devices that contain information which is readable by other devices. But it cannot read information itself. In supermarkets of a mall, we find NFC tags that are the clear examples of passive NFC only.

Active devices are able to collect as well as transmit the information. Smart phones/ mobile phones are good examples of active devices only.

Please note that NFC tags are passive devices that can be used to communicate with active NFC devices i.e., an active NFC reader/writer. The NFC tags can be used within applications like posters. Within the poster the **live area can be used as a touch point** for the active NFC device. The stored data on the NFC tag may contain any form of data. Common applications are to store URLs from where the NFC device may find further information. Here, NFC tags may also be used. As studied, NFC tag is a passive deice with no power of its own. When users touch an NFC device on the tag. **Also note that a small amount of power is taken by the NFC tag from the reader/writer to power the tag electronics. Then the tag is used to transfer a small amount of information to the reader/writer. Data stored in the tag memory is transferred to the NFC enabled device.** There will be a small amount of data in the tag memory that may be used to direct the device to a website URL.

Modes of Operation of NFC

There are three modes of operation of NFC. They are as follows:

(a) **Reader/Writer Mode:** The NFC device is capable of reading NFC Forum-mandated tag types like as tag embedded in an NFC smart poster. This mode on RF interface is compliant with the ISO 14443 and FeliCa schemes.

(b) **Peer-to-Peer Mode:** Two NFC devices can exchange data. **For example,** we can share Bluetooth or WIFI link set-up parameters or we can exchange data such as virtual business cards or digital photos. (Note: It is standardized on ISO/IEC 18092 standard).

(c) **Card Emulation:** Here, the NFC device appears to an external reader much the same as a traditional contactless smart card. This enables contactless payments and ticketing by NFC devices without changing the existing infrastructure.

All these 3 modes are shown in Fig. 2.19 below.

Fig. 2.19: Three Modes of Operation of NFC

7. BLUETOOTH

It has already been discussed in section 2.5 in this chapter.

8. Z-WAVE

Some Main Features of Z-wave are as Follows:

1. It is a **protocol for communication among devices** used for home automation.

2. It uses **RF for signalling and control.**

3. It was developed by **Zensys Inc.**, a company at Denmark.

4. Z-wave was released in 2004.

5. Based on the concepts of ZigBee, Z-wave tries to build **simpler and less expensive devices** than ZigBee.

6. **Z-wave Operates at 908.42 MHz in USA, 868.42 MHz in Europe using a mesh networking topology.**

7. A Z-wave network can contain up to **230 nodes.** Some problems have been, however, reported with networks containing over 30-40 nodes.

8. Z-wave operates using a number of **profiles** but the manufacturer claims they **interoperate.**

9. Z-wave uses **Gaussian Frequency Shift Keying (GFSK) modulation and Manchester channel encoding.**

10. In GFSK, *baseband pulses are passed through a Gaussian filter prior to modulation.* **The process of filtering operation that smoothens the pulses consisting of streams -1 and +1 is known as pulse shaping. Pulse shaping limits the modulated spectrum width.**

11. In data transmission, **Manchester encoding is a form of digital encoding in which data bits are represented by transitions from one logical state to the other.** This is different from the common method of encoding in which bit is represented by either a high state like +5 volts or a low state such as 0 volts.

12. When Manchester code is used then the length of each data bit is set by default. **This makes the signal self-clocking.** The state of bit is determined according to the direction of the transition.

13. In some systems, **the transition from low to high represents logic** 1 **and the transition from high to low represents logic** 0.

14. In other systems, **the transition from low to high represents logic 0 and the transition from high to low represents logic 1.**

15. **Advantage of Manchester Encoding:** The signal synchronizes itself that further minimizes the error rate and optimizes reliability.

16. **Disadvantage of Manchester encoding:** A Manchester-encoded signal requires that more bits be transmitted than those in the original signal.

17. **Architecture of Z-wave:** A *central, network controller device* is needed to setup and manage a Z-wave network. *Each product in the home must be included to the Z-wave network before it can be controlled via Z-wave. Each Z-wave network is identified by a network ID and each device is further identified by a node ID.* Its architecture is shown in Fig. 2.20.

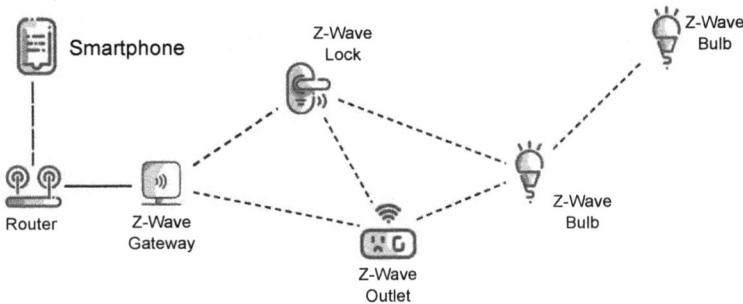

Fig. 2.20: Architecture of Z-wave

The network ID/ Home ID is the common identification of all nodes belonging to one logical Z-wave network. Network ID has a length of 4 bytes and is assigned to each device by the primary controller when the device is added into the network. **Please note that nodes with different network ID's cannot communicate with each other.** Node ID is the address of the device/node existing within the network. The node ID has a length of 1 byte.

18. Z-wave uses a *source-routed mesh network topology.* It has 1 primary controller but secondary controller is optional. **The process in which the devices can communicate to one another by using intermediate nodes to route around and circumvent household obstacles or radio dead spots that might occur through a message called healing is known as the healing process. Also note that delays may be observed during this healing process.**

19. As shown in Fig., the message from a node A can be sent to Node C via Node B if and only if, the intermediate node B can communicate with both Node A and Node C easily.

20. **Also note that if the preferred route is unavailable then the message originator will attempt other routes until a path to the destination node is found. That is why, a Z-wave network can span much farther than the radio range of a single unit.**

21. But with several hops, a slight delay may be introduced between the control command and the desired result. Fig. 2.21 below shows both the direct path and the healing path in Z-wave.

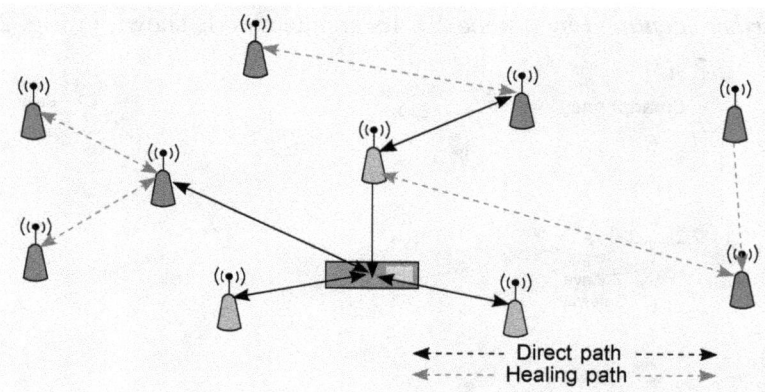

Fig. 2.21: Direct Path and The Healing Path in Z-wave

22. Z-wave units should not be in the **sleep mode** if they have to route messages. **That is why, battery-operated devices are not designed as repeater units.** Z-wave network can use **bridges** to several devices have to be used. **Note that as a source routed static network, Z-wave assumes that all devices in the network remain in their original detected position. Also note that mobile devices like remote controls are therefore, excluded from routing.**

23. New network discovery mechanisms have been developed for better Z-wave too. One new mechanism is **explorer frames- that can be used to heal broken routes caused by devices that have been moved or removed. Also note that a pruning algorithm is used in explorer frame broadcasts.** It is therefore supposed to reach the destination device even without further topology knowledge by the sender. *Explorer frames are used as a last option by the sending device when all other routing attempts have failed.*

24. The differences between Z-wave and ZigBee lies in the point of reference. They are as follows:

Z-wave	ZigBee
User friendly and provides a simple system that users can set up themselves.	Requires little power that devices can last up to 7 years on one set of batteries.
It is ideal for someone with a basic understanding of technology who wants to keep their home automation secure, efficient, simple and easy to maintain.	It is ideal for technology experts who want a system that can customize with their preferences and install themselves.
It is expensive.	It is cheaper than Z-wave.
Nine out of 10 leading security and communication companies in USA use Z-wave in their smart home solutions.	ZigBee Alliance consists of nearly 400 member organizations that use, develop and improve ZigBee's open standard wireless connection.

9. ISA 100.11 A

Some of the main features of ISA are as follows:

1. ISA is an acronym for **International Society of Automation.**

2. Its official explanation is **"Wireless Systems for Industrial Automation: Process Control and Related Applications".**

3. ISA 100.11 A is designed for **large scale industrial complexes** and plants.

4. Today more than 1 **billion devices use it.**

5. Some important features of this protocol include-- *flexibility, support for multiple protocols and applications, use of open standards, reliability that includes error detection, channel hopping* etc., *determinism* that includes TDMA, QoS support and security.

6. The architecture of ISA 100.11 A is shown in Fig. 2.22.

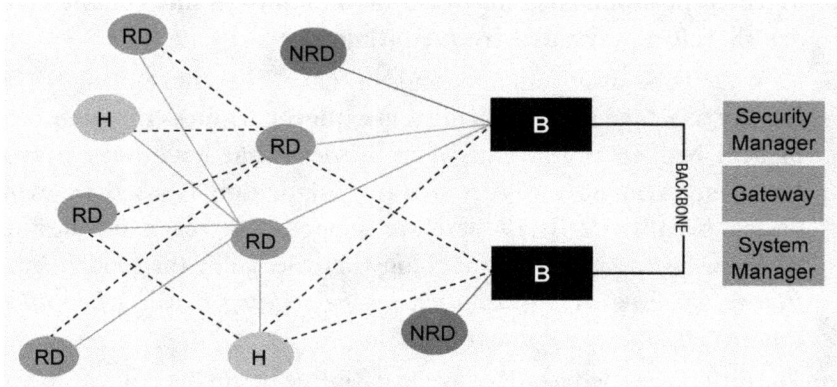

Fig. 2.22: ISA 100.11A

Where, RD- ROUTING DEVICE;

NRD: NON-ROUTING DEVICE;

H: HANDHELD DEVICE;

B: BACKBONE DEVICE.

7. This technology is designed to support **native and tunnelled application layers.**

8. Various transport services like reliable, best effort, real-time are also offered.

9. Network and transport layers are based on TCP or UDP OR IPv6.

10. Data link layer supports **mesh routing and frequency hopping.**

11. **Physical and MAC layer, both are based on IEEE 802.15.4**.

12. In this protocol, the **topologies** involved are star, tree and mesh topologies.

13. Also, the allowed **networks** are radio link, ISA over Ethernet and field buses.

14. **Application Support Layer** delivers communication services to the user and management process. This layer can pass objects, methods, native attributes within ISA 100.11A protocol.

15. A **Tunnelling Mode** is also provided to allow **legacy data** through the ISA 100.11A network.

16. In this standard, security is also in-built. Authentication and confidentiality services are independently available for this standard.

17. A network manager manages and distributes the keys.

18. There are dual security steps in each node. Data link layer encrypts each hop. Transport layer secures peer-to-peer communications.

19. Various usage classes related to this standard are as follows:

Category	Class	Application	Description
Safely	0	Emergency action	Always critical
Control	1	Closed loop regulatory control	Often critical
	2	Closed loop supervisory control	Usually, non-critical
	3	Open loop control	Human-in-the-loop
Monitoring	4	Alerting	Short term operational consequences
	5	Logging/downloading	No immediate operation consequences.

This table gives the category, class, application and its description.

2.9 SOFTWARE COMPONENTS

Various OS for executing software on a particular **"Thing"** exist. This will depend on 3 things:

- Memory footprint the software needs.
- Development environment.
- Real-time requirements.

What is Memory Footprint?

Memory footprint of an executable program shows its **run-time memory requirements while the program executes. Please note here that larger programs have larger memory footprints. Also note that the software themselves don't contribute to the largest portions to their own memory footprints rather structures that are introduced by the run-time environment can increase the footprint. For instance,** in a JAVA program, the memory footprint is made up of JVM (Java Virtual Machine) run-time environment.

A software development environment or an integrated development environment-IDE (like NetBeans, Eclipse etc.) **is a software that provides all facilities to a programmer to develop any type of applications with the help of its APIs** (Application Programming Interfaces). **For example,** a source code editor, debugger.

Example 2: for programming microcontrollers, the Arduino platform provides an IDE.

As far as the "Things" in IoT are concerned, one has to select an IDE that suits your programming needs.

2.10 PROGRAMMING APIS (USING PYTHON) FOR COMMUNICATION PROTOCOLS – MQTT, UDP, TCP

(i) MQTT stands for Message Queue Telemetry Transport Protocol.

Some of the main features of this protocol are:

1. It is an **Open Connectivity** for Mobile, M2M and IoT.
2. It is designed for **high latency, low bandwidth or unreliable networks**.
3. The **design principle minimizes the network bandwidth and device resource requirements.**
4. It is a **light weight broker-based, publish/subscribe messaging protocol** designed to be open, simple, lightweight and easy to implement.
5. This protocol **works by exchanging a series of MQTT control packets in a defined way.** Each control packet has a specific purpose and every bit in the packet is carefully crafted to reduce the data transmitted over the network.
6. A MQTT topology has a **MQTT server and a MQTT client.** MQTT control packet headers are kept as small as possible.
7. Having a **small header overhead** makes this protocol suitable for IoT by **lowering the amount of data transmitted** over constrained networks.
8. MQTT is a **protocol built for M2M and IoT** which is used to provide new and revolutionary performance.
9. **Lightweight message queueing** and transport protocol.
10. **Asynchronous communication model** with messages/events.
11. **Low overhead** (2-bytes header) for **low network bandwidth applications.**
12. **Publish/Subscribe** (PubSub) model.

13. **Decoupling of data producer** (publisher) **and data consumer** (subscriber) through topics (message queues).

14. **Simple protocol,** aimed at **low complexity, low power** and **low footprint** implementations.

15. Runs on **connection-oriented transport** (TCP).

16. MQTT caters for **wireless network disruptions.**

The following Fig. 2.23 shows MQTT:

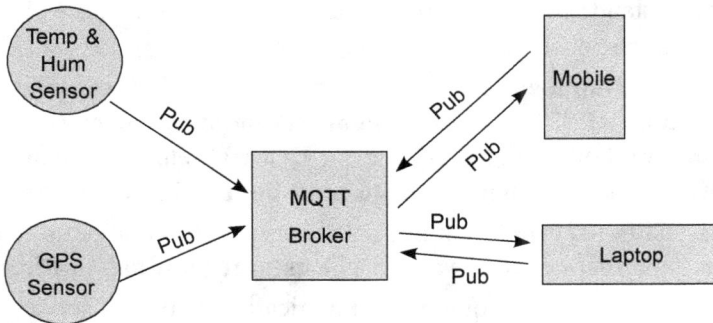

Fig. 2.23: MQTT Protocol

   Working: Sensor continuously sends **sensor data to the broker.** Building **control application** receives sensor data from the broker and decides to activate the blinds. **Applications sends a blind activation message to the blind actor node through a broker.** The **core elements** of MQTT are clients, servers (brokers), sessions, subscriptions and topics. **Clients subscribe to topics** to publish and receive messages. Thus, **subscriber and publisher are special roles of a client. Servers run topics** i.e., receive subscriptions from clients on topics, receive messages from clients and forward these, based on client's subscriptions, to the interested clients.

   The differences between MQTT and HTTP lie in the point of reference.

Parameters	MQTT	FTP
Design	Data centric	Document centric
Pattern used	Publish/Subscribe	Request/Response
Complexity	Simple	More complex
Message size	Small and binary with 2B header	Large and ASCII
Service levels	3	1

(ii) REST and HTTP Restful Protocol

Some of the main features of this protocol are given below:

1. A large part of the **interoperability, scale and control for IoT** can be achieved through API management.

2. **Standards-based design patterns for Web APIs, API management and a RESTful architecture provides tremendous value in simplifying the task of interoperability across heterogeneous systems handling a deluge of data.**

3. REST stands for **Representational State Transfer.** Its APIs follow the request-response communication model.

4. **Note that applications conforming to the REST constraints can be called as RESTful. These systems communicate over HTTP with the same methods** (GET, POST, PUT, DELETE etc) **that browsers use to retrieve the web pages and to send data to remote servers.**

   (a) **Client-server:** Requires that a service offer one or more operations and that services wait for clients to request these operations.

   (b) **Stateless:** It requires communication between service consumer (client) and service provider (server) to be stateless.

   (c) **Cache:** It requires responses to be clearly labelled as cacheable or non-cacheable.

   (d) **Uniform Interface:** It requires all **service providers and consumers** within a REST-compliant architecture to share a single common interface for all operations.

   (e) **Layered System:** It requires the ability to **add or remove intermediaries at runtime** without disrupting the system.

   (f) **Code-on-Demand:** It allows logic within clients like web browsers, to be updated independently from server-side logic using executable code shipped from service providers to consumers.

5. Each **client request and server response** is a message, REST-compliant applications expect each message to be **self-descriptive. Please note that this means that each message must contain all information necessary to complete the task.** Other ways to describe this kind of message are **'stateless' or 'context-free'.** Each message passed between client and server can have body and metadata.

6. **HTTP Restful:** It includes the following request methods and actions:
   GET: return whatever information is identified by the Request-URI.

(a) **HEAD:** it is same as GET except that the server must not return a message body in response, only the metadata.

(b) **OPTIONS:** It returns information about the communication options available on the request/response chain identified by the Request-URI.

(c) **PUT:** It requests that the enclosed entity must be stored under the supplied Request-URI.

(d) **POST:** It requests that the origin server accepts the entity enclosed in the request as a new subordinate of the resource identified by the Request-URI.

(e) **DELETE:** It requests that the origin server delete the resource identified by the Request-URI.

Note: The first three are read-only operations while the last three are write operations only.

(iii) WebSocket-Based Communication Model

WebSocket supports full-duplex, two-way communication between client and server.

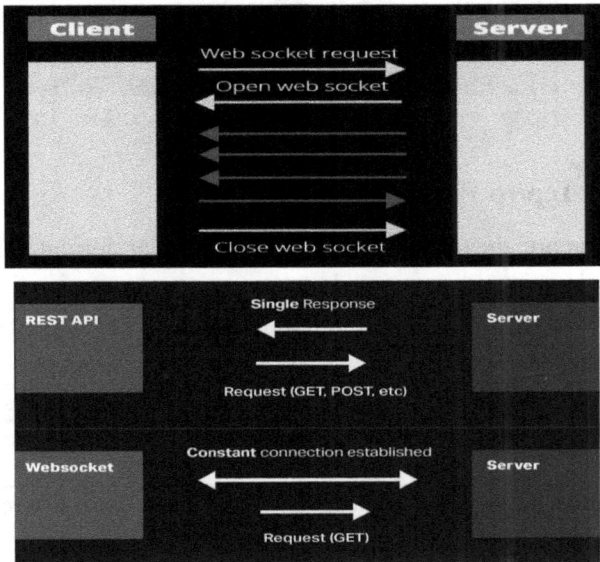

Fig. 2.24: WebSocket-based Communication Model

WebSocket APIs reduce the network traffic and latency as there is no overhead for connection setup and termination requests for each message. Fig. 2.24 shows the WebSocket Model.

WebSocket uses a standard HTTP request-response sequence to establish a connection. When the connection is established, the WebSocket API provides a read and write interface for reading and writing data over the established connection in an asynchronous full duplex manner. Also, WebSocket provides an interface for asynchronously closing the connection from either side.

Now the question is what are the differences between HTTP and WebSocket?

:// HTTP	🐿 WebSocket
Duplex	
Half	Full
Messaging Pattern	
Request-reponse	Bi-directional
Service Push	
Not natively supported. Client polling or streaming download techniques used.	Core feature
Overhead	
Moderate overhead per request/connection	Moderate overhead to establish & maintain the connection, then minimal overhead per message.
Intermediary/Edge Caching	
Core feature	Not possible
Support Clients	
Broad support	Modern languages & clients

(iv) Udp and Tcp/Ip Protocols

We should compare these two protocols in a tabular format. This is shown below:

TCP	UDP
TCP is connection oriented.	UDP is connectionless.
TCP connection is byte stream.	UDP connection is message stream.
TCP does not support multicasting and broadcasting.	UDP supports broadcasting.
It provides error control and flow control.	It does not provide error control and flow control.
It supports full-duplex communication.	It does not support full duplex communications.
TCP is reliable.	UDP is unreliable.
TCP packet is called as segment.	UDP packet is called as user datagram.

Some of the **features of TCP/IP** are as follows:

1. Has a **multi-vendor support** i.e., it is implemented by many software and hardware vendors.
2. **Interoperability:** It supports heterogeneous network. It eliminates cross platform boundaries.
3. **Logical Addressing:** Logical addressing systems used are known as IP address.
4. **Rout Ability:** A router can read logical addressing information and direct data across the network to its destination.
5. **Name Resolution:** We cannot remember so many IP addresses. S, DNS servers are used to resolve such issues.
6. **Error and Flow Control:** TCP/IP defines error checking, flow control and acknowledgement functions.
7. **MUX/DEMUX:** MUX accepts data from different applications and directs the data to different applications. TCP/IP provides a method for delivering packets to the correct application using ports.

Some of the **Features of UDP** are as follows:

1. It is as simple, **datagram-oriented transport layer protocol.**
2. It is a **connectionless protocol** that provides no reliability or flow control mechanisms.
3. Also, it has **no error recovery** procedures.
4. Many **applications layer protocols** like TFTP (Trivial File Transfer Protocol) and the RPC **use UDP only.**
5. UDP makes use of the **port concept to direct the datagrams to the proper upper layer applications.**
6. UDP serves as a simple **application interface** to the IP.
7. **Encapsulation** of a UDP datagram has been done as an IP datagram.

Wireless TCP and UDP

TCP should not care whether IP is running over which media i.e., fibre or radio. Wireless transmission links are highly unreliable. They lose packets all the time. The proper approach to dealing with lost packets is to send them again as quickly as possible. **Please note that when a packet is lost on a wired network, the sender should slow down.** On the other hand, when one is lost in wireless network, the sender should try harder. When the sender does not know what the network is, it is difficult to make the correct decision. *Frequently, the path from the sender to the receiver is inhomogeneous.* It uses both, wired network and wireless network. The wireless TCP is split into two separate connections as shown in Fig. 2.25.

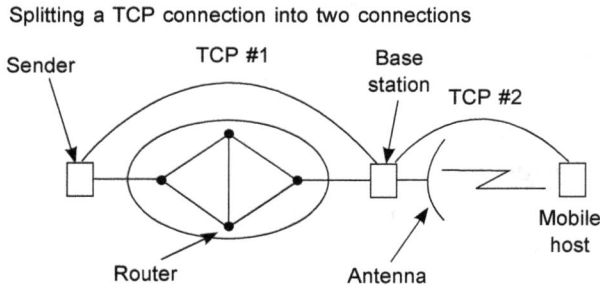

Fig. 2.25: The Wireless TCP is Split Into Two Separate Connections

Working: In TCP-1, the connection goes from the sender to the base station i.e., first stage. Mobile host (receiver) gets data from the base station antenna in TCP-2. **The base station simply copies packets between the connections in both the directions. This scheme solves the time out problem. Please note that both the connections, sender to base station and base station to the receiver are homogeneous. Also note that the Timeouts on the first connection can slow the sender down, whereas time out on the second one can speed it up.** Other parameters can also be tuned separately for two connections.

Disadvantage of This Scheme: The drawback of this scheme is to break the TCP into two segments. UDP does not suffer from the same problem as TCP, wireless communication also introduces difficulties for it. The main trouble is that programs use UDP expecting it to be highly reliable. Wireless communication also affects areas other than just performance.

SUMMARY

We have studied that IoT is a collection of multiple technologies platforms and protocols. MQTT is a light weight protocol that follows publish-scribe pattern. It was made open in 2014. CoAP is another lightweight protocol for IoT. It uses lesser resources than HTTP. Also, we have studied about BLE i.e., Bluetooth Low Energy technology. As we know that any node in the network is uniquely identified by an address, similarly in an IoT infrastructure we do. In this chapter, we have studied about the common IoT connectivity technologies like IEEE 802.15.4, ZigBee, 6LoWPAN, RFID, HART and wireless HART, NFC, Bluetooth, Z-wave and ISA 100.11A. the architecture, features, various communication layers, applications, topologies, workings are also delineated in a better way. These connectivity technologies form the backbone of IoT.

MULTIPLE CHOICE QUESTIONS [MCQS] WITH ANSWERS

1. Microcontrollers/ boards lie on which layer of the IoT stack
   (a) Physical layer.   (b) Control action layer.
   (c) RF layer.   (d) None of the above.

2. BLE belong to which layer of IoT stack
   (a) Physical layer.   (b) Control action layer.
   (c) RF layer.   (d) None of the above.

3. MQTT is related to which layer in the IoT stack
   (a) Message layer.   (b) Control action layer.
   (c) RF layer.   (d) None of the above.

4. Which of the following means that it demands minimal resources for its functioning and needs no more additional resources
   (a) Lightweight.   (b) Heavy weight.
   (c) Medium weight.   (d) None of the above.

5. MQTT was developed by
   (a) Andriy Ray.   (b) Aditya Kumar.
   (c) Andy Standford Clark.   (d) None of the above.

6. On which of the following factor (s) does connecting "Things" is based on
   (a) Amount of data to be transmitted.
   (b) How far data needs to go?
   (c) Power availability.
   (d) All of the above.

7. In IoT ecosystem, at which layer is the largest area of competition
   (a) Session layer.   (b) Data link layer.
   (b) Application layer.   (c) Physical layer.

8. A wireless system that the ZigBee protocol is used to connect to the network is
   - (a) Software patch.
   - (b) Sensium Vitals patch.
   - (c) Hardware patch.
   - (d) None of the above.

9. The full form of LPWAN is
   - (a) Low Power WIFI Able Networks.
   - (b) Low Power Wide Area Networks.
   - (c) Linked Port Wide Area Networks.
   - (d) Low Power Wrong Area Networks.

10. Modern oil and gas platforms are connected by
    - (a) Microwave.
    - (b) WIFI.
    - (c) LoRaWAN.
    - (d) Fibre optic cable.

11. Pick the odd one out
    - (a) IoT Node.
    - (b) IoT LAN/WAN.
    - (c) IoT Gateway.
    - (d) IoT Proxy.
    - (e) None of the above.

12. A protocol that provides connectivity that is embedded between applications and middle-wares on one side and networks and communications on the other side is
    - (a) CoAP.
    - (b) XMPP.
    - (c) AMQP.
    - (d) MQTT.

13. ZigBee supports only
    - (a) Star and mesh topologies.
    - (b) Star, tree and mesh topologies.
    - (c) Cluster tree topology.
    - (d) None of the above.

14. During transmission, if a path fails then the node will find an alternative path to its destination. This property is called as
    - (a) Self-replicating.
    - (b) Self-redundancy.
    - (c) Self-healing.
    - (d) None of the above.

15. A mesh topology is a
    - (a) Single hop network.
    - (b) Multi-hop network.
    - (c) Both of the above.
    - (d) None of these.

16. In the fragmentation header, the first fragment is _____ bits and the subsequent fragment is _____ bits.
   (a) 32, 16.   (b) 16, 32.
   (c) 32, 32.   (d) 64, 64.

17. RFID stands for
   (a) Radar Frequency Identification
   (b) Radio Frequency Identification.
   (c) Rays Frequency Identification.
   (d) None of the above.

18. RPL stands for
   (a) IPv6 Routing Protocol for Low-Power and Lossy Networks.
   (b) Remote Protocol for Lossy Networks.
   (c) Regional Protocol for Low Power Networks.
   (d) None of the above.

19. HART stands for
   (a) Highway Addressable Remote Transducer Protocol.
   (b) Highly Addressable Remote Transducer Protocol.
   (c) Human Addressable Remote Transducer Protocol.
   (d) None of the above.

20. The latest release of HART is
   (a) Cordless HART.   (b) Wireless HART.
   (c) Remote HART.   (d) None of the above.

21. Which of the following tags have their own power supply?
   (a) Passive tags.   (b) Active tags.
   (c) Chips.   (d) None of the above.

22. A form of contactless communication between devices like mobile phones or tablets is
   (a) NFC.   (b) RFC.
   (c) BBC.   (d) None of the above.

23. A LAN with a very limited coverage is
   (a) Piconets.   (b) Internet.
   (b) Scatternet.   (c) None of the above.

24. A Z-wave network can contain up to
    (a) 232 nodes.   (b) 238 nodes.
    (c) 1024 nodes.   (d) None of the above.

25. In Manchester coding, the length of each data bits is set by default. This makes the signal
    (a) Self-healing.   (b) Self-replicating.
    (c) Self-clocking.   (d) None of the above.

26. For large scale industrial plants, which of the following protocols is very useful
    (a) ZigBee.   (b) Z-wave.
    (c) ISA 100.11A   (d) None of the above.

27. A web API executed using HTTP and REST standards is
    (a) RESTful webservice.   (b) RESTful web administration.
    (c) Tranquil web administration.   (d) None of the above.

28. A protocol developed to provide an open, decentralized alternative to the closed instant messaging services
    (a) XMPP.   (b) REST.
    (c) UDP.   (d) None of the above.

29. A protocol that is the new application layer protocol as developed by IETF for smart devices to connect to Internet is
    (a) MQTT.   (b) XMPP.
    (c) MQP.   (d) CoAP.

30. IoT protocol that constitutes for remote interruptions is
    (a) MQTT.   (b) XMPP.
    (c) 6LoWPAN.   (d) None of the above.

Answers

1. b	2. c	3. a	4. a	5. c	6. d
7. c	8. b	9. b	10. d	11. a	12. d
13. b	14. c	15. b	16. c	17. b	18. a
19. a	20. b	21. b	22. a	23. a	24. a
25. c	26. c	27. a	28. a	29. d	30. a

CONCEPTUAL SHORT QUESTIONS WITH ANSWERS

Q1. Define what is Internet of Everything (IoE)?

Ans. IoE is the intelligent connection of people, processes, data and Things.

Q2. Is it must for an IoT application to have an Internet?

Ans. Yes, it is mandatory to have Internet if you want an IoT application to be developed and designed. Otherwise, the system is called as a smart system only.

Q3. Give the names of any two IoT computing boards. Which one to select out of these and why?

Ans. Raspberry Pi, Arduino and Node MCU are some of the computing boards for IoT. There is no hard and fast rule for selection of the board. However, it can be chosen on the basis of the budget, computing power and speed requirements.

Q4. Is cloud essential for IoT?

Ans. No. cloud services are only required if you want to share big data on "pay-per-usage" basis.

Q5. Which is preferred for any IoT application- microcontroller or a microprocessor?

Ans. Microcontrollers are preferred more as compared to microprocessor as microcontroller has everything on board like Arduino is a very good microcontroller. Also, because microcontrollers are meant for a specific application only which is an added advantage. On the other hand, a microprocessor is meant for a general application and hence is not preferred more.

Q6. What is FOG computing?

Ans. There is a deluge of voluminous data today. This data is quite sensitive and what we want is that only the most important data should be analysed in the network's edge. The benefit of this is that data analysis will happen closer to the place from where this data originated. Thus, it will prevent sending of large amount of data on to the cloud. This makes response also faster.

Q7. Give The Roles of MQTT Client and MQTT Broker

Ans. The following are the roles of MQTT Client

- It collects information from the sensors.
- It connects it to the messaging server/broker.

- Topic is used to publish this message to let other clients understand.
- It can also be a subscriber.

The following are the roles of MQTT Broker:

- Protocol is implemented in this case.
- Mediates and facilitates the data based on interest of the subscriber.

Q8. What are the three levels of QoS as given by MQTT?

Ans. The three levels of MQTT are as follows:

1. 0 = At most once (Best Effort, No Ack).
2. 1 = At least once (Acked, retransmitted if ack not received).
3. 2 = Exactly once (Request to send/Publish, clear to send).

Q9. Tabulate the differences between MQTT and CoAP.

Ans. Both are IoT protocols but are different as follows:

MQTT	CoAP
Its underlying protocol is TCP that is connection oriented.	Its underlying protocol is UDP that is connectionless.
Communication is Many-to-Many (M:N).	Communication is One-to-One (1:1).
Power required is higher than CoAP but lesser than other protocols.	Lowest power is required. It consumes less power than MQTT.
It works on Publisher/Subscriber model.	It works on Request-Response, RESTful and not SOAPful model.

Q10. Define Marshalling and unmarshalling.

Ans. Marshalling is defined as the process of converting the data into a byte-stream. On the other hand, **unmarshalling is the reverse process of converting the byte-stream back to their original data.** The benefits of this is that it enables subscribers on multiple (different) platforms to receive the data from the publishers without any problems.

Q11. What is BLE? What is its other name?

Ans. BLE or Bluetooth Low Energy is an open low-energy short-range radio communication technology. It is also called as **Bluetooth Smart.** It is a wireless personal area network. It happens to be an advanced version of Bluetooth. It has reduced power consumption.

Q12. How is BLE superior to legacy Bluetooth?

Ans. BLE is superior to classic Bluetooth as it saves lot of power. Its modules are not costly. The size of BLE chips is also small.

Power consumption is also minimal. BLE is supported by Android OS, Blackberry, macOS, Win 10 and Linux.

Q13. Compare and contrast Bluetooth and BLE.

Ans. Although BLE is an enhanced from of legacy Bluetooth only but still they have some differences as follows:

Bluetooth	Bluetooth Low Energy (BLE)
Its range is 100m.	Its range is more than 100m.
Its data rate is 1-3 Mbps.	Its data rate is 1 Mbps.
Its application throughput is 0.7-2.1 Mbps.	Its application throughput is 0.27 Mbps.
It uses fast frequency hopping.	It uses 24-bit CRC checking.
Latency observed is 100ms.	Latency observed is 6ms.
It is voice capable.	It is not voice capable.

Q14. What is Li-Fi? Who coined this term? Give some of its characteristics along with its advantages and disadvantages.

Ans. **Li-Fi stands for Light Fidelity.** This term was coined by Prof. Harald Haas in 2011. Some of its **features and advantages** are as follows:

1. It has high speed and is bi-directional too. It has a very high speed of 224 GB p/ sec.
2. It uses light to transfer data.
3. Light is generated through light bulbs and hence it is cheaper.
4. As light cannot penetrate through walls, so it very safe. So, data hacking will not occur.
5. It is an efficient and effective technology as compared to RF.

Disadvantages of Li-Fi

1. Due to presence of walls, it could be a short ranger.
2. More time is needed to set up the infrastructure.
3. No clear method of acknowledgements.

Q15. What is FFD and RFD in IEEE 802.15.4?

Ans. A **Full Function Device (FFD) can operate in three modes serving,** namely, Device, Coordinator, PAN Co-ordinator. It must have *memory sufficient to store routing information* as required by the algorithm employed by the network.

Reduced Function Device (RFD) can only operate in a device mode. An RFD is very low-cost device with **minimal memory requirements.** It can only function as a network device.

Network Device: An **RFD or FFD implementation** containing an IEEE 802.15.4 **medium access control and physical interface to the wireless medium.**

Coordinator: An FFD with **network device functionality** that provides **coordination** and other services to the network.

PAN Coordinator: A coordinator that is the **principal controller** of the PAN. A network has **exactly one PAN coordinator.**

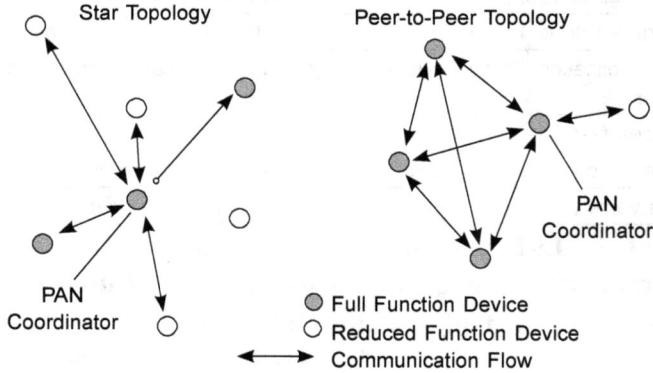

Fig. 2.26: PAN coordinator

Q16. Compare Web of Things and Internet of Things.

Ans. Some of the points of comparisons are as follows:

1. **Web of Things** provides an **Application Layer** that simplifies the **creation of Internet of Things applications.** The web is a system of interlinked documents accessed via the Internet. The term Internet was coined by Tim Berners-Lee in 1990.

2. The web, like email, is one of the services that runs on the Internet. **Key components of the web** are as follows:
   - Uniform Resource Locator (URL) and Uniform Resource Identifier (URI).
   - Hypertext Markup Language (HTML).
   - Hypertext Transfer Protocol (HTTP).

3. **Internet** is the term used to identify the **massive interconnection of computer networks around the world. It refers to the physical connection of the paths between two or more computers.** WWW is the general name for accessing the Internet via HTTP. It is just one of the **connection protocols** that is available in the Internet and not the only one.

4. **Please note here that unlike many systems that exist for IoT, the Web of Things is about reusing the web standards to connect the rapidly expanding ecosystem of the embedded devices built into everyday smart objects.** Well-accepted and understood standards and blueprints like URI, HTTP, REST, RSS etc. are used to access the functionality of the smart objects.

5. **Web of Things (WoT) uses HTTP as an application protocol rather than as a transport protocol as done in the world of web services. It** exposes the **synchronous functionality of smart objects** through a REST interface, also known as RESTful API, and **more generally respects the blueprints of Resource-oriented Architectures.**

6. It exposes the **asynchronous functionality/ events of smart objects** through the use of largely accepted **web syndication standards like Atom or server-push Web mechanisms** such as **Comet.**

7. **Web of Things is the next logical step in this IoT evolution toward global networks of sensors and actuators,** enabling new applications and providing new opportunities.

8. **Web of Things has a flat architecture as compared to the traditional server-client architecture.** To directly integrate things to the web, it is first required that all the things must be addressable i.e., everything must have an IP address or must be IP-enabled when connected to the Internet. **Web of Things also requires connectivity and interoperability at the application layer.**

9. Web of Things applications are Arduino, Japan Geiger Map, Nanode, National Weather Study Project and AgSphere.

   - Arduino is an **open-source electronics platform** based on easy-to-use hardware and software.

   - Regulations as per the **Japanese Nuclear Safety Commission** prescribe some standards that **a monitoring system at a power producing nuclear plant** must adhere to.

   - Nanode is an **open-source Arduino-like board that has inbuilt web connectivity.**

- The *National Weather Study Report (NWSR) is a large-scale environmental study project deploying hundreds of mini weather stations in schools throughout Singapore.*

Q17. Write a short note on satellite IoT.

Ans. Some points to ponder are discussed as follows:

1. A **communication satellite (COMSAT) is a specialized wireless transponder in space, receiving radio waves from one location and transmitting them to another.** Satellite communications are especially important for transportation, aviation maritime and military use.

2. A **satellite is a physical object which revolves around the earth at known height (called as orbit). Artificial satellites are launched into orbits** for various purposes.

3. One of the **major applications of satellite is in communications.** Satellite communication services have become more reliable, affordable and efficient today.

4. Satellite communication systems offer **more flexibility** than submarine cables, underground cables, fibre-optic systems. With the satellite-to-satellite communication, it is possible **to communicate with any point on the globe.**

5. A satellite system basically consists of a **satellite in space and many earth stations on the ground that are linked with each other through the satellite. A ground-based station controls the overall operations of satellite.**

6. A satellite receives the signal transmitted from the earth station. It, then processes or amplifies the signal and then it retransmits the signal back to earth in the desired form. This processing is done by a radio repeater which is also called as a **transponder.**

7. A **communication satellite is a microwave repeater station** that permits two or more users to deliver or exchange information simultaneously.

8. The satellites can be put into 3 different types, based on the location of the orbit. **Also note that these orbits are chosen in such a way that the satellites are not destroyed by the high-energy charged particles present in the two Van Allen belts.**

9. The following Fig. 2.27 shows the satellite orbits with belts.

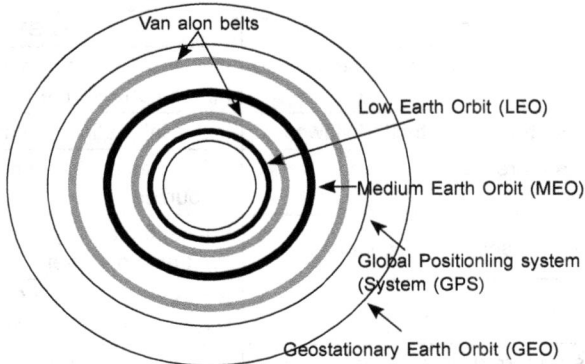

Fig. 2.27: Shows Satellite Orbits with Allen Belts

10. As shown in figure, **the Low Earth Orbit (LEO)** is below the lower Van Allen belt in the altitude of 500 Km to 2000 Km.

11. The **Medium Earth Orbit (MEO)** is in between the lower Van Allen belt and upper Van Allen belt in the altitude of 5000 Km to 15000 Km.

12. Above the upper Van Allen belt is the **Geostationary Earth Orbit (GEO)** at the altitude of about 36,000 Km.

13. **Molniya orbit and Molniya Orbit Satellites:** It has been used by Russia for decades. Molniya orbit is an **elliptical orbit. Please note that the satellite remains in a nearly fixed position relative to the earth for 8 hours. Also note that a series of 3 Molniya satellites can act as a GEO satellite.** It is useful near polar regions.

14. **High Altitude Platform (HAP):** It is the current idea in the satellite communication field. **A blimp or plane around 20 Km above the earth's surface is used as a satellite. Also note that HAPs will have a very small coverage area but would have a comparatively strong signal. It is cheaper to put in position but will require a lot of them in a network.**

15. **One Earth station sends a transmission to the satellite.** This is called as an **Uplink.** On the other hand, the satellite Transponder converts the signal and sends it down to the second earth station. **This is called as a Downlink.**

Q18. Differentiate between the following:

(a) SOAP and REST.   (b) CoAP and HTTP.

Ans. (a) The following tables gives the differences between the two.

SOAP	REST
It is a protocol and hence it cannot use REST.	It is an API or a concept only and hence can use the services only.
Standards should be strictly followed.	It doesn't define much standards.
It requires more bandwidth and resources.	It requires minimal bandwidth and resources.
It has its own security mechanism.	It inherits security mechanism from the transport layer.
It supports XML data format.	It supports different formats like HTML, XML, JSON etc.
It is less preferred as compared to the REST.	It is more preferred as compared to SOAP.

(b) Now we differentiate between CoAP and HTTP in a tabular form

CoAP	HTTP
It uses UDP protocol.	It uses TCP protocol.
In the network layer, it makes use of IPv6 and 6LoWPAN.	It uses IP layer in the network layer.
It supports multicasting.	It does not support multicasting.
It uses both client-server model and publisher-subscriber model.	It makes use of only client-server model.
It is an asynchronous communication.	It is synchronous communication.
It is a simple protocol.	It is a complex protocol.
It has less overhead.	It has more overhead.
It is designed for resource constrained devices.	It is designed for Internet devices.

Q19. How will you classify IoT protocols? Show its multi-layer stack.

Ans. Broadly speaking, the IoT protocols are put under two categories

(a) Infrastructure Protocols.

(b) Messaging Protocols.

Infrastructure Protocols are long range / low power and short -range communications protocols. **For example,** WIFI, ZigBee, Bluetooth, NFC etc.

Messaging Protocols are those that focus on the high-level communication. They concentrate on the interconnection layer.

S. No.	IoT Protocol Stack (Four broad categories)	Position of bask communication protocols in IoT protocol stack & Layered Architechture			IoT Layered Architecture (5-Layered Model)
1	Application Protocols	CoAP	MQTT-SN	AMQP	Application Layer
		DDS	HTTP	REST	
2	Service Discovery Protocols	mDNX	DNS-SD		Network Layer
3	Infrastructure Protocols	RPL			
		6LoWPAN	IPv4	IPv6	Adaptation Layer
		IEEE802.15.4			Data link Layer
		LTE-A	EPC Global	IEEE802.15.4	Physical Layer
4	Influential Protocols	IEEE183.3	IPSec	IEEE 1995.1	

Q20. What was the main reason behind the invention of MQTT protocol?

Ans. MQTT stands for Message Queue Telemetry Transport. It is a M2M or IoT network protocol. In 1999, Dr. Andy Standford-Clark of IBM and Arlen Nipper of Eurotech founded it. **The main reason was to provide optimal (minimum) battery loss and bandwidth efficiency for satellite communications. The main use** of MQTT protocol is to respond for the notifications sent by the sender, pushing of the messages to low power mobile devices. **For example,** The Eclispe Paho is the MQTT implementation for IoT protocol implementations.

Q21. Give some applications of XMPP protocol.

Ans. Some of the applications of XMPP includes:
- Instant Messaging.
- Group Chatting.
- Virtual Classrooms.
- Simple Gaming Applications.
- Vehicle Tracking.
- Updation of Information on Social Networks.

Q22. Can you give some of the examples/cases where XMPP has been used?

Ans. Some examples/cases are Core, Jingle, Multi-user chat, PubSub and BOSH. Core main job is to stream XML over the network. Jingle is for voice and video talks. BOSH is **Bidirectional-streams Over Synchronous HTTP** that is a development for two-route correspondence over the HTTP.

Q23. **Give and explain any one application where AMQP has been applied?**

Ans. **RabbitMQ is one such asynchronous application that is an open-source messaging system and it implements AMQP protocol.** Many RabbitMQ servers can be grouped together. This software enables to scale and connect with the messaging applications. RabbitMQ architecture is quite simple. It consists of producer, consumer and broker. Here, the client applications that create the messages are called as producers. These generate messages and send them to the broker. The broker stores the message. The consumer will connect to the broker and subscribe to the messages which it has to process.

Q24. **Give and explain any one application where REST API protocol is used.**

Ans. **Google glass Mirror API** is one such application. The mirror API allows to push or pull the message and display it on the interface. This is useful in social networking. Another example is Twitter, that also uses REST protocol. Even Amazon uses the REST API.

Q25. **Can you compare some IoT protocols graphically?**

Ans. The following graph gives the comparison of different protocols:

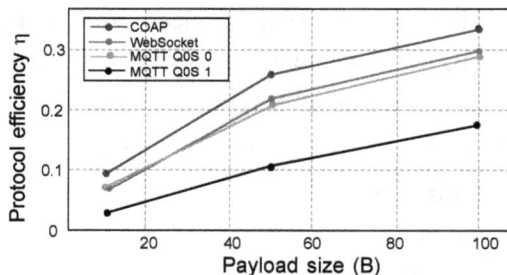

Fig. 2.28: Comparison Graph of IoT Protocol

From the graph, it is clear that COAP protocol has the highest efficiency as the payload increases.

Q26. **Different operating systems can be installed on Raspberry Pi through SD cards. Name some OS that cane be installed on it.**

Ans. Kali Linux, Raspberry Pi Fedora Remix, Rasplex, Runeaudio, Chameleon Pi.

Q27. List some Raspberry Pi commands.

Ans. Some general commands are as follows:

    (a) **raspi-config:** configuration setting menu.

    (b) **clear:** clears data.

    (c) **date:** current date.

    (d) **reboot:** Reboots immediately.

    (e) **shutdown: -h now:** shutdown system immediately.

    (f) **nano py1.txt:** Opens the py1.txtx in the text editor nano.

    (g) **startx:** Opens the GUI.

    (h) **ifconfig:** wireless connection status.

    (i) **ping:** Tests connectivity between two devices connected on a network.

    (j) **free:** shows how much free memory is available.

Q28. Write a simple Python program to run on Raspberry Pi to generate password.

Ans. The following program may be implemented:

```
import string
from random import*
characters = string.ascii_letters + string.punctuation + string.digits
password = " ".join(choice(characters) for x in range(randint(8,16)))
print(password)
```

Q29. Write short notes on IoT tools.

Ans. **Chef is an infrastructure automation and configure management tool.** Chef adopts the infrastructure as a code paradigm. It allows deploying, configuring and integrating of various infrastructure components.

    Puppet is another tool that is also a configuration management tool just like Chef.

Q30. What are MQTT verbs? What is their job?

Ans. **MQTT methods are also called as verbs.** MQTT defines methods to indicate desired actions to be performed on identified resources. These resources can be files or the outputs of an executable program found on server.

Q31. What is Piggybacking?

Ans. When a client sends request using CON type of NON type message and receives response ACK with confirmable message immediately. This is known as Piggybacking.

Q32. What is the basic unit of data in AMQP? Name Them.

Ans. **The basic unit of data in AMQP is a frame.** There are 9 frame types in AMQP that are used to initiate, control and tear down the transfer of messages between two peers. They are as follows:

1. Open the connection.
2. Begin the session.
3. Attach or initiate a new link.
4. Transfer.
5. Flow.
6. Disposition.
7. Detach/Terminate the link.
8. End the session.
9. Close the connection.

Q33. Distinguish between beacon-enabled and non-beacon enabled networks.

Ans. In IEEE 802.15.4 standard, two different operation modes are found.

Beacon-enabled network: In these networks, there will be a periodic transmission of beacon messages. **Please note that here data frames are sent via slotted CSMA/CA with a super frame structure managed by the PAN coordinator.** Beacons are used for synchronization and association of other nodes with the coordinator. The devices in a beacon-enabled network synchronize with each other and the beacon frame which is treated as synchronization signal also provides some extended features. A beacon-enabled device is hard to implement. **Also note that high processing power is needed to meet the constrained timing events and process the beacon packets.** The scope of operation spans the whole network.

Non-beacon network: In these networks, the data frames are sent via unslotted CSMA/CA. Beacons are used only for **link layer discovery.** Non-beacon enabled networks require both source and destination IDs. As 802.15.4 is basically a **mesh protocol,** all protocol addressing must adhere to mesh configurations. In these networks, there is a **decentralized communication** among various nodes.

EXERCISE QUESTIONS

1. Why do IoT systems have to be self-adapting and self-configuring?
2. Differentiate between machines in M2M and Things in IoT.
3. Explain how NFV can be used for virtualizing IoT devices?
4. Write short notes on data storages in IoT.
5. List features of REST.
6. Differentiate between web communication and message communication protocols for connected devices.
7. Comment on media access control in IoT technology.
8. Explain the architecture of Raspberry Pi kit.
9. Distinguish between Raspberry Pi and Arduino platforms.
10. Write short notes on IP addressing in IoT.
11. What is FFD and RFD in IEEE 802.15.4.
12. Compare and contrast Web of Things and Internet of Things.
13. Explain with a neat diagram Cloud-of-Things architecture.
14. With a neat diagram, explain the CoAP architecture.
15. What is BLE technology?
16. Explain MQTT protocol with a neat sketch and also discuss about its characteristics.
17. Differentiate between MQTT and FTP in a tabular form.
18. What is REST? Also explain HTTP Restful.
19. Explain an example of IoT service that uses WebSocket based communication.
20. Write short notes on satellite IoT.
21. The number of customers who enter or leave a mall follow Poisson's distribution. As a software engineer of a mall, you are desired to acquire data about the visitors in a mall. What sort of IoT application can you develop.
22. Suppose you are appointed as a IoT designer in a firm and you have to develop IoT-based machine learning project. What changes would you suggest with respect to design? Which protocol will you use? Draw its complete architectural diagram.
23. Highlight the major technologies that play a vital role in IoT application development. What are the enabling technologies that you know?

24. Differentiate between Edge and fog computing.

[**Hints:** The main difference between edge and fog computing is where data processing takes place. Edge computing is the computing carried out at the device itself where all sensors are connected. **Please note that this means that the computing devices would be physically much closer to the data generation points i.e., sensors.** On the other hand, in fog computing, data processing is moved to the processor that are connected to LAN, making it a little farther from the sensors and actuators. **Also note that the main difference between edge and fog computing is the distance.**]

25. XYZ company wants to have a wireless solution for networking sensors that are installed in the firm. The need is to have an no interference communications. Which of the following is better—Wireless HART or ISA 100.11A and why?

26. An IoT-based smart payment system requires enhanced security measures and even be contactless. Out of RFID and NFC, which one would you prefer and why?

27. A smart home installation requires multiple sensors to be connected in a home. The minimum distance between the devices, if in a mesh configuration or between the device and the hub has to be 80m. then out of ZigBee or Z-wave, which one is more suitable for this type of setup and why?

28. An IoT network setup requires the following:

(a) Communication greater than 600m.

(b) Low power.

(c) No operator costs.

(d) Low bandwidth.

Then in such a scenario, which protocol is best and why?

29. An IoT web-API requires support for WebSocket addressing and WebSocket security and it follows an XML-based structure. Which protocol is best suited for such a case?

30. Specify which protocol is best for the following scenarios:

(a) Reliable queuing, topic-based messaging, publish-subscribe model, flexible routing, transactions and security.

    (b) Resource limited, low bandwidth networks, publish-subscribe model.

31. It is desired to build a multiplayer online game. It is required to have a peer-to-peer implementation of BOTs. Which protocol will you prefer—AMQP or XMPP and why?

32. Two fog nodes are situated at a distance of 50m. the time required to transmit a data packet from one fog node to another is 7ms. Find the propagation speed?

33. Is it possible to program Arduino boards in C and in Python?

34. Can Raspberry Pi read analog signals? If so, how?

35. How will you interface a Gas Sensor to Arduino?

36. How will you interface sensors to a Web Page?

37. It is desired to design an intelligent vehicle management system based on IoT, especially RFID technology. The system should provide automatic payment such that a vehicle can go through an intersection without stopping. When the vehicle exits, the parking charges/fees is deducted automatically.

38. In a healthcare system, the following functions are desired:

    (a) Sensors.

    (b) Wearable devices.

    (c) Real-time monitoring.

    (d) Disease prediction.

    (e) Early disease detection.

    (f) Monitoring system.

    (g) Management system.

    (h) Medical resource distribution.

    (i) Data sharing.

    Explain how will you design such a system?

39. It is desired to use IoT to enhance green agriculture. Also, the requirements are to have real-time collection at farm's temperature, humidity, soil moisture and oxygen levels in a green house, water beds etc. Also needed is the real-time intelligent decision on crop growth. How will you do so?

40. Compare and contrast traditional Bluetooth and BLE protocols.

41. What is Li-Fi? Give some of its features. How does Li-Fi work? Explain its functioning. Also give its advantages and disadvantages. How can it be used in any commercial application? Explain with the help of an example. How is Li-Wi different from Wi-Fi? Which one will you prefer and why so?

42. What is fog computing and fog nodes? Explain its working. What are the benefits of fog computing?

    [**Hints:** All IoT applications need instant data analysis and action on it. The action must be corrective in nature. If the data volume is very high and it is taking time for it to reach the cloud. So, the chances to use it may be lost. So, fog computing will help here. the data that must be analysed out of this voluminous data should be analysed in vicinity/closer to the place where it is generated. Now fog computing helps us to analyse data at a place that is closer to where it was generated. Therefore, we can prevent all data to be sent to the cloud. Even response time will increase and data travel is also reduced. Thus, it becomes a reality now to process data in milliseconds time. Please note that here only the data that is required will be sent to the cloud. This will be based on storage requirements. The data stored in the cloud can also be used to understand the history and to do predictions of the future. Fog computing is shown in Fig. 2.29 below:

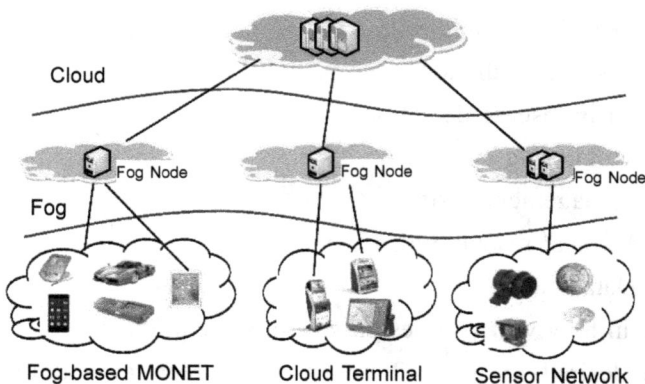

Fig. 2.29: FOG Computing

As shown in this figure, that the fog is below cloud. Also note that this means that it is closer to the elements that generate data. After analysis, only the most sensitive data (as explained above) is stored and pushed on to the cloud. So, a faster response time is provided by fog computing. This also increases efficiency and safety. There are certain applications where the response time is very important like oil and gas line fault analysis, on-flight diagnosis, healthcare, factory manufacturing line etc.

Also shown in the figure is that sensors generate data and transmit it to the middle layer that is very close to the data sources. These nodes in the middle layer are capable of handling data. This requires minimum power and lesser resources. The basic idea is that all data need not go to the cloud at the instant it is generated. Also, sensitive data gets processed very fast which results in an instant response. Note that fog is not meant for hefty storage. it is still the cloud that does the task of storing big data. We can say that fog is just an intermediary layer that enables faster data processing.

Functions of Fog Nodes

(a) It receives the data feed from the sensors in real-time.

(b) Minimum response time (in ms).

(c) Data is stored for a limited time only.

(d) Data is then sent to the cloud in form of a summary. Please note here that the data goes to the cloud.

Function of Cloud

(a) It receives data summary from the fog.

(b) Data prediction, data analytics, data storage etc. all take place here only.

Benefits of Fog Computing

(a) Lesser bandwidth consumption.

(b) Lesser data latencies.

(c) Lesser amount of data sent to the cloud.

(d) Better data security as limited data goes to the cloud.

(e) Faster processing of data in real-time as it is mandatory in industrial applications.

43. Name some platforms that provide cloud computing access for free plus the adaptable interfaces (both).

[**Hint:** Adafruit, Digital Oceans, Thing Speak are some of these platforms].

44. It is desired to develop smart city application that is IoT-based. What IoT devices and platforms may be used?

    [Hints: The following table lists them]

IoT features	Sensor devices needed
For environmental monitoring	Meters, sensors, sensor networks, stations for detection etc.
For traffic intensity monitoring	RFID, GPS receivers etc.
For river, ocean and weather monitoring	pH sensors, flow meters etc.
Outdoor parking	Parking sensors, cameras-cctv, meters etc.
Smart citizens and crowdsensing	Smart phone applications, GPS, twitter etc.
Smart waste management	Sensors in water-bins, garbage trucks etc.

    *crowdsensing occurs due to heavy usage of mobile devices.

45. Compare TCP and UDP in a tabular form. Also explain what is wireless TCP and UDP.

46. Compare Arduino Due and Raspberry Pu Model B.

47. In Raspberry Pi, the term Pi comes from where?

    [Hint: The term Pi comes from the Python programming language only.]

48. What is dynamic machine learning?

49. Throw some light on how IoT and ML can help us in various fields of development.

    [Hint: IoT and ML can be effectively implemented in machine prognostics i.e., an engineering discipline that mainly focuses on predicting the time at which a system or components will no longer perform its intended function. Hence, ML + IoT can be used in System Health Management (SHM) like Vehicle Health Management (VHM). Also, IoT + ML is attracting the attention of defence and space explorations. IoT + ML can also boost growth in agricultural field. As we know that better technologies mean greater yield. According to survey, worldwide food production will need to increase by 70% by 2050 to keep up with the global demand. ML is providing the impetus to scale and automate the agricultural sector. Both IoT + ML ensure better healthcare too. Semantic Web of Things (SWOT) and ML algorithms together, results in less differentiated caregiver.]

50. How the XMPP protocol manages communication between an XMPP client and server?

3

IoT APPLICATION DEVELOPMENT AND DESIGN CHALLENGES

3.0 INTRODUCTION

Design is a general term that is the vital and mandatory part of almost every field now. Even software engineers say that if there in no good software design then your software rests on a shaky condition. Without good and tested design your software will fail. Similarly, in IoT field also design is must. The basic idea is to develop best IoT practices and also these should be available to the end-user/ customer. The need is to have reusable and open-source platforms. Many IoT-IDEs have been designed and implemented for this purpose and are available in markets for lesser costs today. The need is to have a technology independent platform. However, designing of IoT systems is a tedious task as it involves interactions between different components like IoT devices, network resources, analytics components, application and database servers. Keeping in mind the specific product or services desired by the customers, the IoT designers strive to design the systems. sometimes, depending on the customers need, the complete product may be re-designed. The methodology should be such that it suggests reduced design, testing and maintenance times, better interoperability and reduced complexity. The need is of better and better IoT system design methodology.

3.1 IoT DESIGN METHODOLOGY

The rise of Internet-of-Things (IoT) has led to **an explosion of new sensor computing platforms. The complexity and the application domains of IoT devices range from simple self-monitoring devices in vending machines to complex interactive devices with AI in smart vehicles and Drones.**

We must define new guidelines to IoT design and its architecture. Also, we need to provide a reference model for IoT based on quality factors like

DOI: 10.1201/9781003728641-3

scalability, interoperability, security of IoT applications. Better communication means and topologies, a common language and a better domain model.

Some Points to Ponder in IoT Designing are as Follows:

1. As IoT developers wish to meet more aggressive platform objectives and protect market share through feature differentiation, they must choose between low cost and low performance CPU-based Commercial-Off-The-Shelf (COTS) systems and high-performance customer platforms with hardware accelerators like GPU and FPGA.

2. An IoT platform facilitates communication, data flow, device management and functionality of applications. **Please note that the goal is to build IoT applications within an IoT platform framework. The IoT platform allows applications to connect machines, devices, applications and people to data and control centres.**

3. Home automation can be described as introduction of technology within the home environment to provide convenience, comfort, security and energy efficiency to its occupants.

4. A home automation system can involve **switching OFF electrical appliances** like ACs or refrigerators **when a desired temperature has been reached** then switching ON again when the **temperature has crossed a certain value.**

5. The following Fig. 3.1 shows the steps of IoT design methodology.

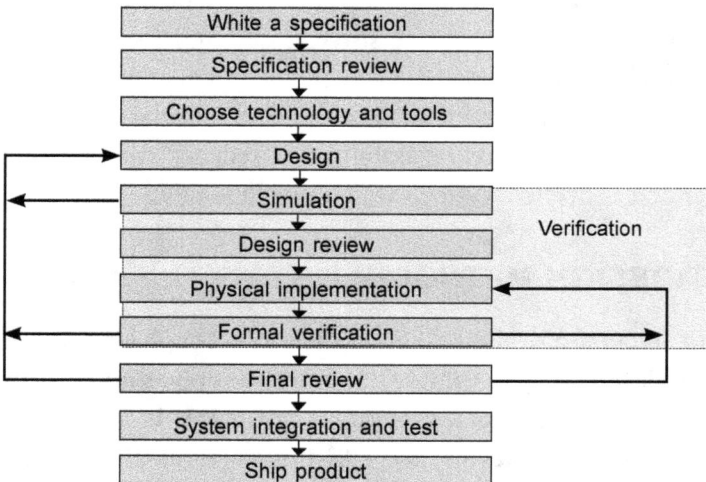

Fig. 3.1: IoT Design Methodology Steps

As studied earlier, that sensors are the eyes and ears of any IoT system. They **see the environment and convert it into an electrical signal that can be measured by a microcontroller or a CPU. Also note that depending on the need and various design considerations, users may need to be able to control the system and appliances remotely too.**

3.2 REQUIREMENT AND PROCESS MODEL OF IoT

The purpose of IoT requirements specifications: Using web application, user can remotely control the home electronic devices (light and air conditioner).

The Behaviour of IoT System: Home automation system will work in two modes, namely, Manual and automatic mode. **In manual mode,** web system provides options of manually and remotely switching ON/OFF the light. On the other hand, **in automatic mode,** sensor is provided in the room. System measures the darkness of the room and light is ON when darkness increases. Room temperature is measured by another sensor, AC is ON when room temperature is increased.

System Management Requirements: Remote monitoring and control function is provided by the system.

Data Analysis Requirements: Data analysis is based on local data.

Application Deployment Requirement: Application is installed on local device but it supports remote operation.

Security Requirement: Basic authentication mechanism must be provided.

3.3 PROCESS SPECIFICATION

Process specification is defined after requirement step. We can draw the use case based on the first stage. The process specification flowchart is the second step in IoT design methodology and is as shown in Fig. 3.2 below:

As shown in fig., in auto mode, system monitors the room temperature and light level and takes the decision for switching ON/OFF. In manual mode, it is the user that performs the operation.

Process Specification

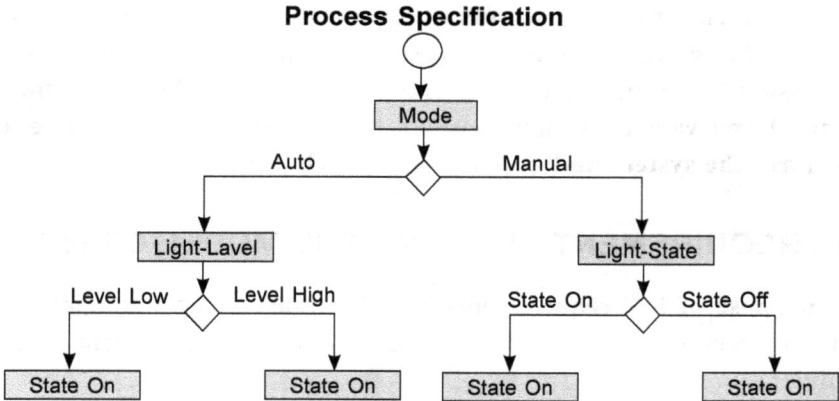

Fig. 3.2: Process Specification Flowchart

Actually, user and a physical entity are the two concepts that belong to the domain model. A user can be a human user and the interaction can be physical. The physical interaction is the result of the intention of the human to achieve a certain goal. A physical entity can potentially contain other physical entities like a building is made up of several floors and each floor has several rooms.

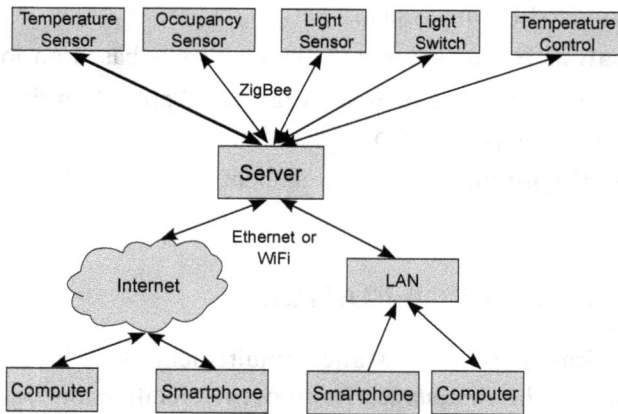

Fig. 3.3: IoT Working for Different Applications

Please note that a physical entity is represented in the digital world as a virtual entity. Also note that a virtual entity can be a database entry, a geographical model, an image or any other digital artifact. The relations between services and entities are modelled as associations. These associations could be static like in case the device is embedded into the entity; **they could be dynamic** e.g., if a device from the environment is monitoring a mobile entity.

NOTE: One physical entity can be represented by multiple virtual entities each serving a different purpose.

3.4 INFORMATION MODEL FOR IoT APPLICATIONS

An **abstract description** (UML diagram or ontology) for explaining information about the **elements or concepts** is defined in the IoT domain model. The information model, models domain model concepts that are to be explicitly represented and manipulated in the digital world. Also, the information model explicitly models **relations** between these concepts. The information model is shown in Fig. 3.4.

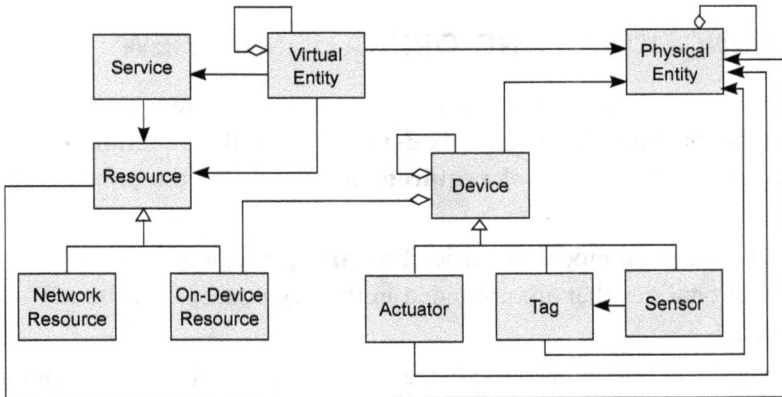

Fig. 3.4: IoT Information Model

This information model is a **meta model** that provides a structure for the information. This structure provides the basis for defining the **functional interfaces.** IoT information model is represented using Unified Modelling Language diagram. IoT information model maintains the necessary information about **virtual entities and their properties or attributes.** The information model for an object can contain information about the objects structure and resource types. This can enable APIs to automatically be composed by the middleware and automatically consumed by the application software. Additional meta data can indicate context like geographical location and bindings like message protocols and event handlers as well as the access control information. The IoT information model describes virtual entities and their attributes that have one or more values annotated with meta information or metadata. The attribute values are updated as a result of the associated services to a virtual entity.

3.5 SERVICE SPECIFICATION

Service specification in IoT defines the list of services provided by the system. It includes service type, I/O, service endpoints, schedulers, service effects and service pre-conditions. State and attributes are defined in process specification and information model. **For instance,** in a home automation system, **mode setting** is an example of mode service. **User can set the auto or manual mode.** Mode services sets the mode to either **auto or manual or retrieves the current mode. In manual mode,** the controller service, retrieves the current state from the database and switches the AC ON/OFF.

3.6 FUNCTIONAL AND OPERATIONAL VIEW

The Functional Model (FM) is derived from the **internal and external requirements. Functional view is derived from the functional model in conjunction with high-level requirements.** Some of the points to ponder are:

1. IoT functional model identifies **Functional Groups** (FG) i.e., groups of functionalities that are grounded in the key concepts of the IoT domain model.

2. Functional model is an **abstract framework** for understanding the main functional groups (FG) and their interactions. This framework defines the **common semantics of the main functionalities** and will be used for the development of IoT-complaint functional views.

3. The functional model is **not directly tied to a certain technology, application domain or implementation.** It does not explain what the different functional components are that make up certain functionality group.

4. The functional model of IoT.

5. From the figure-5, it is observed that the **application, virtual entity, IoT Service and device FGs are generated by starting from the user, virtual entity, resource, service and device classes** from the IoT domain model.

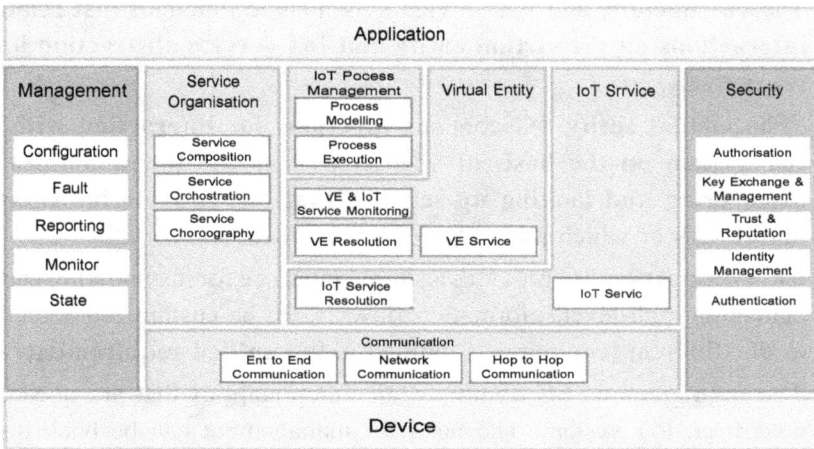

Fig. 3.5: IoT Functional Model View

6. Device functional group contains all **possible functionality hosted by the physical devices. Device functionality** includes sensing, actuation, processing, storage and identification components, the complexity of which depends on the device capabilities.

7. Communicational functional groups support all communications used by the devices. It uses **wired and wireless technology.**

8. **IoT Service Functional Group:** It supports functions like directory services which allow discovery of services and resolution to resources.

9. **Virtual Entity Functional Group:** It is related to the virtual entity class in the IoT domain model. **Also note that the associations between virtual entities can be static or dynamic depending on the mobility of the physical entities related to the corresponding Virtual Entities.**

10. **IoT service Organization Functional Group:** To host all functional components that support the composition and orchestration of IoT and virtual entity services.

11. **The Management Transversal FG** is required for the management of and/or interaction between the functionality groups.

12. **The IoT Process Management FG** relates to the conceptual integration of process management systems with the IoT ARM.

13. **The** service organization FG is a central functionality group **that acts as a communication hub between several other Functionality Groups.**

14. The virtual entity and IoT service FGs include functions that **relate to interactions on the virtual entity and IoT service abstraction levels** respectively.

15. **The virtual entity FG** contains **functions for interacting with the IoT system on the basis of VEs as well as the functionalities for discovering and looking up services that can provide information about VEs** or which allow the interaction with VEs.

16. **Communication FG** provides a simple interface for instantiating and for managing high-level information flow. It can be customized according to the different requirements defined in the **unified requirements list.**

17. **The management FG** combines all functionalities that are needed to govern an IoT system. The need for management can be back traced to at least four high-level system goals i.e., **cost reduction, attending unexpected usage issues, fault handling and flexibility.**

18. **The security functionality group is responsible for ensuring security and privacy of IoT-A-Compliant system.** It is in-charge of handling **the initial registration of a client to the system** in a secure manner. **Please note that this ensures that only legitimate clients may access services provided by the IoT infrastructure.**

19. On the other hand, **Deployment and Operational view** depends on the specific actual use case and requirements. Smart objects in the IoT system uses various methods for communication using a different technology.

20. So, the **deployment and the operational view** is very important to address how the actual system can be realized by selecting technologies and making them **communicate and operate in a comprehensive way.**

21. **It provides an IoT reference model with asset of guidelines to the application users.** The different design choices that they have to face while designing the **actual implementation of their services.**

22. Some of the viewpoints used in the deployment and operation view lie in the point of reference:
    - The IoT domain model diagram is used as a guideline to describe the specific application domain.
    - The functional model is used as a reference to the system definition.
    - **Network connectivity diagrams can be used to plan the connectivity topology to enable the desired networking capability**

of the target application, at the deployment level, the connectivity diagram will be used to define the hierarchies and the type of the sub-networks composing the complete system network.

- **Device descriptions** can be used to map actual hardware on the service and resource requirements of the target system.

3.7 PRINCIPLES AND SECURITY CHALLENGES OF IoT

Principles of Security of IoT

1. **Identity: Trust is always tied to an identity.** Hence, **every device needs a unique identity that cannot be changed.** The device must also be able to prove its identity at all times.
2. **Positive Intention:** The device and linked service have positive intentions.
3. **Predictability and Transparency:** The functional scope of the service provided by the devices is known to its full extent. There are no undocumented functions/ secret functions. **Also note that the behaviour of the system can be checked at any time by independent third parties.**
4. **Reputation:** An increasing number of positive interactions between the things gradually from a **reputation- based intelligent network.**
5. **The security challenges** are as follows**:**
   - Devices are **not reachable.**
   - Devices can be **lost and stolen.**
   - **Devices are not crypto-engines**—strong security is difficult without processing power.
   - **Devices have finite life.** Credentials need to be tied to lifetime.
   - **Devices are transportable** and will cross borders.

3.8 VULNERABILITIES OF IoT

Some of the vulnerable points in IoT system are as follows:

1. Today cars are equipped with **high-end technologies like Bluetooth, GPS mounted dashboard, automatic transmission and remote start by smart phones and many more different apps preinstalled in the**

car's dashboard monitor. All these technological advances are **the cause of serious vulnerabilities also.**

2. Even medical devices are not away from critical vulnerabilities with IoT. At a research at University of Alabama, the students were able to **hack into the WIFI system of a pace-maker implanted inside an iStan** i.e., a robotic dummy patient used to train medical students. **Also note that the heart rate can be increased or decreased from a conceptual Pacemaker by an external adversary.**

3. **Two nuclear power plants monitoring systems** were infected by a virus. It is called as **Slammer Worm. Slammer worm is a SQL worm if injected then it would cause a denial-of-service (DoS) attack.**

4. **Household appliances are also vulnerable** from different types of external attacks. **Security breach** on these IoT objects can take place in 2 ways—either the system will be physically compromised or the central serve monitoring devices could be compromised.

5. One of the **biggest applications of cloud computing and IoT is in the area of personal fitness tracking through smart phones and smart devices.** The 3 biggest smart device OS i.e., Apple iOS, Google Android and Microsoft phone, have their own apps connecting to a central cloud network to track a user's daily fitness goals and progress update. This service requires a user account in the device but if the app on the phone and watch are identical then these devices can be synced automatically, if either one had a pre-existing account. Here, **the vulnerable point is if the smart watch is stolen or lost then there lies a possibility of consumer's data retrieval even if the data is residing within the phone.**

3.9 UNSTRUCTURED DATA STORAGE ON CLOUD/ LOCAL SERVER

The evolution of cloud computing is very interesting. **The roots of cloud computing lie and start from cluster computing where homogeneous computing nodes work together.** They are connected loosely or lightly. Then we came to **Grid Computing where heterogeneous computing nodes are distributed over a wider area to perform larger tasks.** Then, **Ubiquity computing** was the successor of grid computing in which packaged resources are available for computing and storage. at least, the cloud computing model emerged that has a shared pool of configurable computing resources that are ubiquitous, dynamic and provides on-demand access. That is to say, the cloud services mean services on rental basis/ pay-per-usage basis.

The issues of transferring large amount of data / big data to the cloud as well as data security, once the data is in the cloud, initially hampered adoption of cloud for big data. But now that much data originates in the cloud and with the advent of bare-metal servers, the cloud has become a solution for use cases including business analytics and geospatial analysis. Solutions will range from Hadoop hosting in the cloud to end-to-end analytics.

Several tools like R, Python and MATLAB can be used to move data into a local system and also for building the model. But the model will not be able to any real-time prediction. **Please note that the cloud space can be configured with big data platform in which storing, processing and retrieving of data becomes faster, simpler and more efficient.** The traditional big data platform is HADOOP and its file system named as HADOOP DISTRIBUTED FILE SYSTEM (HDFS). **Also note that cloud is not necessarily a single system rather it can be a network configured to a single contact point.** As far as big data is concerned, like IoT, distributed systems are very efficient in handling it. And HDFS is a distributed storage space for this application. Hadoop is a master-slave architecture wherein **master is called the name node and the slaves are called as data nodes. The name node is connected with all of the data nodes.** In HDFS, every file is split on the basis of **block size** and stored in different **data nodes** so as to achieve **distribution of data and parallel processing.** By default, a block size is 64MB. **The given file is divided into blocks of size lesser than or equal to 64MB and placed in different data nodes.** So, distribution, parallelism and cost of the architecture controlled are all important here. So, all data nodes are made up of commodity hardware. **Please understand that when the data nodes are made with commodity hardware and every node has a lot of data to process then there are chances that the nodes turn down due to excessive load.** This leads to a huge risk of losing data when a data node is down. **Also note that to increase the fault tolerance, the cluster is configured with a replication factor (bby default, replication factor = 3, which means that every data block is replicated 3 times at the time of storage and placed in three different data nodes.** So, when one node goes down then the data can be recovered from another node. **And this process of dividing the data, replicating and selecting the data**

nodes is done at the name node. The selection of data point is done on the basis of features like the amount of free space, new node and nodes' age (calculated from its last down time). **Also note that the replications of the data block are placed in three dissimilar data nodes to further increase fault tolerance.** Name nodes play a very vital role in maintaining where the blocks of file are stored. **Note that if the name node fails but all data nodes are high, then the data will be safe in the data nodes.** While retrieving the data, the request is sent to the name node. **One instance of every data block is chosen by the name node and the same is retrieved, merged and finally returned.** The selection of a block out of these three replicas is based on the features like which node is comparatively free. Some times a data node may also fail due to some external features. **But as the data node fails, then the name node should be able to identify the same immediately.** Then the **name node takes the list of data blocks that were present in that node and the replicas of the same present in other active nodes are identified.** All those data blocks are then replicated and placed in another data node. Hence, the **name node** can ensure that any data block always has three instances. For the name node to identify the active data nodes, a **heartbeat along with a block report is sent from every data node to the name node at regular intervals. Also please understand that the heartbeat signifies that the data node is active and the block report updates the name node with the details of data node** like amount of space available, process status etc. when a heartbeat from a data node is not received then the name node immediately notes it and initiates the recovery process. Some of the main highlights of Hadoop are as follows:

1. Hadoop is a **master-slave architecture.**
2. **Master is a name node and slaves are data nodes.**
3. **Data file** is divided into **small blocks** of 64MB and **saved in different data nodes.**
4. It is the **name node that decides in which data nodes**, the data block is to be saved.
5. **Every block of data is replicated three times and stored in different data nodes for fault tolerance.**
6. **Every process is submitted to the name node to get a Job Tracker. The Job Tracker** sends sub-tasks to each data node that has the corresponding data blocks. This creates Task Trackers in the data nodes.

7. **Pipelines like Flume and Kafka bring in the data from real-time streams.**
8. **Sqoop is used to integrate data from the relational database.**
9. **Hive is a database tool of Hadoop, where we can write SQL to fetch data and analyse it.**
10. **Pig scripting language** is used to process dumped data in HDFS.
11. **Mahout** is a tool for executing ML algorithms in Hadoop.
12. **AVRO** is a tool for representing **online data.**
13. **Drill** is a large-scale **data analysis visual tool.**
14. Many other **utility tools** also run-on Hadoop and these tools along with HDFS layers constitute the Hadoop ecosystem.
15. All these process and utility tools are monitored from the **Ambari view.**
16. **Zookeeper** is a server that coordinates jobs within this ecosystem.

3.10   IoT APPLICATIONS

Designing of smart street lights in smart city, smart metering, city automation, automotive applications, home automation, smart cards, e-health, communicating data with hardware units, mobiles, tablets.

The application domain of IoT is not limited. It touches the sky. Some of the applications of IoT are discussed below:

1. Smart City Streetlights Control and Monitoring

The number of urban residents is growing by nearly 60 million every year. Also, more than 60% of the world's population will be living in cities by 2025. As a result, people occupying just 2% of the world's land will consume about three-quarters of its resource. Also, more than 100 cities of 1 million people will be built in next 10 years. Over the past decade, the city of Amsterdam, Netherlands has developed **a vision for collaborating, envisioning, developing and testing many connected solutions that cloud pave the way to a smarter, greener urban environment.** Many projects were launched (in 2006) as Amsterdam identified the ways to improve sustainable living, working, public spaces and mobility. Currently, the city has been exploring the potential for **a connected public lighting infrastructure. Innovations will aim to improve the quality of life in cities, encompassing security issues and energy resourcefulness.** Smart city includes the following:

1. **Smarter management of city infrastructure** using Big Data Analytics.
2. Collaboration across multiple and disparate agencies **using the cloud technologies.**
3. **Real-time data collection, enabling quick response** using mobile technologies.
4. **Improved public safety and law enforcement** and more efficient emergency response.
5. **Better city planning, improved schematics, project management and delivery.**
6. **Networked utilities smart metering and grid management.**
7. **Building developments, more automation and better management.**

Research challenges for smart city IoT applications are:

1. To overcome the **traditional organization of the cities.**
2. **Creating algorithms and schemes** to describe information created by sensors in different applications to enable **useful exchange of information between different city services.**
3. Mechanisms for **cost efficient deployment** and even more important maintenance of such installations including energy scavenging.
4. Ensuring reliable readings from a plethora of sensors and efficient calibration of a large number of sensors deployed everywhere from lamp-posts to waste bins.
5. Development of **low energy protocols and algorithms.**
6. **Algorithms for analysis and processing of data** acquired in the city.
7. IoT large scale **deployment and integration.**
8. With smart city applications producing continuous large data from heterogeneous sources, **existing relational-database technologies are inadequate to handle** such huge amounts of data given the limited processing speed and the significant storage expansion cost.
9. To solve this problem, **big data processing technologies** that are based on **distributed data management and parallel processing** have provided enabling platforms for data repositories, distributed processing and interactive data visualization.
10. Smart grids are an advancement of electricity grids that are being used currently. **A smart grid is an electrical grid that uses modern technology to collect and communicate electricity related information of both the suppliers and consumers.**

11. **It** not only increases the **efficiency and reliability** but also improves the **production and distribution of electricity** to the customers.

12. **The process of installing a smart grid necessarily means technical re-designing of the infrastructure at different levels.** One such measure means **replacing the existing electronic meters with smart meters** so as to increase the sustainability and efficiency of the entire electrical system.

13. It uses IT to improve **how electricity travels from power plants to customers and allows its consumers to interact with the grid.** It integrates new and improved technologies into the operation of the grid.

14. **The smart grid will require wide, seamless, real-time use of applications and tools** that enable grid operators and managers to make decisions rapidly.

15. **Decision support and improved interfaces will enable more accurate and timely human decision making at all the levels of the grid** including the consumer level while also enabling more advanced operator training.

16. **Energy storage systems are highly versatile.** This is a technology that can meet the needs of various users and be utilized in diverse fields. These include power generators that use renewable energy, grid equipment like energy transmission, distribution equipment as well as facilities, factories and homes.

17. **The street lighting is one of the largest energy expenses for a city. The street light section** comprises of all the light lamps in an area with current sensors and RF module.

18. The 'N' street lights communicate with the local controller unit wirelessly through RF module (ZigBee). 'N' local controller unit communicates with main server through IoT due to its global coverage area.

19. **Smart light infrastructure is the backbone of IoT in smart cities.** Smart and wireless street light luminaries can act as service gateways for other street level IoT devices.

20. **Please note that the smart street lights are intelligent lights that gather dynamic data** (data that keeps changing dynamically by time) through some sensors and generate required information for the request claimed by a citizen on road.

21. Smart street light saves energy by sensing the surrounding through their sensors expecting some other sensor in some other device.

22. **Smart meters** provide the smart grid interface between the customer and the energy service provider. **These meters operate digitally.** They allow for automated and complex transfers of information between the two. **Also note that it helps to reduce the energy costs of the customers and provides information about the usage of electricity in different service areas to the energy service providers.**

2. Home Automation

1. Technologies that help for smart lighting include solid state lighting like LED lights and IP-enabled lights.

2. Domestic lighting solutions are made smart to sense human movements and environment conditions like cloudy or sunny weather and control the lights accordingly.

3. Hence, smart home lighting means huge energy savings.

4. **Mobile devices or web-based IoT applications** can be used to remotely control wireless-enabled Internet connected lights.

5. **Smart thermostats, smart refrigerators and smart TVs** are some of the devices used in our homes today.

6. **Security cameras** are also used today for home security.

7. **Fire alarms** are also used that do smoke detections.

8. **Smart parking** makes the search for parking space simpler.

9. **Smart lighting** for roads, parks and buildings can save energy too. Smart lights connected to Internet can be controlled remotely to find out **lighting schedules and lighting intensity. Also note that smart lights fitted with sensors can communicate with other smart lights without sensors and can exchange information on the sensed ambience of the surroundings so that lighting can be adapted.**

10. Smart roads are made smart by adding sensors that collect information like traffic congestions, driving conditions and accidents. This information can be used by the drivers to estimate the travel time. Also note that even cloud-based services and applications may be used to communicate this information to other drivers, or on to the social media.

11. **Smart meters** provide the smart grid interface between the customer and the energy service provider. **These meters operate digitally.** They allow for automated and complex transfers of information between the two. **Also note that it helps to reduce the energy costs of the customers and provides information about the usage of electricity in different service areas to the energy service providers.**

3. E-health

1. IoT in health care monitoring has a very important role. **Health care devices may be wearable devices like smart watches, belts or wrist bands. Various body parameters** like its temperature, oxygen level, blood pressure, ECG etc. can also be monitored.

2. **With smart watches,** the users can search the Internet, play audio/video files, make calls etc. **Smart glasses** allow users to take photos and record videos, get map directions, check flight status and so on.

3. **Simultaneous reporting and monitoring:** Real-time monitoring via connected devices can save lives in case of emergency like heat attack, diabetes, asthma attacks etc.

4. In a report by Centre of Connected Health Policy, it is stated that there was a 50% reduction in 30-days readmission rate because of remote patient monitoring on heart failure patients.

5. **IoT devices collect and transfer health data** like oxygen level, blood pressure etc. These data are stored in the cloud and can be shared with an authorized person like a doctor, external consultant, to allow them to look at the collected data regardless of their place, time or device.

6. **IoT can automate patient care workflow** with the aid of healthcare mobility solutions. IoT enables *interoperability, M2M communications information exchange and data movement* that make healthcare service delivery effective.

7. IoT devices can **collect, report and analyse data in real-time** and cut the need to store raw data.

8. IoT allows devices **to collect vital data and transfer it to the doctor for real-time tracking. Reports and alerts** give firm opinion about a patient's condition wherever he is. Even notifications are dropped to people about critical parts using mobile apps. **Hence, we can say that IoT provides real-time alerting, tracking and monitoring that**

allows hands-on timely treatments with better accuracy and better doctors intervention.

4. Smart Dust

1. The concept of tiny sensors (the size of a grain of sand) with the ability to detect everything from chemicals to vibrations was first thought in in 1990s.

2. However, the interest in this nascent technology has recently become quite active. According to Gartner report, smart dust will be very active in next 5 to 10 years.

3. Applications of these smart dust particles in IoT are virtually endless, ranging from oil exploration companies spreading smart dust to monitor rock movements to small sensors all over factory equipment continually looking out for changes and problems.

4. The challenge of smart dust sensors are its miniaturization and the prohibitive cost of producing huge quantities.

5. But they are slowly and securely becoming cheaper to manufacture.

5. Smart Farming

1. Implementation of smart and connected IoT projects enables farmers to make use of the massive amount of data generated on their farms.

2. Many IIoT programs have been deployed to increase productivity and quality of the food in food supply chain. It may use satellite imaging to monitor all of the farming operations.

3. In precision agriculture domain, real-time data about soil, weather and hydration levels can help farmers to make better decisions about crop harvesting.

6. Automation and Automotive Applications

According to the US Department of Transportation, National Highway Traffic Safety Administration (NHTSA), **"Fully automated and, autonomous or self-driving vehicles are those in which the operation of the vehicle occurs without direct driver input to control the steering, acceleration and braking and are designed so that the driver is not expected to constantly monitor the roadway while operating in self-driving mode."** Recently, the area of **intelligent transportation, pedestrian and transport infrastructure** are connected to the communication network to improve the **driver safety and traffic efficiency and this is known as Intelligent Connected Vehicle (ICV).** Some of the main features of automated, connected vehicles are:

1. Automated and connected vehicle technologies are among the most heavily researched automotive fields today.

2. Please note that the emerging technologies from the consumer electronics and IT fields crossover to the automotive domain, so modern vehicles are being equipped with powerful sensors and networking and communication devices that can communicate with other vehicles and exchange information with the external environment.

3. Today, we need to have connected modern devices at both intra and inter levels.

4. **Also note that the way in which we interact with our vehicles is rapidly changing, driven by the increased use of mobile devices, cloud-based services and advanced automotive technology.** *This implies that the machine interface between automobiles and humans must allow for the seamless integration of several types of personal devices* that support various software and hardware standards to allow the drivers to use their smart phones while driving.

5. **Internet-integrated vehicles are already on roads.** The **future of automotive industry** needs newer applications and technologies related to electric powering, automation and connected services.

6. The **future vehicle should have the capability of surround sensing** and should be able to establish connections between vehicles and surrounding infrastructure.

7. The **concatenation of cloud computing and IoT provides a promising automotive domain.** However, IoT-based vehicular data clouds must be *efficient, scalable, secure and reliable.* This is must before we apply it to larger systems.

8. Please note that IoT-based vehicular data clouds are the backbone of the system. But still this research is in its infancy stage. Also note that to ensure that the vehicular data clouds are useful, many services like road navigation, traffic management, remote monitoring, business intelligence etc. need to be developed and deployed based on these vehicular-data clouds.

9. Several challenges like *security, scalability, reliability, vulnerability, lack of global standards etc* still exist.

10. **IoT connectivity to vehicles** has two driving forces

11. The connected vehicle to communicate via mobile network with the connected house.

12. To adjust any connected devices in the home remotely.

13. *Future automotive IT infrastructure and interaction specifications should follow on from general human-computer interaction guidelines with the understanding that there will be a high heterogeneity required to manage these contents.*

14. **High speed Internet** is the current demand even in the running vehicles as it improves security. Applications are Google MAPS, YouTube etc. are very common on a moving vehicle.

15. **Better GUIs** like speech interfaces are becoming very popular now a days.

16. The Industrial IoT (IIoT) has power to revolutionize the transport industry. It provides access to new data streams and has made self-driving vehicles a reality.

17. IIoT will help reduce pollution, optimize people's mobility and goods and save lives.

18. Fleet management is another application of IoT. It enables intelligent tracking and monitoring of vehicles through data from GPS sensors. **Vehicles can be routed and scheduled automatically. Also note that fleet management through IoT, results in benefits like more safety, better productivity and time as well as cost savings.**

19. IoT automates **revenue collection, bill generation and toll metering.**

20. IoT sensors monitor **train speed in real time.**

21. **Smart parking** is also possible with IoT sensors that can detect whether the parking space is available or not.

22. IoT is helpful in **finding structural problems** in bridges, tunnels and roadways.

SUMMARY

This chapter starts with a generic IoT system design methodology that has been found to be independent of the specific product, service or programming language. The IoT design methodology is a step-by-step process as follows:

- To define the purpose and the requirements of the system
- Develop use cases for the IoT system.
- Define the domain model.
- Define the information model.
- Define the functional view.
- Define the service specifications.
- Define deployment and operational view specifications.
- Integration of devices and components.
- Finally, develop the IoT application.

This chapter deals with domain-specific applications of IoT. Several applications of IoT are discussed and explained in a simpler way.

MULTIPLE CHOICE QUESTIONS [MCQS] WITH ANSWERS

1. _____ are the eyes of a home automation system.
   - (a) Mobiles.
   - (b) Sensors.
   - (c) Water purifiers.
   - (d) None of the above.
2. In which mode, the sensor is provided in the room?
   - (a) Manual mode.
   - (b) Automatic mode.
   - (c) Both 'a' and 'b'.
   - (d) None of the above.
3. A physical entity is represented in the digital world as a
   - (a) Sensor.
   - (b) Virtual entity.
   - (c) Compound entity.
   - (d) None of the above.
4. The relations between services and entities are modelled as
   - (a) Associations.
   - (b) Compositions.
   - (c) Derivations.
   - (d) None of the above.
5. If the device is embedded into an entity, then the association is
   - (a) Static.
   - (b) Dynamic.
   - (c) Mobile.
   - (d) None of the above.
6. If the device from the environment is monitoring a mobile entity then the association is
   - (a) Static.
   - (b) Dynamic.
   - (c) Mobile.
   - (d) None of the above.

7. One physical entity can be represented by

(a) A graph. (b) A tree.

(c) Many virtual entities. (d) None of the above.

8. The model that is a meta model and provides a structure for the information is named as

(a) Domain model. (b) Information model.

(c) Application model. (d) None of the above.

9. UML stands for

(a) Uniform Modeling Language. (b) Unified Master Language.

(c) Unified Modeling Language. (d) None of the above.

10. The central functionality group that acts as a communication hub between several other Functional Groups is named as-

(a) The virtual entity FG. (b) The management traversal FG.

(c) The service organisation FG. (d) None of the above.

11. To plan the connectivity topology to show the desired networking capability, the diagrams drawn are

(a) Network connectivity diagrams.

(b) Class diagrams.

(c) Collaboration diagrams.

(d) None of the above.

12. Trust is always tied to

(a) An entity. (b) An identity.

(c) An object. (d) None of the above.

13. An increasing number of positive interactions between the "Things" gradually form a

(a) Client-based intelligent network.

(b) Reputation-based intelligent network.

(c) Artificial Intelligent network.

(d) None of the above.

14. _____ prevents IoT device from being compromised

(a) Hardware patching. (b) Software patching.

(c) Both "a" and "b". (d) None of the above.

15. What minimizes the risks of data loss or interference with the business operations
    (a) Software patching.
    (b) Hatching.
    (c) Caching
    (d) None of the above.

16. IoT software analytics must be designed on the basis of
    (a) Threat detection.
    (b) Anomaly detection.
    (c) Disease detection.
    (d) None of the above.

17. Home automation is also known as
    (a) Small home technology.
    (b) Smart home technology.
    (c) Simple home technology.
    (d) None of the above.

18. Two most common home automation communication protocols are
    (a) ZigBee and TCP/IP.
    (b) Z-wave and UDP.
    (c) ZigBee and Z-wave.
    (d) All of the above.

19. For control applications, which of these is a networking platform
    (a) WIFI.
    (b) LonWorks.
    (c) WLAN.
    (d) None of the above.

20. HAN stands for
    (a) Home Area Network.
    (b) Happy Area Network.
    (c) Huge Area Network.
    (d) None of the above.

21. Smart grid is also known as
    (a) Electronet.
    (b) Piconet.
    (c) Internet.
    (d) None of the above.

22. The energy management in smart grid can be more efficient if we use
    (a) Grid computing.
    (b) Soft computing.
    (c) Cloud computing.
    (d) None of the above.

23. Using cloud in smart grid, what type of data can be analyzed
    (a) Big data.
    (b) Smaller data.
    (c) Block chained data.
    (d) Real-time data.

24. With the explosion of IoT, _____ is gaining momentum
    (a) Smart phones.
    (b) Smart cities.
    (c) Cyber cities.
    (d) None of the above.

25. Smart city is also known as
    (a) Business cluster.
    (b) Smart community.
    (c) Urban agglomeration.
    (d) All of the above.

26. If cities establish institutions and community-based problem solving then the intelligence is named as
    (a) Intelligent IoT.
    (b) Orchestration Intelligence.
    (c) Instrumentation Intelligence.
    (d) None of the above.

27. To enhance the data quality and decision making, what can be done with different type of data
    (a) Data division.
    (b) Data compression.
    (c) Data fusion.
    (d) None of the above.

28. The mathematical model for data fusion may be
    (a) Probability based.
    (b) AI based.
    (c) Both "a" and "b".
    (d) None of the above.

29. Data fusion and IoT can help in
    (a) Solving big data problems.
    (b) Making information more intelligent, decisive and precise.
    (c) Hiding critical information.
    (d) All of the above.

30. Smart parking and intelligent transportation are based on a basic
    (a) Ecological principle.
    (b) Huygen's principle.
    (c) Security principle.
    (d) None of the above.

31. The backbone of the vehicle systems is
    (a) Good vehicle.
    (b) Faster vehicle.
    (c) IoT-based vehicular data clouds.
    (d) None of the above.

32. ICV stands for
    (a) Intelligent Connected Vehicle.
    (b) Internal Common Vehicle.
    (c) Indian Connected Vehicle.
    (d) None of the above.

33. The fourth industrial revolution is referred to as
    (a) Industry 4.0
    (b) Industry 4.1
    (c) Industry 4.2
    (d) Industry 4.3

34. The intersection of IoT and Industry 4.0 is nothing else but
    (a) IIoT.
    (b) COT.
    (c) BOT.
    (d) None of the above.

35. Industry 4.0 creates
    (a) Smart Objectory.   (b) Smart Factory.
    (c) Smart Library.   (d) None of the above.
36. IIoT is also known as _____ while IoT is also known as _____
    (a) Internal, External.   (b) External, Internal.
    (c) Enterprise IoT, Consumer IoT.
    (d) None of the above.
37. The time for which the IoT device can operate with limited power supply is known as
    (a) Latency.   (b) Energy.
    (c) Topology.   (d) None of the above.
38. The time required for transmitting the data to the cloud or any other processing centre is known as
    (a) Latency.   (b) Redundancy.
    (c) Energy.   (d) None of the above.
39. IoT use cases are derived from
    (a) SDD.   (b) DFD.
    (c) Requirements Specification.   (d) None of the above.
40. The number of IoT system levels is
    (a) 3   (b) 4   (c) 5   (d) 6

Answers

1. a	2. b	3. b	4. a	5. a	6. b
7. c	8. b	9. c	10. c	11. a	12. b
13. b	14. b	15. a	16, b	17. b	18. c
19. b	20. a	21. a	22. c	23. d	24. b
25. d	26. b	27. c	28. c	29. d	30. a
31. c	32. a	33. a	34. a	35. b	36. c
37. b	38. a	39. c	40. c		

CONCEPTUAL SHORT QUESTIONS WITH ANSWERS

Q1. Explain the following:
   (a) Application development.
   (b) Device and component integration.

Ans. (a) **Application Development:**

1. It is the final stage in developing an IoT application. In web application, it displays mode control: Auto and manual.

2. Two modes are provided—auto mode and manual mode.

3. **If auto mode is enabled,** the light control in the web application is disabled and it reflects the current state of light.

4. **If auto mode is disabled,** the light control is enabled and it is used for manually controlling light and air conditioner.

(b) **Device and Component Integration:**

1. In this step, we have to integrate the devices and components. The devices and components used in home automation examples are Raspberry Pi, sensor, laser pointer, light dependent resistor etc.

2. When developing an innovative solution for this device, Raspberry Pi, you will need to come up with a software design solution that addresses your end-use requirements. You can accomplish this more easily when you have a sense of Raspberry Pi capabilities being demonstrated out in the field now.

   From controlling the room lights with your smartphone to scheduling events to occur automatically, home automation has taken convenience to a whole new level. Instead of using mechanical switches, you can now conveniently control all of the devices in your home from your fingertips.

Q2. Define a virtual sensor.

Ans. Virtual sensor is a software sensor as opposed to a physical or hardware sensor. Virtual sensors provide indirect measurements of abstract conditions by combining sensed data from a group of heterogeneous physical sensors.

Q3. How can we achieve feasible solutions in IoT?

Ans. It is said that IoT, sensors and data analytics can provide feasible solutions. This can be stated in form of an equation also

   IoT + Sensors + Data Analytics = Feasible Solutions

The sensor collects data, microcontroller processes it and the data is stored in the cloud for future predictions.

Q4. **It is desired to build an IoT-based application to monitor the water quality. Suggest some steps that you will follow to accomplish the same.**

Ans. The following are the proposed four steps:

1. Data collection and communication.
2. Cloud and data analytics.
3. Data visualization and presentation.
4. Water status report generation.

Q5. **Using IoT, how can we develop a system to measure the impact of collision of an automobile accident and its location of accident so that help can be provided?**

Ans. The collision severity measuring system is built on IoT only. For detecting the pressure applied on the vehicle during collision, force-sensitive resistors are mounted on the vehicles at places where the collision is likely to occur. Also the vehicle is fitted with collision sensor to detect collision. When the collision happens, the data obtained from the sensors is processes and the alert is sent to the hospitals along with the Google maps link that has details of the location where the accident has occurred.

Q6. **How IoT-based solutions can be provided for air pollution?**

Ans. We have heard about acid rains. That is, factories and automobiles emit huge amounts of harmful gases like CO_2, NO, CO etc. that when mixes with outer environment or even water, may be consumed by animal and this can cause deaths. So, **IoT-based air pollution monitoring systems can be used along with the gaseous and meteorological sensors to monitor the emission of these gases. Several such distributed monitoring stations can then be connected over internet. Also, they can communicate with other peers. Note that this distributed network of monitoring nodes can be controlled by a real-time air quality monitoring system.**

Q7. **Write a short note on Home Area Network (HANs).**

Ans. Some of the **main points to ponder on HANs** are as follows:

1. It is a network that is deployed and operated within a **small boundary** (a small house or small office.
2. It enables **communication and allows the sharing of resources** like the Internet between computers, mobiles and other devices over a network connection.

3. Even HAN may be **wired or wireless.**

4. HAN consists of a **broadband Internet connection** that is shared between multiple users through a vendor or 3rd party wired or wireless modem.

5. **User host devices** may be standard computers, laptops, mobiles and tablets.

6. Generally, the modem has **network switch capabilities** that provide wired LAN network switch capabilities that provide wired LAN ports or wireless connectivity to host users.

7. HAN may also include other devices like FAX, printer, scanner or small network attached storage that is **shared by all host devices.**

Q8. Write a short note on Local Operation Networks (LonWorks).

Ans. LonWorks is **a networking platform that has been specifically created to address the needs of control applications.** Some of the main points on LonWorks are as follows:

1. The platform is built on a protocol created by Echelon Corp. for networking devices over media like twisted pair, power lines, fibre optics and RF.

2. It is used for automation of various functions within buildings like lightning, heating, ventilation and air conditioning.

3. Every device includes a Neuron chip, a transceiver and the application electronics.

4. Neuron chip is a System-on-Chip (SOC) with multiple processors, RAM, ROM and I/O INTERFACE PORTS.

5. LonWorks splits device groups into intelligent elements that can communicate through a physical communication medium.

Q9. HAN has two architectures. Name them. Write short notes on them.

Ans. HAN has two architectures—DomoNet and Jini.

DomoNet: DomoNet architecture uses XML for description and web-services for control and follows a SOA-Service-oriented Architecture. **Please note that this is not tied to any software, programming language or architecture. Also note that in this, a central gateway connects different technologies.** The tech manager for each technology provides web services for control and access.

Jini: It is a network architecture concept that SUN Microsystems call as **"spontaneous networking"**. Using Jini, users will be able to plug printers, storage devices, speakers and any kind of device directly into a network. **Note that each pluggable device will define itself immediately to a network device registry. Also note that there is no need of a device driver in an OS as the OS will know about all accessible devices through the network registry only.** Jini architecture connects various devices sharing their resources with **auto-configuration and auto-installation.** It is based on Java by SUN Microsystems and follows an object-oriented paradigm.

Q10. **"Smart grid is also known as electricity with a brain." Justify this statement.**

Ans. Smart grids achieve **high reliability in power systems.** It is a **cyber-physical system** equipped with sustainable models of **energy production, distribution and usage.** Smart grid is conceptualized as a planned nation-wide network that uses IT to deliver electricity efficiently, reliably and securely. So, **smart grid is also named as electricity with a brain or the energy Internet or electronet.** Smart grid is a modernized grid that enables **bidirectional flow of energy and uses two-way communication and control capabilities** that will lead to an array of new functionalities and applications.

Q11. **Give some advantages of smart grid to customers and stakeholders.**

Ans. **Benefits to customers are:**
1. Reduced operations and management.
2. Low power costs for consumers.
3. Reduced peak demand that further lowers the electricity rates.
4. Better integration of customer + owner power generation systems like renewable energy systems.
5. Rapid restoration of electricity after power disturbances.
6. More security.
7. Updated information on their energy usage in real-time.
8. Enables electric cars, smart devices etc to be charged.
9. Many pricing options available.

Benefits to stakeholders are:
1. It increases the grid reliability.
2. Reduces the frequency of power backouts and brownouts.

3. It provides infrastructure for monitoring analysis and decision making.
4. It increases the grid resiliency by providing detailed information.
5. It reduces inefficiencies in energy delivery.
6. In integrates the sustainable resources of wind and solar.
7. Better management of distributed energy sources like micro-grid operations.

Q12. What are smart meters?

Ans. Smart meters provide the smart grid interface between the customer and the energy service provider. **These meters operate digitally.** They allow for automated and complex transfers of information between the two. **Also note that it helps to reduce the energy costs of the customers and provides information about the usage of electricity in different service areas to the energy service providers.**

Q13. Define what is Distribution Intelligence?

Ans. Distribution Intelligence means the energy distribution systems that are quipped with smart IoT devices. For example, smart meter is an example of distributed intelligence.

Some of the points to ponder are:

1. The identification of the source of a power outage.
2. To ensure power flow automatically.
3. It optimizes the balance between the real and reactive power.
4. There are devices that store and release energy.
5. This may cause increased electrical currents without consuming real power.
6. Intelligent distribution system maintains the proper level of reactive power in the system.
7. It controls and **protects the feeder lines.**

Q14. Write short notes on Plug-in Electric vehicles (PEVs).

Ans. Plug-in Electric vehicles (PEVs) use smart grids only for efficient working. PEVs reduce the **oil dependency and pollution -less** when it runs of electricity. They rely on **power plants to charge their batteries** and this is done during **off-peak hours.** They can also be used as **an energy source during on-peak hours.** PEVs also get incentives from energy service providers for providing energy to the grid through discharging.

Q15. What challenges do you face in smart cities?

Ans. The following challenges are faced when smart cities are developed:

1. **Security:** Data that is collected from consumers/ end-users need to be secured. This collected data can be exposed to attacks, vulnerabilities and multi-tenancy that includes the risk of data leakage.

2. **Heterogeneity:** Various hardware platforms, radio specifications and software platforms need to be integrated. Different user requirements must be accommodated and this is a challenge.

3. **Reliability:** As communication can be unreliable in smart cities and this happens due to vehicle mobility. Delivery failures are still found in smart cities. Delay in receiving of data as deployed nodes are mobile.

4. **Legal and Social Aspects:** Legal aspects of smart cities include services based on user provided information while social aspects is that individual and informed consent is required for using humans as data sources.

5. **Big Data:** Big data has many challenges like its storage, management, fusion, consistency, its volume, velocity, variety, vulnerability etc. In smart cities also, transfer, storage and maintenance of huge volumes of data are expensive. **Please note that data cleaning and purification of data is time consuming. Also note that data analytics on this deluge of data is process intensive.** Embedded intelligence to support AI on IoT to build the smart city infrastructure is also a challenge.

6. **Sensor Selection:** The choice of proper sensors for energy planning is also critical. **Note that device placement and network architecture is also important for reliable end-to-end IoT implementation.**

7. **Communication Medium** also plays a vital role in seamless function of IoT in smart cities.

Q16. What is single hop and multi-hop data fusion? What are the different levels of data fusion? Explain its mathematical model.

Ans. In **single-hop,** every sensor transmits data to the data fusion centre directly. On the other hand, in **multi-hop process** data passes across adjacent sensors.

This is shown in figure below:

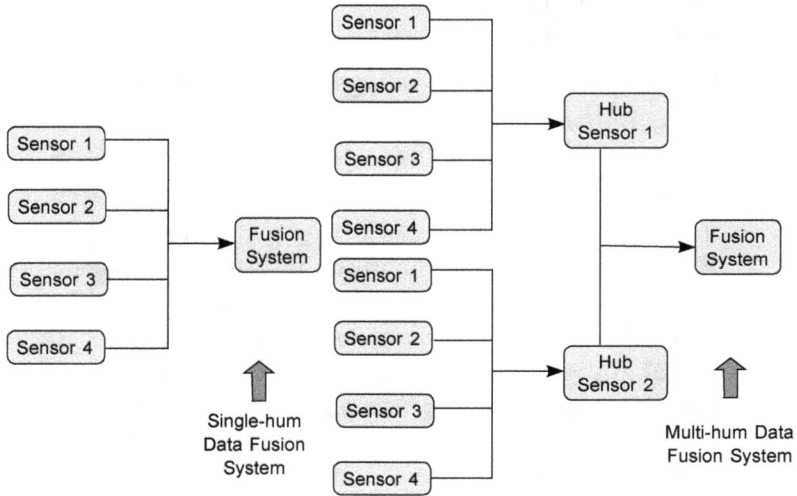

Fig. 3.6: Single-hop and Multi-hop Data Fusion

As is crystal clear from this figure that in case of single hop all sensors data is brought to one fusion system only while in a multi hop data fusion system, multi-hub data fusion is done.

Various stages of data fusion include decision level, feature level, pixel level and signal level. **In signal level data fusion,** the fusion of information takes place at the sensor node or within the local network itself. **In pixel level data fusion,** the fusion of data takes place at the imaging device level itself. **In feature level data fusion,** fusion of information takes place prior to decision making. However, data fusion at the **decision level is an ensemble of decisions.**

Mathematical models of data fusion: It includes probability-based, AI-based or Theory of Evidence based models. **Probability-based models** include Bayesian analysis, statistical methods and recursive methods while **AI-based models** include Artificial Neural Networks (ANN), ML etc. **Theory of Evidence based** models include belief functions, transferable belief model etc.

Q17. How can data fusion in IoT paradigm be useful?

Ans. Data fusion + IoT paradigm can play a very important role in its success due to the following reasons:

1. Data fusion makes information more intelligent, decisive, sensible and precise (as information from a single source make not be very meaningful).
2. Data fusion can handle big data issues of IoT **because we are fusing data from many sensors into more precise and accurate information.**
3. **Data fusion hides critical information** like in military applications, medical domains and in intelligent buildings.
4. Data fusion creates a very accurate information.
5. A statistical benefit of fusion is obtained by computing the N-independent observations. One can analyse that the data are amalgamated in an optimal manner.

Q18. Data fusion has many challenges. What are they?

Ans. Some of the challenges are listed below:

1. Sensor data is imprecise, inaccurate and uncertain many times. **Hence, this data imperfection must be dealt effectively and this can be achieved with the help of data fusion algorithms only.**
2. Outlier detection, replacement and data imputation are significant in an IoT ecosystem.
3. The conflicting nature of data is needs to be treated. Hence, data fusion algorithms must take care of this.
4. Data correlation and alignment is a common problem in WSNs. This may result in over or under confidence in a data fusion algorithm. **Please note that an alignment problem or sensor registration problem occurs when sensor data is transformed from every sensor's local frame to a common frame prior to data fusion.**
5. The huge amount of data that is collected by sensors from industries may be trivial or non-trivial data. **Also note that the processing of trivial data may affect the data fusion accuracy.** Therefore, only most relevant features need to be selected before data fusion process.
6. **Data fusion is not a static process in nature** rather it is a **dynamic iterative process.** Now dynamic iterative needs **regular refinement of the estimates** in a fusion environment.

7. In IoT, **environment information fusion** can be used in various areas to enhance the IoT ubiquitous aspect.

Q19. **What factors should be taken care of when smart parking systems are deployed?**

Ans. The following factors must be taken care of when smart parking systems are deployed:

1. Robustness of Sensor Devices.

2. Stability of Sensor Networks.

3. Timeliness of Sensor Networks.

4. Level of Service Quality.

5. Driver-centric Information Dissemination.

Q20. **Throw some light on the smart parking ecosystem with respect to IoT.**

Ans. As Internet is becoming more and more dynamic, dense and heterogeneous, so the conventional system architectures cannot satisfy the vehicle drivers. Parking conflicts are endless. So, we need a smart parking ecosystem. This ecosystem must include 2 flows— information and traffic. Once a vehicle arrives or departs from a parking space, the parking availability information changes and this must be communicated to the drivers for a parking space availability. **And the parking information, from the moment when they are detected by sensors to the moment when they appear on the drivers' terminal is called as the information flow.** To know about the vacant parking space, sensors are installed to detect vehicular movements. These sensors form a network and sends the latest updates to the data storage devices.

(i) **Information Collection in a Smart Parking System:** Information collection takes a technical overview of all existing sensing techniques to identify the parking spaces status. It involves **information sensing, sensor connectivity, parking meter, crowdsensing and gaparking/ shared parking.** Let us define these all.

Information Sensing: It relies on **sensors to collect real-time parking availability information.** There are two methods used—**stationary and mobile collections. Mobile sensors can detect the parking occupancy status. For example,** in *ParkNet, that is a smart parking system,* a cab collects data from GPS receivers and ultrasonic sensors and then transmit it over a cellular uplink to the central server. Such a system needs much lesser installation. But different sensors have different ways to detect a vehicle's presence. **Passive infrared sensors** receive heat radiated from the human body. On the other hand, **active infrared sensors** measure the distance to any obstacle in front. These infrared sensors are very sensitive to sun. similarly, we have ultrasound sensors that use sound (and not light). They provide a more complex signal pattern with a possibility pf multiple detections in fixed or mobile scenarios. Optical sensors detect the change in light and must be installed where light can be obscured by a parked vehicle. **But please note that these optical sensors are vulnerable to any light source and hence their accuracy is still an issue.** Yet another common **stationary parking detection sensor is magnetometers** that measures the current magnetic fields and detects huge metal object's presence.

Cameras and acoustic sensors provide a **more complex signal pattern. Inductive loops and piezoelectric sensors** are both, contactive and installed on the road surface. Piezoelectric sensors are similar to inductive loops. Also, RFID is many a times proposed in a smart parking payment solution. **Laser range finder** is often used to build a 1D/ 2D/ 3D map for environmental perception. **Intelligent robots** cruising on the street can also be used to recognize available parking spaces. **Also note that mobile crowdsourcing via smart phones is the most economical way to obtain parking availability information from the drivers themselves.**

Sensor Connectivity: Once networked sensors are installed on the parking spaces, they can form a network to send out their messages. There are 2 communication methods used:

(a) **Short-range communication** like Bluetooth/BLE, 802.11ah, ZigBee.

(b) **Long-range** communication like SigFox, LoRa, weightless.

The long-range communication benefits from the existing radio access network that can communicate with infrastructures anytime and anywhere. On the other hand, **short-range communication** is often implemented by WSN where messages have to be re-transmitted several times via relays (like parking meters) until they reach cities infrastructures.

Parking Meter: With the growth of networked sensors, **parking meters are turned into parking helpers** that establish **a link between drivers and parking data.** Single-space and multi-space meters are the two vital automated payment machines.

Crowdsensing: In some **smart parking applications,** like in gathering the sensed available parking information from the smart phone users gave rise to crowdsensing term. The designers must design a smart parking app and must motivate the users to willingly share information. **This is called as participatory crowdsensing.**

Gaparking/Shared Parking: Gaparking or shared parking takes the idea of gap and parking to share one parking spot to more than one motorist at a different time. **Its principle of working is that the parking spot owners registers their spare parking spots on a website / an app with the proposed price and service time and then the drivers book one suitable space that meets their needs. For example, ParkingAuction, Mobypark and JustPark are some of the popular gaparking/ shared parking apps.**

(ii) **System Deployment in a Smart Parking System:** It deals with the software system exploitation. Also, it deals with the statistical analysis of the collected data. Software functionality includes e-parking, reservations, guidance and monitoring information for the users. **Please understand that with the collected data, the data scientist often performs its analysis in order to study the driver's behaviour for improving the system performance.**

(iii) **Service Dissemination:** In this step, the **relationship between information and social features** is investigated. It includes information dissemination and parking competition. Service dissemination includes dynamic pricing, infrastructure-based information, parking options and other vehicular activities.

(iv) **Energy Management:** It involves energy efficient solutions like light-weight protocols, scheduling optimization, predictive models for energy consumption, cloud-based approach, low power transceivers and cognitive management frameworks. **Energy harvesting solutions include ambient energy harvesting and dedicated energy harvesting. Ambient energy harvesting includes wind, sun, heat, RF sources, and vibrations.** On the other hand, in dedicated energy harvesting, energy sources are intentionally deployed near IoT sources.

Also note that the amount of energy harvested will depend on the sensitivity of the harvesting circuit, distance between the device and the source and environment.

Q21. What are the different levels of automation of vehicles?

Ans. Vehicles are divided into levels based on "who does what, when" and are as follows-

Level 0: The human driver does all of the driving.

Level 1: An advanced driver assistance system (ADAS) on the vehicle can assist the human driver with either steering or braking or accelerating.

Level 2: An ADAS on the vehicle can control both steering and braking under some circumstances. The human driver must continue to pay full attention at all times and perform the rest of the driving task.

Level 3: An automated driving system (ADS) on the vehicle can perform all aspects of the driving task under some circumstances. The human driver must be ready to take back control at any time the ADS requests the human driver to do so. In all other conditions, the human driver performs the task.

Level 4: An ADS on the vehicle can itself perform all driving tasks and monitor the driving environment, do all driving in certain circumstances. The human need not pay attention in those circumstances.

Level 5: ADS on the vehicle can do all driving in all situations. The human occupants are just the passengers and need never be involved in driving.

Q22. CASE STUDY: A Home Automation System has to be developed using IoT. Explain how to apply the different steps of IoT design methodology for this application.

Ans. Different steps that are used in IoT system design can be applied to the Safe Home Automation System as follows:

Step 1: Requirements Specification

For Safe Home Automation System, the purpose and requirements for the system may be defined-

Purpose: A Safe Home Automation System that allows controlling of the lights in a home remotely using a **web application.**

Behaviour: The Safe Home Automation System should have **both manual and auto modes. In auto mode,** the system measures the light level in the room and switches on the light when it gets dark. **In manual mode,** the system provides the option of manually and remotely switching on/off the light.

System Management Requirements: The system should provide remote monitoring and control functions.

Data Analysis Requirement: The system should perform local analysis of the data.

Application Deployment Requirement: The application should be deployed locally on the device but should be accessible remotely.

Security Requirements: The system should have basic user authentication.

Step 2: Process Specification

In this step, the **use cases of the IoT system are defined** in a formal way and derived on the requirements specification step (step-1) of the design phase.

Step 3: Domain Model Specification

In this step, a **confined list of entities, objects and concepts** are defined. Some of these entities include:

Physical Entity: In Safe Home Automation System case study, **the physical entities involved are room in the home,** wherein the lighting conditions need to be monitored and other is the **light appliance** to be controlled.

Virtual Entity: In Safe Home Automation System, there is **one virtual entity** for the room to ne monitored, another for the appliance to be controlled.

Device: In Safe Home Automation System, device is **a single board mini computer that has light sensor and actuator** attached to it.

Resource: In Safe Home Automation System, the **on-device resource is the OS** that runs on the single-board minicomputer.

Service: In Safe Home Automation System, there are **three services** as follows:

Service 1: A service that sets mode to auto or manual or retrieves the current mode.

Service 2: A service that sets the light appliance state to on/off or retrieves the current light state.

Service 3: A controller service that runs as a native service on the device. **Note that during auto mode, the controller service monitors the light level and switches the light ON/OFF and updates the status in the status database. During manual mode, the controller service retrieves the current state from the database and switches the light ON/OFF.**

Step 4: Information Model Specification

In Safe Home Automation System, there are two virtual entities, one is for the light specification and another is for the room.

Step 5: Service Specification

It includes the definition of services in the IoT system like service types, service I/O, service endpoints, service schedules, service preconditions and service effects. **Also note that from the process specification and information model, identify the states and attributes, for each state and attribute define a service, these services either change the state or attribute values or retrieve the current values.** The state service sets the light appliance to ON/OFF or retrieves the current light state. The controller service retrieves the current state from the database and switches the light ON/OFF in the manual mode. In Safe Home Automation System,

The mode service is a Restful web service that sets mode to auto or manual or retrieves the current mode. The mode is updated to or retrieved fom the status database.

The state service is a RESTful web service that sets the light appliance to ON/OFF or retrieves the current light state.

The controller service runs as a native service on the device. **In auto mode,** the controller service monitors the light level. **During manual mode,** the controller service retrieves the current state from the database and switches the lights ON/OFF.

Step 6: IoT Level Specification

In this step, we define the specifications of IoT levels. There are 5 levels:

IoT Level 1: It contains a **single node that does the operation of sensing and actuation, stores data, performs analysis. In level-1**

of the Safe Home Automation System, the system consists of single device that controls the light and appliances with switches. The **status information** of each device is stored in a local database. REST services are deployed locally and it allows retrieving and updating the state of the light and activates the relay switches depending on the need. A **local application will have a GUI** for controlling the lights or appliances. The application can be accessed remotely since the device is connected to the Internet.

IoT Level 2: A level-2 IoT system has a single node that performs sensing and actuation. **Data is stored in the cloud and the entire application is cloud-based only.** IoT level-2 systems are suitable for solutions where the data involved is big, the primary analysis requirement is not intensive and can be done locally itself.

IoT Level 3: has a single node and they are suitable for solutions where the data involved is big and the analysis requirements are computationally intensive.

IoT Level 4: contains local and cloud-based observer nodes that can subscribe to and retrieve information collected in the cloud from IoT devices. **Note that the observer nodes can process information and they do not perform any control functions. Level-4 IoT systems are suitable for solutions where multiple nodes are required.**

IoT Level 5: consist of **multiple nodes placed at different locations** for monitoring humidity, temperature and other levels. The **end nodes** are equipped with various sensors like temperature, humidity etc. **Please note that the coordinator node collects the data from the end nodes and works as gateway that provides Internet connectivity to the IoT system. The controller service** on the coordinator device **sends the collected data to the cloud the analysis of data is done in the computing cloud to aggregate data. Also note that a cloud-based application is used for visualizing the data.**

Step 7: Functional View Specification

The functional view defines the functions of the IoT systems grouped into various Functional Groups. The IoT **device maps** to the Device FG that are sensors, actuators, computing devices and the Management FG. **Resources map to the Device FG** (on-device resources) **and Communication FG** (Communication APIs and protocols). **Please note that the Controller service maps to the service FG and Web**

services map to services FG. also note that the Database maps to the Management FG which is for the database management and security FG is used for database security. Application maps to the Application FG (web application, application and database servers). Management FG is used for the app management and Security FG is used for app security.

Step 8: Operational View Specification

In this step, different options pertaining to the IoT system deployment and operation are defined namely service hosting options, storage options, device options, application hosting options etc. **In Safe Home Automation System in IoT, the operational view specifications are as follows:**

- **Devices:** Computing device is Raspberry Pi. **Light dependent resistor is sensor. Relay switch is actuator.**
- **Communication APIs:** REST APIs.
- **Communication Protocols:** Link Layer-802.11, Network layer – Ipv4/IP v6. Transport layer- TCP Application layer-HTTP.
- **Services:** Controller service-hosted on device, is implemented in Python as a native service.
- **Mode of Service:** RESTful web service, hosted on device, it is implemented with Django-REST Framework.
- **State Service:** RESTful web service, hosted on device, it is implemented with Django-REST Framework.
- **Application:** Web application—Django web application, Application server—Django App Server, Database Server—MySQL.
- **Security:** Authentication-web apps and database.
- **Authorization: web app and database.**
- **Management: Application Management**—Django App **Management; Database Management**—MySQL DB **Management; Device Management**—Raspberry Pi Device management.

Step 9: Device and Component Integration

In this step, we do integration of the devices and components. In Home Automation IoT system, the devices and components used may be Raspberry Pi minicomputer, LDR sensor and relay switch actuator.

Please understand that there are three basic components in an IoT node i.e., intelligence, sensing and wireless communications. Also note that wireless connectivity is significant as it will allow the sensor nodes to be deployed quickly and easily without the requirement to route network cables to each location.

Step 10: Application Development

A home automation web application, for instance, has some controls for the mode that are auto On or auto OFF and the lights are ON/OFF. During the auto mode, IoT system automatically controls the light appliance based on the lighting based on the lighting conditions in the room. **If the auto mode is enabled,** then the light control in the application is disabled and it gives the current state of the light. On the other hand, **when the auto mode is disabled,** light control is enabled and is used manually for controlling the light. An efficient IoT platform design is needed that embeds devices, computing devices, management level, services offered in IoT that can be native to an application of a web app. **Also note that the application can be built using the frameworks like Django and security concerns towards the IoT deployment levels.** The need is to map functional groups to the operational view for home automation systems.

EXERCISE QUESTIONS

1. What is the main goal of IoT design methodology?
2. Distinguish between physical and a virtual entity.
3. Show the purpose and requirements specifications depicting any one of the applications of IoT like smart cities or a safe home security system.
4. What is the use of virtual entities in the information model specification of IoT design?
5. Design a generic framework showing all levels for an application in the domain of smart cities.
6. Determine the IoT levels for designing home automation IoT systems that includes features like smart lighting and threat detection.
7. Find out the IoT levels for designing a health monitoring system (HMS).
8. Explain how IoT can be used in smart city street light control and monitoring.

9. Write short notes:
   - (a) Logical and physical design of IoT.
   - (b) Applications of IoT.
   - (c) Challenges of IoT.
   - (d) Design issues related to IoT.
   - (e) IP addressing in IoT.
10. Explain the IoT design methodology in details with a neat flowchart.
11. Draw and explain the functional view model of IoT.
12. What is operational view specification? How viewpoint is used in deployment operational view?
13. Write short notes on:
    - (a) Application development.
    - (b) Device and component integration.
    - (c) Security challenges of IoT.
    - (d) Vulnerabilities of IoT.
    - (e) Key elements of IoT security.
    - (f) IoT software analytics.
    - (g) Security model of IoT.
    - (h) Smart energy.
    - (i) Smart grid.
    - (j) Research challenges for smart city IoT application.
    - (k) Smart lighting.
    - (l) Virtual sensors and virtual entity.
    - (m) IoT cloud-based services.
    - (n) Importance of satellites in agricultural IoT.
14. Design a case study to develop an IoT-based agricultural planter. In this case study, apply all the steps of IoT design methodology.
15. Which one will you prefer more for a vehicular IoT system—cloud computing of fog computing and why?

    [**Hints:** In vehicular IoT system, fog computing handles the light-weight processes that are closer to the vehicles than the cloud. But for faster decision making, fog computing is used in vehicular IoT systems. for a heavy-weight process, cloud computing is more useful. **Please note** that cloud computing provides more scalability of resources as compared to fog computing. So, we can say that the choice of cloud or fog computing depends on the situation. For example, short on-road congestion can be managed by fog computing with the help of sensed data. While for determining regular on-road congestion, cloud computing is used for predictions. And for regular congestion prediction, cloud may do data analytics].

16. How clouds and sensors work?

    [Hints: The sensors attached to different parts of a vehicle like battery and fuel pump will transmit data to the cloud for analysing the requirements for the maintenance of those parts. It is the evolution of IoT that enables a user to lock/unlock, locate their cars even from a remote location.]

17. Design a use case for developing an IoT-based driver's sleep detection system [DSDS]. Also mention the different types of sensors that you will use for developing such a system.

18. Why is cloud computing vital for a healthcare IoT system?

19. It is desired to build an IoT-based healthcare system where we can do fingerprint based on the sensor. Design such a system concept and ideas.

20. Throw some light on the new evolving paradigms as a result of the use of IoT in various fields.

21. What is the role of AI/ML in IoT?

22. Discuss the following pillars of IoT:

    (a) Big data.

    (b) Cloud or fog or edge Computing.

    (c) 5G and beyond.

    (d) AI/ML.

    (e) Communication Networks.

    (f) NFV.

    (g) SDN.

    (h) Phantom Networks.

    [Hints: phantom networks paradigm tries to develop intangible communication infrastructures. This paradigm depends on the Terahertz (THz) band for communication between aerially diffused nano-relays. This paradigm involves the operational knowledge of

nanotechnology, communications, networking etc. its applications are like military communications.]

23. Write short notes on:
    (a) Internet of Drones (IoD).
    (b) Internet of Space (IoSpace).
    (c) Internet of Services (IoS).
    (d) Internet of People (IoP).
    (e) Internet of Nano Things (IoNT).
    (f) Internet of Underwater Things (IoUT).
    (g) Internet of Vehicles (IoV).
    (h) Internet of EveryThing (IoE).

24. Explain how IoT level 2 works for smart irrigation?

25. Explain how IoT level 4 works for noise monitoring?

26. How will you develop a home automation web application?

27. It is desired to develop a blast furnace in a chemical factory. The temperature of the furnace is very high. Develop an IoT based solution for it giving details of which all sensors will you use.

28. Design an intelligent healthcare system that consists of body sensors and wearable devices to collect human physiological signals, real-time monitoring, disease prediction etc.

29. Design an intelligent vehicle management system in a mall based on IoT, using RFID. The system should enable automatic payment so as to allow easy movement of vehicles at the intersection point. Also, when the vehicle exits a mall, the parking fee is automatically deducted.

30. Design an IoT-based application to monitor water quality. Use nodal network method or electronic sensor monitoring.

    [Hints: Sensors may be placed at different points of the river and the water quality is gathered by these sensors at regular intervals. This data is then uploaded to the Internet. This nodal network method / electronic sensor monitoring method addresses the short comings of the traditional manual method by collecting data in real-time. For this wireless sensor networks may be used. But keep in mind that sensors are costly. Water sensor networks can gather data in real-time but most of the sensors lack mobility because they are fixed in their positions. Natural calamities like earthquakes, floods

etc may also damage these sensors. To overcome this problem, by building a water quality monitoring system by using the capabilities of IoT, unmanned surface vehicles (USVs), sensors and data analytics. The selection of sensors is based on parameters like sensitivity, cost, accuracy, latency etc. random water samples are chosen. Data collected is sent to the cloud via WIFI/GPRS/GSM module. In cloud, the geo-tagged sensor data is stored as a history of the corresponding water body. To analyse the data in the cloud, ML techniques like clustering and regression are used. Using this analysed data, the algorithm plots the choropleth map of the water body. These maps are also stored on the cloud. The end user gets the updated information about the water body using the applications developed for mobile and web platforms. Continuous monitoring makes prediction also more accurate. Also, parameter trend can be noted to generate this map for future conditions.]

4 IIoT-INDUSTRIAL IoT

4.0 INTRODUCTION

When we say IIoT we mean the use of IoT technologies in manufacturing industry. It is also known as **Industrial Internet.** IIoT also includes ML, Big data, sensor data, M2M communications and automation technologies existing in industry settings for years and years. It is said that IIoT believes that smart machines are better than humans as far as accuracy, data capturing and data communications are required. IIoT in industry holds a great potential for quality control, green practices, supply chain traceability and overall SCM efficiency. **IIoT is also known as Enterprise IoT while IoT is also known as Consumer IoT. Enterprise IoT is not equal to Consumer IoT. IIoT is supported by a huge amount of data collected from sensors and is based on wrap-and-reuse approach rather than rip-and-replace approach.** IIoT is a network of physical objects, systems, platforms and applications. In IIoT systems, there will be a large number of sensors ingesting millions of messages per second. This is known as **time series data.** IIoT data streams are highly varied and voluminous.

4.1 IIoT REQUIREMENTS

First of all, we should know what are cyber-physical systems? **Industrial systems that interface the digital world to the physical world through sensors and actuators that solve complex control problems are known as cyber-physical systems.** Today, these systems are being combined with big data solutions to gain deeper insights through data and analytics. The objective is to have a large number of industrial systems that are communicating with each other so as to improve the industrial performance. By making machines smarter, by local processing and communication, IIoT could solve problems in newer ways. **Please understand that as the innovation grows so does**

DOI: 10.1201/9781003728641-4

the complexity, which makes the IIoT a very large challenge that no company can achieve in isolation. **Also note that at its root, IIoT is a vast number of connected industrial systems that communicate and coordinate their data analytics and actions to improve performance and efficiency and minimize downtime.** This can save millions of dollars.

The possibilities in industry are limitless like smarter factories, greener energy generation, self-regulating buildings that minimize energy usage, cities that can adjust traffic patterns so as to avoid congestions on roads.

IIoT Requirements are Cloud Computing, access anywhere/anytime, security, Big Data Analytics, user experience, assets management and smart machines.

Service is a collection of data and associated behaviors to accomplish a particular function of a device. **Service management in IIoT refers to the implementation and management of the quality of services that meets the user demands.** Services are of two types:

(a) Primary Service.

(b) Secondary Service.

Primary services are the basic services that are responsible for the primary node functions. On the other hand, **the auxiliary functions that provide services to the primary service are termed as secondary services.**

4.2 DESIGN CONSIDERATIONS OF IIoT

Some of the design objectives that are to be met for IIoT are as follows:

1. **Energy: It is defined as the time for which the IoT device can operate with limited power supply.** There is a power limitation for IoT devices. **Also note that the more the IoT device could work with little power supply, the more energy efficient is the IoT device.**

2. **Latency: It is defined as the time required for transmitting the data to the cloud.** While designing an IoT network, latency should be kept in mind and it should be as low as possible.

3. **Throughput: It is defined as the maximum data transmitted across the network in unit time.** Design should be such that it increases the throughputs.

4. **Scalability:** The number of IoT being connected everyday is increasing. But at the same time the IoT network should be able to scale well to adjust for these devices.

5. **Topology:** It refers to the network topology used by IoT networks. Interoperability is the major concern as these networks have devices that are of different standards, different vendors etc.

6. **Security:** Data being communicated or collected must be safe. It should not be vulnerable to cyber-attacks. So, test this data, if possible. Use encryptions.

4.3 APPLICATIONS OF IIoT

Ranging from ML, M2M to AI, IIoT takes IoT technologies and apply them directly to the industrial applications. This further improves efficiency and productivity. Let us now discuss some of the applications of IIoT.

(i) Manufacturing Industry includes several areas like:

(a) **Digital Factory: IoT-enabled** machines can transmit operational data to the field engineers. This helps them in remote operation of factories and to take the advantages of process automation and optimization. **Also note that a digitally connected unit will establish a better line of commands and helps in identifying the Key Result Areas (KRAs).**

(b) **Facility Management:** IoT sensors can actively monitor machines and send alerts when the device deviates from its normal parameters. **Note that by ensuring the prescribed working environment for machinery, the manufacturers can conserve energy, reduce costs, eliminate machine downtime and increase the operational efficiency.**

(c) **Production Flow Monitoring:** IoT can monitor the production lines starting from the refining process to the packaging of the final products. This monitoring if done in **real-time** can provide new scopes for adjustments in operations for better management of **operational costs.**

(d) **Inventory Management:** IIoT allows the monitoring of the events across the supply chain (SC). Using these systems, the inventory can be tracked and traced globally, cross-channel visibility into inventories, work in progress, real estimates to managers and the **estimated time of arrival of new items.** This **optimizes the supply and also reduces shared costs** in SCM.

(e)   **Plant Security:** (IoT + Big Data Analytics) can improve the overall worker's security in the plant. The **Key Performance Indicators (KPIs)** of health and safety includes the number of injuries and illness rates, short and long -term absences, vehicle incidents, property damage etc. that can be easily monitored.

(f)   **Quality Control:** IoT sensors collect the product data during IoT life cycle. This data like raw materials used, temperature and working environments, wastes, transportation and finally the **customer sentiments collected** on using of the product can further be analyzed to handle quality issues.

(g)   **Smart Tracking Mechanisms** can trace product deterioration during their transit due to weather conditions, road and other factors on the product. So, we can **re-engineer the product and packaging** for better performance in the cost of packaging.

(h)   **Supply Chain Optimization (SCO):** IIoT can provide access to real-time Supply Chain information by tracking materials, equipment and products. **Also note that effective reporting enables manufacturers to collect and feed delivery information into ERP**. We connect plants to the suppliers. By doing this, all parties involved in the supply chain can trace interdependencies, material flow and the manufacturing **cycle times.**

(ii) Healthcare Industry

Some of the IIoT Applications are as Follows:

1. **Real-time monitoring using connected devices can save human lives in case of critical conditions like heart failure, diabetes, asthma etc.** it is the combination of real-time monitoring, smart medical device and smart phone app that connected devices can collect medical data. This collected information is then sent to the doctor. It has been observed that there is 50% reduction in readmission rate as remote patient monitoring was done. Furthermore, this data is stored on cloud and hence can be shared with a doctor or medical insurance dealer etc.

2. **IIoT automates the hospital workflow and also enables interoperability, M2M communication, information exchange and data movement in a better way.** This type of technology-driven model actually reduces its cost, reducing not required visits to hospital and better allocation and planning can be done.

3. Data deluge is found in a healthcare system also. Here, also data is aggregated that comes from different multiple devices. **But please understand that IoT device can collect, report and analyze the data in real-time.** Then, later data analytics may be performed that will help in better and faster decision making with minimal errors.

4. In emergency situations, alerts about patient's critical health can be sent via mobiles. IoT allows *real-time alerts, tracking, monitoring that gives patients on-time treatments, more accuracy and better results.*

5. Remote medical assistance is also possible, if patient or doctor wants to communicate from far-off places. Many **healthcare delivery chains** exists and IoT will improve the patient's care using these linked devices.

(iii) **IIoT Can Revolutionize The Transport Industry Too.** It has made self-driving vehicles possible. some of the applications of IIoT includes fleet management, transport logistics, smart toll revenue collection, railways, smart parking and roadways.

(iv) **Monitoring Air Quality is A Very Serious Job Today. IIoT** can automate air and poisonous gases and generate alerts for them.

(v) **Networks Using IoT Technologies** like fire engines acting as the wireless hotspot for each IoT-linked devices in a fire department's inventory.

(vi) **Smart Dust** refers to the concept of tiny sensors like that of a grain size of sand. These connected smart dust particles in IIoT has a huge number of applications. **For example,** oil exploration companies spread dust to monitor rock movements to small sensors, so as to make changes and problems.

(vii) **Drones:** They are also called as **"Unmanned Aerial Vehicles".** They can carry all types of sensors that are capable of gathering huge amount of data. Builders/constructors can use them to do every day land surveys. They can feed this data into the software to ensure timely construction. One drone can communicate with other drones in IIoT to work in a cohesive way.

(viii) **IIoT-based Agriculture**

Using smart devices and connected IIoT projects enables farmers to make use of huge amounts of data generated on their farms. **For example,** Oyster Aquafarms, Verizon, has implemented an IIoT program to maximize productivity and increase the quality of the food in SCM, uses satellite imaging and **IIoT track-and-trace technology** to simulate on the farming operations, running from harvest to delivery. **Collection of real-time data** like soil, weather, air quality and hydration levels can help farmers to take decisions regarding planting and harvesting of crops.

(ix) Airspace Industry

A joint venture by GE and Accenture, named as Taleris, develops IoT solutions for airlines. It minimized delays and disruptions by analyzing data collected from sensors fixed on airplanes. Using analytics programs will monitor airplanes will improve turnaround times for them and will satisfy customer too.

(x) Energy Networks

Several spikes are seen in energy consumption-based companies. **But please remember that effective energy demand management through IIoT will reduce the costs.** Utility firms (power plants) use **smart meters to unveil the price information on these smart devices** which can be very useful if it can interact with other IoT devices to use energy in an effective and efficient way. Now-a-days new **oil and gas pipelines** (IGL-pipelines) are **fitted with sensors** that detects gas leakages. With the help of IIoT, Energy Supply Chain (ESC) will become more precious.

4.4 MERITS OF IIoT

The following are the advantages of IIoT:

1. IIoT has made the **device connectivity more easy,** improved efficiency, more scalability, smaller operation time, remote diagnosis and cost effective.

2. The connected (Ecosystem + IIoT) would be very beneficial to us.

3. If we see the traditional supply chains in industries then we find that they are **linear in nature. The focus is now shifting from products to the results (outcomes). Hence, a new ecosystem should be followed. And for this digital ecosystem is better as it can easily adapt to ever changing environments.**

4. In IIoT, **machines become more intelligent because it integrates both digital and traditional human workforce. Also, note that now automated tasks can be done in industries at minimum costs and better quality.**

5. IIoT will redefine and reform the skills of the workers.

6. IIoT increases new job openings too. Like, precision agriculture, digital healthcare system, digital mines, driverless vehicles and so on.

7. More skilled workers are needed now.

8. In IIoT, Robots are developed with three *sensing, thinking and acting* capabilities. Robots have become very intelligent today and can be reprogrammed also.

4.5 CHALLENGES OF IIoT AND ITS SOLUTIONS

Some of the challenges faced by IIoT are as follows:

1. **Identification of Things,** big data, interfacing IIoT and existing infrastructures, storing data etc. into a new IIoT platform is a big challenge.

2. The worker health, environmental protections, regulations and minimal operations are also some of the issues to be addressed.

3. Hazardous challenges like storage of poisonous substances, O_2 deficiency, radiations and so on.

4. Standardization of systems will increase the interoperability of various systems so that better performance can be achieved. The problems related to standardization are interoperability, semantic operability, security and vulnerability.

5. IIoT has to take care of **data security** also.

Solutions: Many factors like **lack of leadership, costly sensors and bad infrastructure** are some of the issues related to IIoT. To overcome these problems/challenges we need **miniaturization (smaller) devices, good quality sensors, lesser cost and energy consumptions** etc. Furthermore, we can do **predictive maintenance,** minimal maintenance costs, minimal number of breakdowns etc.

SUMMARY

In this chapter, we have studied what is IIoT, what are the challenges faced, merits and demerits of IIoT. Many applications of IIoT are also dealt with in this chapter. Also, we have seen the possible solutions for the same.

MULTIPLE CHOICE QUESTIONS [MCQS] WITH ANSWERS

1. The intersection of IoT and Industry 4.0 is called as
   - (a) IOP
   - (b) IoT
   - (c) IIoT
   - (d) None of the above.

2. Industry 4.0 creates
   - (a) Smart phones.
   - (b) Smart pens.
   - (c) Smart factory.
   - (d) None of the above.

3. The systems that monitor the physical processes by creating a virtual copy of the physical world are known as
   - (a) Cyber-cyber systems.
   - (b) Cyber-physical systems.
   - (c) Cycle systems.
   - (d) None of the above.

4. IIoT is also known as
   - (a) Consumer IoT.
   - (b) Enterprise IoT.
   - (c) Cyber IoT.
   - (d) None of the above.

5. At its root, IIoT is
   - (a) Collection of connected industrial systems.
   - (b) Collection of sensors.
   - (c) Collection of data.
   - (d) None of the above.

6. The time required for transmitting the data to the cloud is known as
   - (a) Energy.
   - (b) Throughput.
   - (c) Latency.
   - (d) Security.

7. The maximum data transmitted across the network in unit time is called as
   - (a) Throughput.
   - (b) Energy.
   - (c) Latency.
   - (d) Security.

8. The IoT devices can collect, report and analyze data in real-time also. (True/False)
   - (a) TRUE.
   - (b) FALSE
   - (c) Sometimes.
   - (d) None of the above.

9. A joint venture of GE and Accenture is Named as

   (a) Telris   (b) Taleris

   (c) Tales   (d) None of the above.

10. Robots can be reformed to do

    (a) Repetitive tasks.   (b) Smaller tasks.

    (c) Newer tasks.   (d) None of the above.

Answers:

1. c	2. c	3. b	4. b	5. a	6. c
7. a	8. a	9. b	10. a		

CONCEPTUAL SHORT QUESTIONS WITH ANSWERS

Q1. What is data fusion? What is its need?

Ans. Data Fusion is defined as the theory, techniques and tools that are used for combining sensor data and data derived from it, into a common representational form. IoT is itself responsible for data deluge. A timely fusion of data to enable efficient, effective, reliable and accurate decision making is of prime importance. Computational intelligence will aid in this process. Data volume, data veracity, data velocity, data variety and data vulnerability are the major challenges to be addressed. **Also note that data fusion enables optimization of big data that is collected by sensors from multiple sources and from multiple platforms.**

Q2. How is IoT different from IIoT?

Ans. IoT applications meant for industry is different. It is at bigger scale and mostly all are critically real-time applications. **For example,** monitoring an oil pipeline for the fuel leakage is an intense, real-time IIoT application. Monitoring the functioning of the industrial motors involves the usage of many sensors to monitor the equipment. But normal IoT application does not involve that many sensors. Also, while **the data to be processes in normal IoT application may not be that intensive, it would be dense in** IIoT.

Q3. What is the core of ICV? How will you classify it based on its domains?

Ans. The core of ICV is the VANETs. VANET domains are classified into three categories:

(a) In-Vehicle Domain.

(b) Ad-hoc Domain.

(c) Infrastructure Domain.

In-Vehicle Domain is composed of one or more on-board units (OBUs). Additional presence of Advanced Driver Assistance Systems (ADAS) sensors like cameras, proximity sensors, engine sensors, radars and actuators are the part of this type of domain. **Also note that in this domain the communication is mainly through Controller Area Network (CAN), Vehicular Power Line Networks (VPLN) and Ethernet.**

Ad-hoc Domain consists up of vehicles and road side units. **The vehicle's on-board-units are mobile, however. The road side units (RSUs) are static. Communication mode** may be either Vehicle-to-Vehicle (V2V) or Vehicle-to-Internet (V2I). Communication takes place through Dedicated Short-Range Communication (DSRC) technology stack (IEEE 802.11p).

Infrastructure Domains consists of Road Side Units (RSUs) that are connected to the Internet by means of **gateways.** In presence of RSUs, the vehicles may communicate to the Internet via Vehicle-to-Internet (V2I) interfaces. In absence of RSUs, the vehicles may communicate with each other or the Internet through cellular networks like 3G, 4G, 5G, LTE etc.

Q4. What is CupCarbon? Can we simulate smart city with it?

Ans. As we have seen that it was a diverse range of devices interconnected through wireless technologies that gave birth to IoT and when applied to industrial domain it became IIoT. Across the world, devices enjoy all-time connectivity because of IoT only. As per the research reports from Statista.com, sales of smart home devices in US went up from US$ 1.3 billion to US$ 4.5 billion in year 2019. As per another latest report by The Economic Times, there will be around 2 billion units of e-SIM based devices by 2025. It enables subscribers to use the digital SIM card for smart devices. These services can be activated without a physical SIM card. It is one of the secure applications of IoT. In industry also, IoT has several applications, like

- Smart grids.
- Machine-to-machine (M2M) communications.
- Machine auto-diagnosis.

- Indoor Air Quality.
- Industrial Disaster Prediction.
- Temperature Monitoring.
- Ozone Presence.
- Indoor Location.
- Agriculture Robots (Agribots).

Simulators for IoT

CupCarbon is a multi-featured simulator that is used for the simulation of smart cities and IoT based advanced WSNs. It has a very simple GUI for the integration of objects in a smart city with wireless sensors. In CupCarbon, the sensor nodes and algorithms can be programmed in the SenScript Editor. SenScript is the script that is used for the programming and control of sensors used in the simulation environment. It uses many programming constructs so that the smart city environments can be simulated.

Many other simulators for IoT integrated smart city implementations do exist. Some of them are **Contiki, InterSCity, OpenIoT, Zetta, SCSimulator, DSA, CitySim. Node-RED, IoTivity and KAA.**

Q5. Name some IoT operating systems.

Ans. Ubuntu core, RIoT, Contiki, TinyOS, Zephyr are some of the OS for IoT.

Q6. What is IoT analytics?

Ans. Analytics for IoT is the science and art of trying to find the matching patterns in huge quantity of data like big data. It simply means monitoring trends and finding abnormalities, if any. Many types of analytics exist like descriptive analytics, diagnostics analytics, predictive analytics, prescriptive analytics and so on.

Q7. What are edge analytics? Name some IoT tools for the same.

Ans. Edge analytics is the analysis done at the source by processing, collecting and analyzing the data instead of sending it to the cloud or server for processing and analysis. This saves a **lot of time and reduces latency.**

Tools for Edge Analytics are:

- **EdgeX Foundary:** It is an open-source project that is hosted by the Linux Foundation. It provides interoperability. It can be hosted within the hardware. The EdgeX ecosystem can be used as plug-and-play with support for multiple components. This can be easily deployed as an IoT solution with edge analytics. EdgeX Foundary can be deployed using microservices also.

- **Eclipse Kura:** It is also an open-source edge framework. It is Java-based. It offers API to access underlying hardware interface of IoT gateways for serial ports, watchdog, GPS, I2C etc.
- **Eclipse Kapua:** It is a modular IoT cloud platform that is basically used to manage and integrate devices and their data.

According to Gartner's report, edge analytics is the leading tech trend today.

Q8. What are the two main challenges faced by sensors?

Ans. There are two main challenges as follows:

1. **Sensor performance** values vary widely.
2. Basic **testing** by manufacturers is lagging.

Q9. Which all methods are needed to ensure safety of workers in IIoT?

Ans. This is so because many industries generate poisonous gases like sulphur, methane and their compounds that are bad for humans and animal's health. Using sensors, we can achieve our goals.

Q10. Demand for open-source is sky rocketing. Why is it so?

Ans. The technology ecosystem of IoT is complex and includes hardware, connectivity, platforms middleware, analytics, OS applications and services. As Per IDC reports, there will be 41.6 billion connected IoT devices or Things generating 79.4 Zettabytes (ZB) of data in 2025. 64% of the participants in IDC Global IoT Decision Maker survey think that open-source is mandatory in IoT development cycle. In another report by W3.org, 91% of IoT developers use open-source software, open hardware or open data in at least one part of the development stack. **Believe it or not, in coming years IoT market will move towards an open-source and open standards ecosystem that enables collaborative innovation, interoperability, flexibility and modularity.**

Some open source IoT development platforms include- Kaa, Sitewhere, DeviceHive, Zetta and Thingsboard.io.

Q11. Name some open-source databases available for IoT-based applications.

Ans. MongoDB, MySQL, Redis, Cassandra, Hadoop, CrateDB, GridDB, InfluxDB, BigChainDB etc.

Q12. Name some key open-source cloud platforms.

Ans. OpenStack, Cloud Foundary, OpenShift, Cloudify are some examples.

Q13. Name some open-source hardware platforms for IoT.

Ans. rduino, Raspberry Pi, mangoOH are some examples.

Q14. Name some open-source OS.

Ans. RIoT (Real-time IoT), Zephyr, Ubuntu Core are some examples.

Q15. Give an example of edge computing.

Ans. Alexa, is an example for edge computing as it uses NLP at the edge to reply to queries from a human being. AI on edge is not just data processing but also deriving trends and patterns or intelligence by applying ML algorithms to give use a response. An example of this is a smart camera installed in a smart city.

Q16. Is edge computing more secure?

Ans. Some users might not be willing to share their data on the cloud. It may sound a little oxymoronic because when you have distributed computing resources in the edge network then you are exposed to data attacks. But AI-edge is considered to be more secure for our data.

Q17. What is the full form of SMART? Who coined this term?

Ans. **SMART refers to Specific Measurable/Measurement Achievable Relevant Time-Oriented.** It refers to the computing to perform calculations easily and quickly. This term was coined by **Andrew Barlets.** the components of SMART Computing are as follows:

• Ubiquitous Computing.
• Virtual Computing.
• Cloud Computing.
• A. I.
• Human Computer Interaction (HCI).

Q18. What is Ambient Intelligence? Explain with examples.

Ans. **Ambient Intelligence is a type of intelligent, smart and sensitive electronic environment which responds as per human presence and action.** Like AI, Ambient Intelligence is also a large umbrella of technologies like ubiquitous computing, cloud computing, fog computing, AI, ML, DL, IoT, Networking, telecommunication, embedded systems, HCI and vision. Ambient Intelligence algorithms recognize the state of the environment and users with sensors that are embedded in the environment and reasons about the data using different types of AI techniques. Ambient Intelligence is embedded in our daily life as IoT and Internet of Humans (IoH). **For instance,** this technology will make refrigerators intelligent and can maintain a list of vegetables for us.

Q19. What is IIoT made up of?

Ans. Industrial IoT is made up of a multitude of devices connected by communications software. The resulting systems and even the individual devices that comprise it, can *monitor, collect, exchange, analyze and instantly act* on information to intelligently change their behavior or their environment—al without any human interventions.

EXERCISE QUESTIONS

1. What is considered at the intersection of IoT and Industrial 4.0?
2. Explain what is "smart factory".
3. What are cyber-physical systems?
4. What are IIoT requirements?
5. What are the design objectives to be considered for IIoT design?
6. Give some applications of IIoT.
7. How can IIoT help in critical healthcare service industry?
8. Write short notes on-
   (a) Smart Dust.
   (b) Drones and IIoT.
   (c) Futuristic Farming.
   (d) Airspace and IIoT.
   (e) Energy Networks.
   (f) Automotive IoT.
9. Give some advantages and some disadvantages of IIoT.
10. What challenges will you face when implementing IIoT in your company?

5 FOG COMPUTING

5.0 INTRODUCTION

The extension of cloud computing to the edge of an enterprise's network is known as Fog Computing/Edge Computing/Fogging. Fogging facilitates the operation of compute, storage and networking services between end devices and cloud computing data centres. This term was created by Cisco. In Jan. 2014. By handling these services that constitute IoT at the network edge, data can in many cases be processed more efficiently than if needed to be sent to the cloud for processing. **Please understand that Fogging/edge computing/ fog computing is a concept of a network fabric that stretches from the outer edges of where data is created to where it will eventually be stored, whether that is in the cloud or in a customer's data centre. Also note that we can say that FOG is another layer of a distributed network environment and is closely associated with cloud computing and IoT.** Public infrastructure as a service (IaaS) cloud vendors can be thought of as a high-level, global end-point for data. **The edge of the network is where data from IoT devices is created. Therefore, we can say that FOG is an intermediate layer between cloud and devices that generate data** as shown in Fig. 5.1.

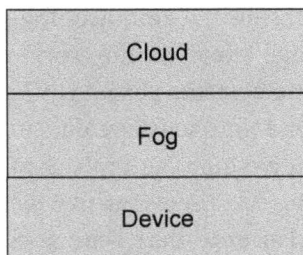

Fig. 5.1: Fog Layer in-between Cloud and Device

DOI: 10.1201/9781003728641-5

By bringing cloud computing services to the edge of the network and hence closer to this rapid growth of number of connected devices and applications that consume cloud services and generate vast amount of data. According to recent survey, it is reported that 40% of the whole world's data will come from sensors by 2020-21. Also, it reports that 90% of the world's data were generated only during the period of last 2 years. 2.5 quintillion of data, in terms of bytes, is generated per day and the total expenditure on IoT devices will be $1.7 trillion by 2020-21. The total number of connected vehicles worldwide will be 250 million by 2020-21 and there will be more than 30 billion IoT devices. Furthermore, the amount of data generated is so large that even cloud computing is unable to handle this vast data and hence IoT requirements.

5.1 NEED OF FOG COMPUTING

Cloud computing has several issues like volume, latency and bandwidth of data. In cloud computing, devices generate data and send this data for analysis and storage in the cloud. On request or after analysis, data is sent back to the devices or to execute an action.

1. **Volume of Data:** *As reported, data explosion and device density are increasing exponentially.* Current cloud models are not able to process this huge amount of data. This huge amount of data, needs to be filtered before storing.

2. **Latency: It is defined as the time taken by a data packet for a round trip. Please note that this means the time taken by the data to travel from the devices to the cloud and back to the devices. Latency is an important aspect for handling time sensitive data.** One of the main reasons to embrace fogging/edge computing/ fog computing is to manage latencies. **Fog services have smaller latencies that enables real-time systems** (like AI, VR, AR, Data Analytics etc.). if the edge devices send time sensitive data to the cloud for analysis and wait for the cloud to give a proper reply then it may result in irrelevant results. When handling this time-sensitive data, a millisecond can make a huge difference. **Also note that time sensitive data is send to the cloud for analysis, latency will be increased.** We can use this formula to calculate latencies:

$$\text{Latency} = \text{T (from device to cloud)} + \text{T (data-analysis)} +$$
$$\text{T (from cloud to device)}$$

Where, T = Time

So, when the action reaches the device, it may not be meaningful or in situations like connected vehicles accidents may also occur.

3. **Bandwidth: If this huge amount of data is sent to the cloud, then a huge amount of traffic may be generated by these devices. This will consume almost all of the bandwidth.** This is quite challenging. Also, **if all of the devices become online,** then even IPv6 will not be able to provide facility to all devices. Furthermore, data may be confidential and the company may not want to share. In these scenarios, **fog computing/edge computing is the best solution.**

5.2 REQUIREMENTS OF IoT

If any organization wants to implement IoT successfully the the requirements to be met are as follows:

1. **Minimize Latency of Data:** Latency reduction is the most vital part of IoT requirement. **Please note that latency can be reduced by analysing the data close to the data source.** As far as real-time systems are concerned, we cannot have delay in decisions as it may result in big differences and disasters.

2. **Data Security:** IoT data must be secured from hacks. Preventive measures may be taken.

3. **Reliability:** IoT device generated data can be used to solve real-time problems. Availability of data is a must in IoT systems.

4. **Data Sensitivity:** Data may be time sensitive data, less time sensitive data and non-sensitive data. **Note that extremely time sensitive data must be analysed very near to the data source. And the data that is not time sensitive will be analysed in the cloud itself.**

5. **Monitor Data Across Large Geographical Area:** IoT connected devices may be spread all across the country or even state. **For example, monitoring the railway track of a country or a state.** Sometimes the devices are also exposed to harsh environmental conditions like winds, rain, snowfall etc.

In nutshell, fog computing is used in four situations as follows:

1. If data need to be analysed within a fraction of a second.
2. If the number of IoT devices are huge.
3. If the devices are separated by a large geographical distance.
4. If the devices are subjected to extreme conditions.

5.3 ARCHITECTURE OF FOG

By architecture of fog, we mean an arrangement of physical and logical network elements, hardware and software to implement a useful IoT network. There are some key architectural decisions involved in fog i.e., *the physical and geographical positioning of the fog nodes., their arrangement / hierarchy, the numbers, types, topology, protocols and data bandwidth capacities of the links between fog nodes, things and the cloud, hardware and software design of individual fog nodes and how a complete IoT network is managed.* The procedure is to firstly, understand the critical requirements of the general use cases that will take the advantage of fog and specific software applications that will run on them. Then these **requirements are mapped onto a partitioned network of fog nodes.** If we see from a systematic perspective then the fog networks provide **a distributed computing system** with a **hierarchical topology.** These fog networks provide *reduced latencies, reduced power consumptions of end devices, real-time data pro cessing and control with localized computing resources and reducing the load of backhaul traffic to centralized data centres.* Figure 5.2 shows the architecture of FOF COMPUTING.

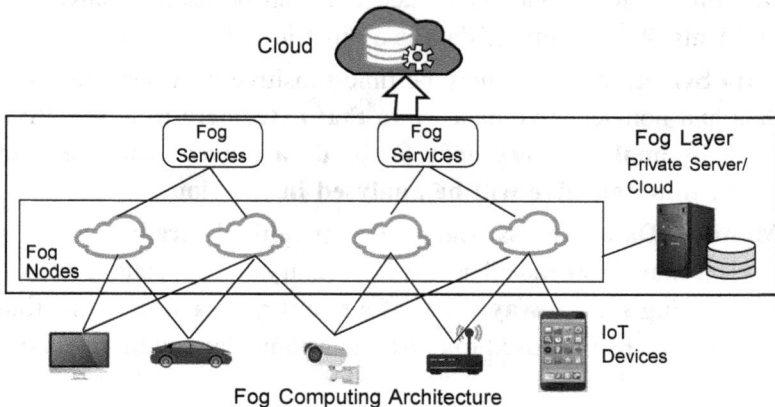

Fog Computing Architecture

Fig. 5.2: Fog Architecture

From this figure, it is crystal clear that:

1. Storage to provide **transient storage.**
2. **Computing facility** to process data before it is sent to the cloud.
3. To take **fast decisions.**
4. **Network connectivity** to connect with IoT devices, other fog nodes and cloud.
5. **Deployable** anywhere inside the network.
6. Each fog node has its own **aggregate fog node.**
7. It receives data from the **sensors in real time** scenarios.
8. **Response time** is **minimal** (in ms).
9. **Fog computing is transit** where data is stored for a limited time period only.
10. Then, data is sent to the cloud as a summary. **Also note that not all data goes to the cloud.**
11. So, cloud receives data summary from the fog.
12. Data analytics, data prediction, data storage all take place at cloud platform only.

5.4 WORKING OF FOG

Sensors generate data and transmit it to the middle layer that is quite close to the data source. These nodes in the middle layer are capable of handling data. This requires minimum power and lesser resources. **Please note that the point is that the all data need not go to the cloud at the instant it is generated. Also note that sensitive data gets processes very fast which results in an instant response.** Fog is not meant for heavy storages. This is so because it is still our cloud that stores big data. **Fog is just an intermediary layer that enables faster data processing and hence faster response times.** Only the data that is less time-sensitive is sent to the cloud for predictions, big data analytics and long-term storage.

Fog nodes work according to the **data that they receive. An IoT application should be installed to each fog node. The nearest fog node ingests data from the devices** (see Fig. 5.3).

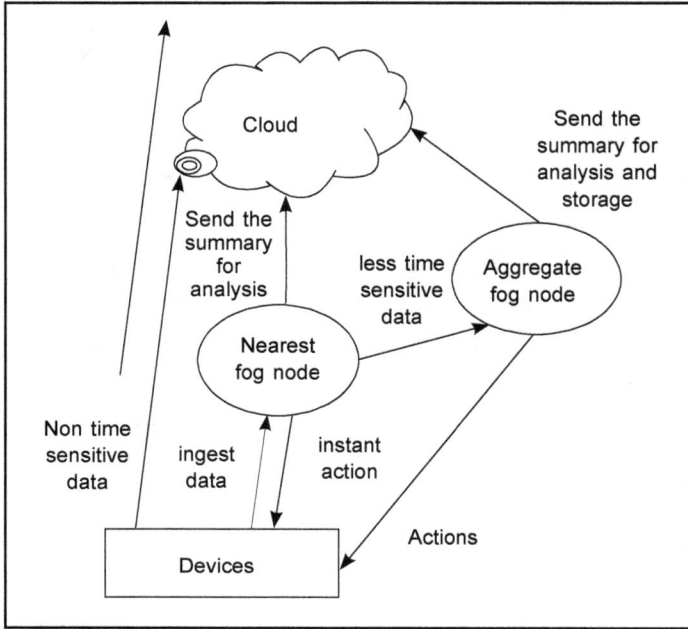

Fig. 5.3: Working of Fog Computing

Three Cases Arise:

Case 1: If the data is time-sensitive data then data needs to be analysed within a fraction of a second. Then it needs to be analysed **at the nearest node itself.** After analysing the data, the decision is sent to the devices. After that it sends and stores the summary to the cloud for future analysis.

Case 2: If data is less time-sensitive data then data can be analysed after seconds or minutes. Sensed data is sent to the **aggregate node for analysis.** After analysis, the aggregate node sends the decision to the device through the nearest node. The aggregate node then sends the summary to cloud for storage and future predictions.

Case 3: The data which is not time-sensitive can wait for hours, days or weeks. In such a case, data is sent to cloud for storage and future predictions. **Also note that those summaries from fog nodes can be considered as less-time sensitive data.**

We can compare various attributes for three types of data (Case-1 to Case-3) as follows:

Table 5.1: Compares Various Attributes for 3-types of Data

Attributes/ fog nodes	Fog nodes closest to devices	Fog aggregate nodes	Cloud
Analysis duration	Fraction of a second	Seconds to minutes	Hours to weeks
IoT Data Storage Duration	Transient	Hours to days	Months to years
Geographical Coverage	Very local	Wider	Global

5.5 ADVANTAGES OF FOG

1. **Minimal amount of data** is sent to the cloud.
2. **Reduced bandwidth consumption** as it processes selected data locally, instead of sensing it to the cloud for analysis.
3. **Reduced data latency.** This results in fast decision making and avoids unwanted accidents also.
4. More and **improved data security.**
5. As limited data goes to the cloud, it is **easier to protect** it.
6. **Immediate processing of data in real-time** and this is mandatory in IIoT.
7. Fog computing provides **better security.**
8. **Fog nodes can be protected** using the same procedures, controls and policies that you use in other areas of IoT.
9. **More privacy as the sensitive data can be analysed locally** instead of sending it to the cloud for analysis. The IT team can keep track and control the devices that collect, analyse and store the data.
10. By using a better set of tools, developers can develop fog applications and deploy them too. **Fog applications drive the machine to function in a way according to the customers need.**
11. Fog nodes can be **mobile** too. **This means that nodes can join and leave the network at any time.**
12. **Fog nodes can be deployed in remote places also.** The nodes can be subjected to harsh environmental conditions or in places like under sea, railway tracks, vehicles etc.
13. **Better data handling** by fog nodes and hence fog computing.

5.6 APPLICATIONS OF FOG

Some of the applications of FOG Computing are discussed below.

1. **Smart Homes: N**ewer and newer smart devices, real-time data, limited hardware capability are some of the reasons that make working with IoT harder. In order to solve these problems, we **use fog computing to integrate all debris into a single platform** and empower those Smart Home Applications with **elastic resources.** Incompatibility among various IoT devices is a greater challenge. Fog computing can provide home security applications:

   - A unified interface to integrate all kinds of independent devices.
   - Flexible resources to support computation and storage.
   - Real-time processing.
   - Low latency response.

   Once the fog platform is set up, each **secure sensor** is connected as a client. The corresponding **server application can be installed on independent virtual machines. Advanced processing logic** can also be implemented on VMs in which it can process data shared by those secure monitor applications.

   For example, a motion sensor detects a suspicious motion in a certain room and then a cleaning robot with video camera will be commanded to check out the exact location. **Real-time video analytics** will process those videos and confirm whether it is a false alarm. **Notification and report** will be sent to house owner and the system will call cops, if required.

2. **Smart Grid:** As already defined, *a smart grid is an electricity distribution network with smart meters deployed at various locations to measure the real-time status information.* A **centralized server** called as SCADA System gathers and analyses the status information and sends command to respond to any demand change/emergency to stabilize the power grid. But fog computing can benefit smart grid also. With fog computing, the smart grid will turn into a **multi-tier hierarchical system** with an interplay between the FOG and SCADA. Herein, a FOG is in charge of a **micro-grid** and communicates with **neighbouring fogs and higher tiers. Please note that the higher is the tier, the larger will be the latency and the wider will be the geographical coverage. Also note that the final global coverage is**

provided by SCADA that is responsible for long-time repository and economic analytics.

3. **Smart Vehicle:** Both fog and vehicle networks can also be integrated. Vehicular fog computing is put under two categories- infrastructure-based an autonomous. **In infrastructure-based fog computing,** fog-nodes are responsible to send or retrieve information to or from the driving vehicles. On the other hand, **in autonomous vehicular fog computing,** vehicles on-the-fly are used to form a Fog or cloud to support ad-hoc events. Herein, each fog can communicate with its client and other fogs. Many applications for vehicular fog computing exist like traffic light scheduling, congestion reduction, precaution sharing, parking facility management, traffic information sharing etc.

4. **Smart Cities:** Problems of larger cities like safety, sanitisation, traffic congestions, MCD services etc can be solved if we use a **single IoT network by installing a network of fog nodes.** Deploying fog computing architecture, **fog nodes allow local storages and processing.** This **optimizes the network usage.** Smart cities also try hard with safety and security issues. To solve these problems **real-time applications**, require **real-time analytics.** The network may transmit traffic and data along with life-critical systems. **Fog computing resolves security issues, data encryption and distributed analytics requirements.**

5. **Smart Building:** Fog computing allows free local operations for optimized control functions. Not only a single floor bur also individual rooms can have its own fog node, allowing emergency monitoring and response functions, climate control, lighting control and supplementing the limited capacity of computers and smart devices.

6. **Health-care Data Management:** Using fog computing, it is possible to realize the goal that a patient will take possession of their own **health data locally.** This health data will be stored in fog nodes such as a smart phone or a smart vehicle. The calculation will be outsourced in a private-preserving manner when the patient is seeking help from a medical lab or a physician's office. **Also note that modification of data also takes place directly in the patient-owned fog node.** Real-time health analysis can be done for patient with chronic illness. This data is analysed in real-time and during emergency situations. The doctors and the ambulances will be altered automatically. **Note that the historical data analysis of these patients can predict future dangers of the patient.**

7. **Visual Security:** The bandwidth if the visual data like video cameras used at parking places, makes it impossible to move this data to the cloud and collect real-time views. **Please note that fog computing aids in real-time, latency sensitive distributed surveillance systems that uphold privacy. Also note that with the help of fog computing and its architecture, video processing is logically divided between fog nodes located with the cloud and the cameras.** It helps in real-time tracking, anomaly detection and collection of results from the data collected over a period of time.

8. **Rail Monitoring:** Fog nodes can be deployed in the railway tracks for real-time monitoring of the track conditions. Again sending data from a high speed train to the cloud for analysis is not efficient. **Note that fog nodes provide a faster data analysis in such a scenario and this further improves safety and reliability.**

9. **Pipeline Optimization:** We also know that the gas and petroleum products that are transported through pipelines can be monitored in real-time. In such a scenario, real-time monitoring of pressure, flow and compression is mandatory. **And this can be achieved with the help of fog computing.** So, fire alarms may be altered accordingly.

5.7 CHALLENGES OF FOG

Fog computing has several challenges also. Some of them are listed below:

1. **Data Security and Privacy:** Even IoT and fog computing have many security issues. **Please note that both are heterogeneous in nature, so security and privacy of data is usually cast aside in order to achieve general functionality and interoperability.** In other words, even encryption and strict security policies make it difficult for arbitrary devices to exchange data. Even with these encryption algorithms, several data breaches have been reported. **Also note that fog computing applications in future, should also preserve user privacy, data security, security promises and to listen to the customer needs.**

2. **Data Consistency: The cloud servers in the data centres must coordinate with each other so as to achieve data consistency.** But in fog computing, things become more complicated. **The need is to invalidate the cached data on the fog nodes as well as on the client devices, if strong data consistency is required.** So, the

write performance may reduce further. This will reduce the benefits of using fog nodes as the write-cache servers. **Also note that fog computing provides opportunities of achieving data consistency more efficiently than cloud computing.** Consider an **example now.** *If the write requests on a data object are sent to only one fog node during a certain period of time (common in fog) then the system may temporarily transfer the ownership of the data object from the cloud to the fog node.* **Note that by doing this, the data consistency can be achieved on the fog node which promises better write performance than cloud computing. This is so because the fog nodes reside at the edge of the network.** Still, this is in its infancy stage.

3. **Management of Data:** The end-users aim is to get a **global-storage which can always be accessed, has infinite size and yet performs as with the information stored locally.** And this is possible with fog computing. But certainly, there are some challenges associated with it like need of efficient algorithms for data shuffling among these devices, using pre-fetching to get lowest latency, the namespace scheme used, data security and energy consumption and network usage **conservation on mobile devices** as they are limited by the batteries.

4. **Scheduling: In fog computing, the tasks can be moved between different physical devices** like client nodes, fog nodes and back-end cloud servers. Hence, **scheduling is much more complex.** But many challenges and issues arise here. If the fog nodes have heterogeneous hardware, is it acceptable to trade energy for reduced latency? A process running on one fog node, should be interrupted if it moves onto another fog node? Have you considered factors like latency, energy consumption, mobility and existing workloads for task scheduling? Is inter-task scheduling possible? **Also note that security issues are complex in fog computing. Traditional scheduling algorithms may not be ideal for fog computing as the fog nodes may have different hardware resources and different tasks priorities.**

5. **Programming Architecture: Fog computing is a new computing paradigm that needs a new programming model.** The need is to design newer, innovative and effective tools and frameworks for developers and helping them to use dynamic, hierarchical and heterogeneous resources to build compatible applications on diverse platforms. Again, task scheduling and migration are open to challenge.

What migration rules are to be followed? Is there any standard? **Also note that we should avoid forcing of developers to re-implement functionalities that will likely to be common like** distributed caching, load balancing, system monitoring etc.

6. **Service Discovery Protocols:** Cloud computing can provide automatic discovery of services. **But please note that fog nodes differ from location to location, users can arrive at a new location and take advantage of different services provided by the fog nodes in that particular location. Also note that service provisioning is usually done dynamically in fog computing.** This means that new virtual machines are orchestrated on the spot when a particular service is needed. Here also many services like when should they be stopped or started? What is the best workload? It may also be possible to do pre-service requirements finding before the user arrives. How can millions of users be serviced? Some services are deployed on the fog nodes to aggregate the information from the nearby client devices. How to split task workloads so that energy efficiency is retained on the client side?

7. **Latency:** Many reasons are there that increases the latency time of the fog computing platforms. **Please note that high latency will spoil the user experience and their satisfaction level because fog computing targets at delay-sensitive applications.** The factors that result in this latency may be data aggregations, resource provisioning and node mobilities.

8. **Power Consumption: In fog computing, fog-nodes power consumption is also high.** Fog uses more number of nodes and hence the power consumption is also high than a centralized cloud applications.

SUMMARY

Fog computing is IIoT + Industry 4.0. The term fog was defined by Cisco. What we learnt in this chapter is shown in a flow below:

Things→huge vol. of data → to cloud for analysis → services to end -users

In IoT, billions of things or devices are connected through wired or wireless connectivity. These Things produce a deluge of data that is then transmitted to the cloud for analysis. This may take lot of time and is very crucial for several real-time applications like airplanes, healthcare etc. Hence, providing real-time services is a challenge in cloud computing. So, the concept of fog was introduced to overcome these problems of latencies in cloud architecture. Fog computing follows a distributed architecture that enables processes to execute near the edge of the devices to avoid service latency. **Please note that the fog layer is an intermediate layer between the physical IoT device and the cloud.**

MULTIPLE CHOICE QUESTIONS [MCQS] WITH ANSWERS

1. Fog computing is also known as
   (a) Cloud computing.
   (b) Edge computing.
   (c) Parallel computing.
   (d) None of the above.

2. A network fabric that stretches from the outer edges of where data is created to where it will eventually be stored whether that is in cloud or in a customer's data centre is called as
   (a) Cloud computing.
   (b) Fogging.
   (c) Parallelism.
   (d) None of the above.

3. _____ is an intermediate layer between cloud and devices that generate data
   (a) Log.
   (b) Fog.
   (c) Blog.
   (d) None of the above.

4. The time taken by a data packet for a round trip is called as
   (a) Frequency.
   (b) Latency.
   (c) Consistency.
   (d) None of the above.

5. When time sensitive data is sent to the cloud for analysis, then the latency will be
   (a) Increased.
   (b) Decreased.
   (c) Constant.
   (d) None of the above.

6. If data is analysed closed to the data-source then _____ is reduced
   (a) Bandwidth.
   (b) Volume of data.
   (c) Latency.
   (d) None of the above.

7. Fog computing works best in
   (a) Distributed environment.
   (b) Cloud-based control environment.
   (c) Multiprocessor environment.
   (d) None of the above.

8. A centralized server called as _____
   (a) SCALA.
   (b) SCADA.
   (c) SMALLA.
   (d) None of the above.

9. Fog nodes reside at the edge of
   (a) Computers.
   (b) Vehicles.
   (c) Network.
   (d) None of these.

10. _____ is done dynamically in fog computing
    (a) Store provisioning.
    (b) Cloud provisioning.
    (c) Service provisioning.
    (d) None of the above.

11. What can bring latencies in fog computing
    (a) Data aggregation.
    (b) Resource provisioning.
    (c) Node mobility.
    (d) All of the above.

12. What makes fog computing better is
    (a) Sensitive data is analysed in vicinity closer to the place where it is generated.
    (b) It prevents all data to be sent to the cloud.
    (c) Much faster response as data travel is reduced.
    (d) All of the above.

13. Data is processed in milliseconds time in
    (a) Cloud computing.
    (b) Fogging.
    (c) Jogging.
    (d) None of the above.

14. The use of cloud computing is
    (a) Only voluminous data is stored.
    (b) Only required data will be sent to the cloud.
    (c) No use in fogging.
    (d) None of the above.

15. In fog computing design, fog nodes are closer to
    (a) Devices that generate data.
    (b) Cloud.
    (c) Sensors.
    (d) None of the above.

16. Fog is not meant for bulky storage then bulky storage is done by
    (a) Sensors.
    (b) Actuators.
    (c) Clouds.
    (d) None of the above.

17. Cloud receives data summary from the
    - (a) Sensors.
    - (b) Fog nodes.
    - (c) Cloud nodes.
    - (d) None of the above.
18. One of the best benefits of fogging is that
    - (a) It improves data security.
    - (b) Lesser bandwidth consumption.
    - (c) Immediate data processing in real-time.
    - (d) All of the above.
19. The computing that is done at the device itself is called as
    - (a) Vertex computing.
    - (b) Virtual computing.
    - (c) Edge computing.
    - (d) None of the above.
20. The main difference between edge and fog computing is
    - (a) Speed.
    - (b) Distance.
    - (c) Time.
    - (d) Inertia.
21. Which of the following is a cloud platform?
    - (a) Thing Speak.
    - (b) People Speak.
    - (c) No one Speak.
    - (d) None of the above.
22. Because fog nodes are heterogeneous, so the communication protocols may also vary from a fog node to another
    - (a) True.
    - (b) False.
    - (c) Sometimes true.
    - (d) None of the above.
23. Fog computing supports _____ for seamless execution of processes
    - (a) Stability.
    - (b) Reliability.
    - (c) Mobility.
    - (d) None of the above.
24. This allows directly to access every machine and device on the shop-floor through
    - (a) Edge computing.
    - (b) Distributed computing.
    - (c) Parallel computing.
    - (d) None of the above.
25. To increase the speed of service accessibility, fog applications use
    - (a) Accelerators.
    - (b) Demodulators.
    - (c) Simulators.
    - (d) Monitors.

Answers

1. b	2. b	3. b	4. b	5. a	6. c
7. b	8. b	9. c	10. c	11. d	12. d
13. b	14. a	15. a	16. c	17. b	18. d
19. c	20. b	21. a	22. a	23. c	24. a
25. a					

CONCEPTUAL SHORT QUESTIONS WITH ANSWERS

Q1. Discuss the factors that bring latency in fog networks.

Ans. There are 3 main factors to bring latency in fogging-

1. **Data Aggregation:** It is the **geo-distributed nature of fog paradigm** that finds out that there will be a delay if **data aggregation is not finished before data processing.** Many methods exist to reduce this problem. For e.g., data partitioning, utilizing locality in hierarchy to reduce computation volume on higher layer.

2. **Resource Provisioning:** There will be delay in provisioning resources for certain tasks for resource-limited fog nodes. So, better scheduling may be designed using priority and mobility models.

3. **Node Mobility: Fogging** must be resilient to node mobility, churn and failure. **Also note that both system monitoring and location service will work together to provide information to help on choosing mitigation methods like check-pointing, rescheduling and replication.**

Q2. Distinguish between the cloud computing and fog computing.

Ans. In traditional **cloud computing,** all of the data from the devices are **transmitted to the cloud directly.** Then, it is processes so as to get the final end-user services. These end services may be in form of results of analytics, visualizations etc. On the other hand, **in fog computing/ fogging,** real-time-sensitive data (from different devices) are transmitted to the fog devices at the fog layer. Then, data are processes to serve an end-user application. And if long-term storage is required, then the remaining data is sent onto the cloud.

Q3. **What are the similarities and differences between edge and fog computing?**

Ans. Both fog and edge computing are concerned with the computing capabilities to be executed locally, before passing it to the cloud. Also, both aim at reducing the complete dependency on the cloud to perform computation. **Please note here that analysing data and processing it at the cloud is to be avoided and both edge and fogging helps in achieving it. Also note that the main difference between fog and edge computing is where data processing is taking place.** It means that edge computing is done at the device itself where all sensors are fixed. In fogging, data processing is moved to the processors that are connected to the LAN, making it farther from the sensors. **That is why we say that the main difference between edge and fogging is the distance only.**

Q4. **Throw some light on fog node deployment model.**

Ans. The deployment model of fog nodes is put under four categories (NIST Report):

1. **Private Fog Node:** These fog nodes are allocated and dedicated for a single-user organization. For e.g., a hospital uses a private fog node for analysing the patient's data.

2. **Community Fog Node:** These fog nodes are used for a set of functionality similar organizations. For e.g., a set of hospitals use fog nodes for analysing patient's data. But in this case, only those hospitals that are associated with the deployed fog nodes can access the services. The community fog nodes are owned and maintained by a single or multiple organizations.

3. **Public Fog Node:** The fog nodes that can be used by different organizations is a public fog node. For e.g., a fog node at one particular instance of time may be used by hospital and at some other time may be used by the road transportation company. **Note that a public fog node is owned and managed by multiple organizations.**

4. **Hybrid Fog Node:** It consists up of **a single or multiple public, community or public fog nodes that are logically** combined to provide services to multiple organizations.

Q5. Why is edge computing called with the name "Edge"?

Ans. In fog computing, a large area is sub-divided into smaller sub-areas. These sub-areas take data from the smart IoT devices and process them at the fog nodes fixed at these sub-areas. Because the data is analysed near the edge, so it is called as edge computing. It also reduces the latency of data transmission as is found in the cloud applications.

Q6. Why we need Industrial 4.0?

Ans. At the high level, Industrial 4.0 is aimed to-:

(a) Track the operations, avoid accidents, reduce time and cost.

(b) Enhance employee (worker) productivity.

(c) Make better decisions.

(d) Adapt to different business models.

Q7. What is the main vision of Industry 4.0? What is its core?

Ans. Vision of Industry 4.0 is "to realize the vision of smart factory". It connects machines, people and physical assets into an integrated digital ecosystem that seamlessly generate, analyse and communicates data.

Core of Industry 4.0 is "Combining Internet with Manufacturing." It consists of three parts—Cyber-physical systems (CPS), IoT and cloud computing. In larger manufacturing plants, CPS have been used to integrate the manufacturing processes and the M2M communications.

It suggests vertical integration which allows directly to access every machine and device on the shop-floor through **edge or cloud computing. Also, it suggests intelligent user interfaces** i.e., that is information can be provided in real-time to the operator based on AR/VR.

Q8. Name some IIoT usage in different markets section.

Ans. Today, IoT makes its mark in every industrial sector. The business ideas are infinite. Some of the fields where IIoT is employed are:

• Automobile manufacturing industry.

• Chemical industry.

• Mining industry.

• Paper industry.

• Aerospace industry.

• Food and beverage industry.

- Healthcare industry.
- Utilities.
- Wind energy.
- Power generation.
- Semiconductor industry.
- Glass industry.
- Marine.
- Oil and gas company.
- Tyre manufacturing.
- Cement industry.
- Transport and logistics.
- Parking.
- Cities and municipalities.
- Agriculture industry.
- Construction machinery.
- Machines.
- Pharma industry.
- Water and wastewater industry.
- Insurance.
- Hotel.
- Real estates.
- Service industry.
- Plat engineering.
- Building constructions.

Q9. Show how big data and edge computing are related?

Ans. A diagrammatic view of IoT -enabled system design is as shown below:

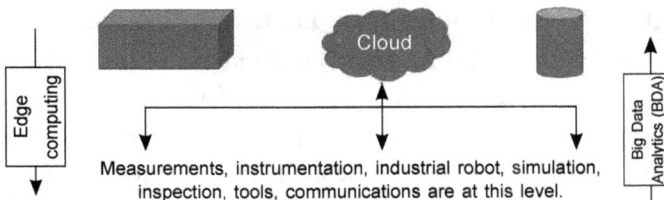

Edge computing

Cloud

Measurements, instrumentation, industrial robot, simulation, inspection, tools, communications are at this level.

Big Data Analytics (BDA)

This figure shows how Things/ Devices get the responsibilities of handling data. The downward arrow shows edge devices processing sensitive data. On the other hand, when data is moved to the cloud, there big data analytics is done to do predictions based on this data. This shows the role of Industry 4.0 on the floor.

Q10. Show the complete ecosystem of IIoT.

Ans. The figure below shows the complete IIoT ecosystem.

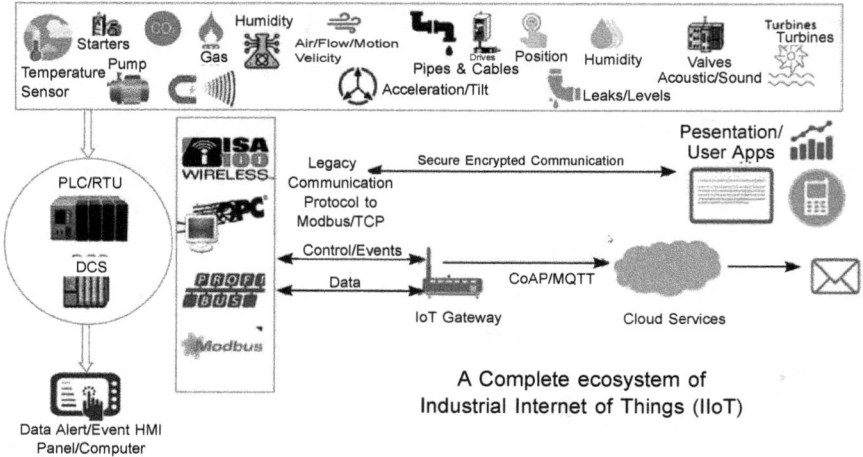

A Complete ecosystem of
Industrial Internet of Things (IIoT)

Q11. What could be the possible drawbacks of Industry 4.0?

Ans. Although the main focus of Industry 4.0 was **the availability and use of Internet and IoT, Edge/fogging, integration of technical and business processes, digital mapping, virtualization of the real world (Digital Twin)** and to realize the vision of **"Smart Factory".** At the same time, Industry 4.0 factory will result in:

1. Decrease in production costs by 10-30%,

2. Decrease of logistic costs by 10-30%.

3. Quality management costs by 10-20%.

Also note that in general, Industry 4.0 can be interpreted as the integration of two things- "automation + "informationization".

Q12. Keeping Industry 4.0 in mind, write short notes on Industry 5.0.

Ans. Some of the salient features of Industry 5.0 are as follows:

1. It is the revolution by which **"man" and "machine" merge** and work together to improve the efficiency of production.

2. It also covers four design principles- **interoperability, transparency, technical assistance and decentralizations.**

3. Industry 4.0 was based on automations **while Industry 5.0 will be a greater synergy between Humans and Autonomous machines.**

4. It will change the definition of the word **"Robot". Robots will not only be a programmable machine that can perform repetitive tasks but will also transform into an ideal human friend for different scenarios.**

5. **Also note that humans might handle the work lighter while machines take care of more active operations.**

6. **Networked Sensor Data Interoperability: Interoperability is the main gist of Industry 5.0** that will cover CPS, humans and autonomous machines communicating with each other.

7. Sensing and collection of big data is the part of Industry 5.0.

8. It will enable **error-free transmission and translation** in Industrial 5.0 development process.

9. Push is towards more advanced **human-machine interfaces.** This implies improved integration, faster and better automation paired with the power of human brains.

EXERCISE QUESTIONS

1. Differentiate between the following:
   (a) Cloud and fog computing.   (b) Edge and fog computing.
   (c) IoT and IIoT.

2. What challenges will you face when you select cloud storage with IoT?

3. "With fogging, it becomes possible to analyse the data at a place closer to where it is generated." Justify this statement.

4. Explain the concept of fog computing, edge computing/fogging with a neat diagram. Also give its advantages, disadvantages and its applications.

5. Why should you opt for fogging? Give three main reasons.

6. How do you calculate the latency? Give the formula used.

7. The fog computing is mainly used in four situations. What are they?

8. What are the main characteristics of fog nodes?

9. Explain the working of fog computing for three cases:
   (a) Time-sensitive data.   (b) Less time-sensitive data.
   (c) Non-time sensitive data.

Also compare different attributes for these three types of data.

10. Discuss some applications of fog computing.

11. What challenges are faced in fog computing?

12. Why is scheduling more complex in fogging?

13. How is service provisioning done in fog computing?

14. Explain the following with respect to fogging-

    (a) Private fog node.   (b) Public fog node.

    (c) Community fog node.   (d) Hybrid fog node.

15. What are run-time engines?

    [**Hints:** Engines that provide the execution environment for the services that includes VMs, containers, platform and programming libraries.]

16. Can we use fog computing in a smart city?

17. How is fog computing model useful in aerospace?

18. Two fog nodes are situated at a distance of 50m. the time required to transmit a data packet from one fog node to another is 10 ms. Find the propagation speed?

19. Assume that there is an IoT device, d1 that wants to transmit a data packet to the fog node but d1 is not directly connected to the fog node. So, d1 has to select the best suitable IoT device as an intermediate hop, among its neighbour IoT devices to deliver the packet to the fog node. **Please note that the neighbour IoT devices of d1 are those that are within their communication range.** Design a mechanism that helps d1 to select the most suitable neighbour IoT device to forward the sensed data.

20. In a fog network, there are 'm' number of IoT devices and 'n' number of fog devices. Two devices d2 and d2 produce data of 16 MB and 32 MB per minute, respectively. As d1 and d2 have a limited computation capability, these devices select fog nodes to process their data. Devices d1 and d2 choose f1 and f2 to transmit the data through different medium. The propagation speed of these medium are $1.5 * 10^6$ m/s and $3.5 * 10^5$ m/s, respectively. It takes 40 ms for a data packet to travel from d1 to f1 and 80 ms to travel from d2 to f2. Find the distance between d1 and f1, and d2 and f2.

6 FLYING AD HOC NETWORK

6.0 INTRODUCTION

Flying Ad Hoc Network (FANET) is a small group of nodes flying in the sky which is also known as unmanned aerial vehicles (UAVs). The term FANET is used for UAVs continuously flying over the sky with the intervention of humans. The movement of FANET in space is 3-D with a speed of 30-40 Km/h [1]traditional omnidirectional antennas are deployed on UAV nodes which result in reduced spatial reuse and limited network capacity. Alternatively, deployment of directional antennas can significantly increase the capacity, spatial reuse and communication range of FANETs. In addition, being aware of the exact locations of the neighboring nodes in a FANET is vital especially for directional ad hoc multi-UAV scenarios. In this paper, we present a novel MAC protocol, LODMAC (Location Oriented Directional MAC. It basically, comes under ad hoc network families such as mobile ad hoc network (MANET) and vehicular ad hoc Network (VANET).

The purpose of FANET is to provide some activities like surveillance, disaster monitoring, security, military, terrain, etc. [2]. We can operate it from some distance such as ground-based infrastructure. The communication between FANET and ground-based infrastructure is centered on the communication standards like IEEE 802.3, 802.11, 802.15.4, etc. These are the band used for communication of the node with infrastructure in a particular network. Figure 6.1 depicts the difference between the traditional and latest trends in the field of communication concerning MANET, VANET, and FANET.

Below understanding the complete information of upcoming technology I want to discuss the previous technologies such as MANET and VANET. Let us discuss the following concept of MANET and VANET.

DOI: 10.1201/9781003728641-6

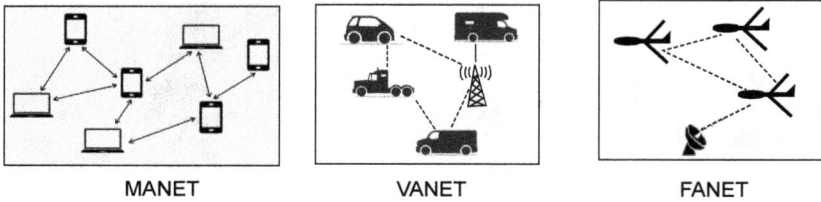

| MANET | VANET | FANET |

Fig. 6.1: MANET, VANET and FANET

6.1 MOBILE AD HOC NETWORK (MANET)

MANET stands for Mobile Ad hoc Network, it's also called a wireless ad hoc network that has generally used for a routing network routable networking situation. It comprises a pair of mobile nodes that are connected wirelessly in the self-configured, self-healing network without having a stable arrangement. In MANET nodes that are open to passage movement randomly as the network topology changes simultaneously. Every node acts as a networking device such as a router which is forwarded passage to another specified node connected in the network.

MANETs is a mobile node that communicates with each other via mobile gadgets for example mobile phones, laptops, and other electronic appliances depicted in Fig. 6.2.

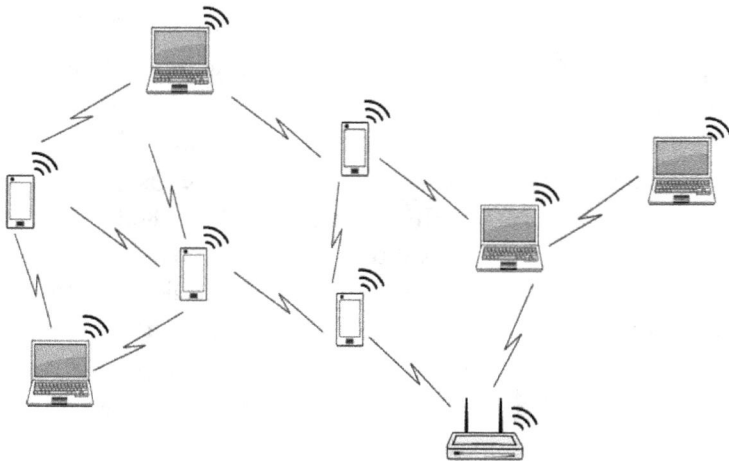

Fig. 6.2: Mobile Ad Hoc Network (MANET)
(source: *https://www.comm.upv.es/en/lines-adhoc/*)

In MANETs the position of nodes, their speed, and acceleration alter from time to time due to the continuous movement of nodes. MANET is very close to sensor network but as compared to them, sensor network has a much larger number of nodes, transmission power, and less radio range. Topology change is frequent in sensor networks which attribute to node mobility and failure, falling in sleep, being blocked by environmental interference, etc.

6.2 CHARACTERISTICS OF MANET

The characteristics of MANET are discussed below:

1. **Dynamic Topologies:** Due to moving from one place to another it typically forms a multihop network randomly. This feature makes the mobile ad hoc network is dynamic.

2. **Low Bandwidth Issue and Variable Capacity Links:** In this network, the bandwidth range are the issue while communicating. Whenever the node is beyond the range it will not communicate correctly and the capacity power of the link also slows down.

3. **Independent Behavior:** Every node in this network works as autonomous because there is no such router to handle the communication between two or more connected devices.

4. **Energy Constrained Issue:** As we know the batteries or other exhaustible means provide the energy to some or all of the nodes. After some time the batteries are drain frequently and required to charge or replace. Typically, mobile nodes have less memory, power, and lighter features.

5. **Restricted Security:** Whenever communication is taking place the security threats pose a greater threat in a wireless network. Because the security, routing, and host configuration are distributed, there is no centralized firewall.

6.3 VEHICULAR AD HOC NETWORK (VANET)

In VANET, nodes are moving in different tracks and roads which are continuously interacting via Wi-Fi IEEE 802.11 [1] such as buses, own cars, etc. VANET was first launched in the year 2001 as '*Car to Car* Ad Hoc Mobile Communication and Networking' purposes, to enable relay of information among cars. The Vehicle to Vehicle and Vehicle to Roadside communication system that co-existed in VANETs provided safe and secured road transport, navigation, and other roadside facilities, depicted in Figure 1.3, VANET is a significant feature of *Intelligent Transportation Systems* (ITS) architecture. VANET consists of numerous microprocessors, an EDR which is useful for crash reconstruction, and a GPS receiver to provide the location and a clock.

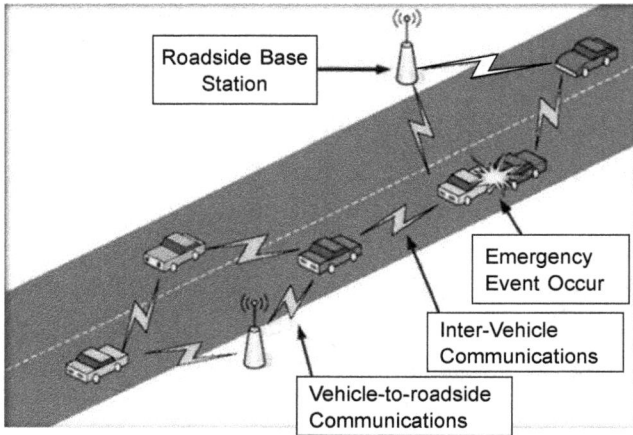

Fig. 6.3: Different communication occurs in VANET
(source: https://www.researchgate.net/figure/A-VANET-consisting-of-vehicles-and-road-side-base-stations-that-exchange-primarily-safety_fig1_288171216)

6.4   COMPARISON BETWEEN MANETS, VANETS, AND FANETS

Table 6.1: Comparison between MANETs, VANETs, and FANETs

S.No	Based on Different Standards	MANETs	VANETs	FANETs
1.	Topology Changes	Slow and Steady	Average	Rapid, Fast
2.	Node Density	Low thickness	Medium	Low thickness
3.	Node Mobility	Low compression	Medium compression	High compression
4.	Mobility Model	arbitrary	steady	Predefined
5.	Radio Propagation	Very Close to the ground, LoS	Close to the ground, LoS	High above the ground level, LoS (line of sight)

Contd.../(Table 6.1)

S.No	Based on Different Standards	MANETs	VANETs	FANETs
6.	Power Consumption	Need of energy-efficient protocols	Not needed	Needed for mini UAVs but now needed for small UAVs
7.	Computational Power	Low	Average	High
8.	Localization	GPS, AGPS,DGPS, IMU	GPS, AGPS,DGPS	GPS, AGPS, DGPS, IMU

6.5   CHARACTERISTICS OF VANET

The characteristics of VANET are discussed below:

1. **High Mobility:** Due to the high speed of VANET it has a high mobility power. When the vehicle movement is supposed to be very high this makes it difficult to find the exact position of other nodes.

2. **Network Topology:** In this network of VANET the movement of nodes are at random speed and continuously changing the position. Due to the high node mobility and random speed of vehicles, the position of the node changes frequently.

3. **Boundless Size of Network:** There is no limit to the network it could be connected within one city, some cities, or in the countries.

4. **Recurrent Interchange of Information:** Since VANET is an ad hoc network, the nodes gather information from other vehicles and roadside equipment.

5. **Cellular Connection:** Nodes in VANET are connected wirelessly and exchange information via a wireless channel, making them suitable for wireless environments.

6.6   VARIOUS COMMUNICATING STANDARD PROTOCOLS

There are some standard protocols such as ZigBee IEEE 802.15.4, Bluetooth, IEEE 802.11 b/g, and UWB (Ultra-wideband), etc., that are used for wireless communications shown in Table 6.2.

Table 6.2: Various Communicating Standards Protocols

Standard	ZigBee/IEEE 802.15.4	Bluetooth	Wi-Fi IEEE 802.11 b/g	UWB (Ultra-Wide Band)
Working frequency	868/915 MHz, 2.4 GHz	2.4 GHz	2.4 GHz	3.1-10.6 GHz
Range (m)	30-75+	30-Oct	30-100+	~10
Data Rate	20/40/250 kbps	1 Mbps	2-54 Mbps	100+ Mbps
Power consumption	~1 mW	~40-100mW	~160mW-600W	~80-300mW

6.7 NETWORK ARCHITECTURE OF FANET

The complete structure of FANET is composed of satellites, flying UAVs, and infrastructure. These three components are very useful to design flying ad hoc networks as is shown in Figure 6.3. In this scenario, the two types of possibilities are encountered in the ad hoc network. First is the satellite and the unmanned aerial vehicle both communicating with each other and sending the information to the ground station, second is satellite UAV to infrastructure. All connected UAVs communicate with each other and send the information to the ground station.

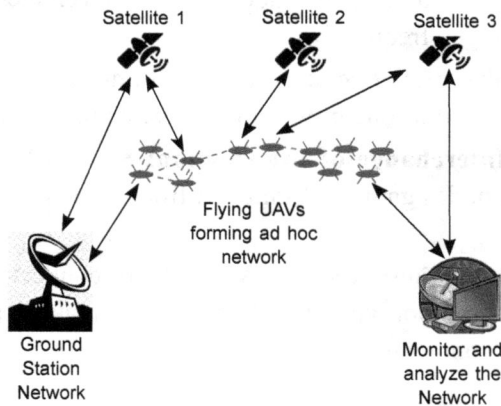

Fig. 6.3: Network Architecture of FANETs

6.8 CLASSIFICATION OF UNMANNED AERIAL VEHICLE NETWORKS

There are two scenarios in the unmanned aerial vehicle (UAV) networks. The first is a single UAV and the second is a multi UAV (represented in

Figures 1.4 (a) and 1.4 (b)). In a single UAV, the flying nodes communicate directly with the ground-based infrastructure and do not communicate with each other. But, in a multi UAV system, the communication takes place in between the flying UAV nodes with the ground-based infrastructure. In this methodology, UAV-to-UAV connectivity is seen through the ground station.

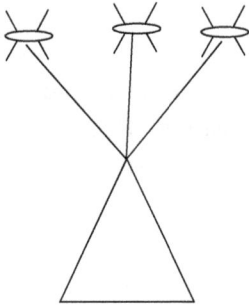

Fig. 6.4: (a) Single UAV   **Fig. 6.4:** (b) Multi-UAV

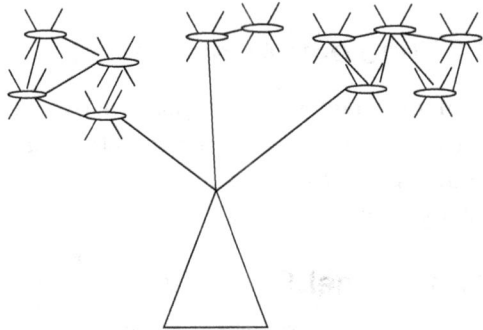

6.9 CHALLENGES IN UNMANNED AERIAL VEHICLE AD HOC

Different challenges are encountered which are discussed below. In Fig.1.5 FANET challenges represent seven different challenges and are discussed below.

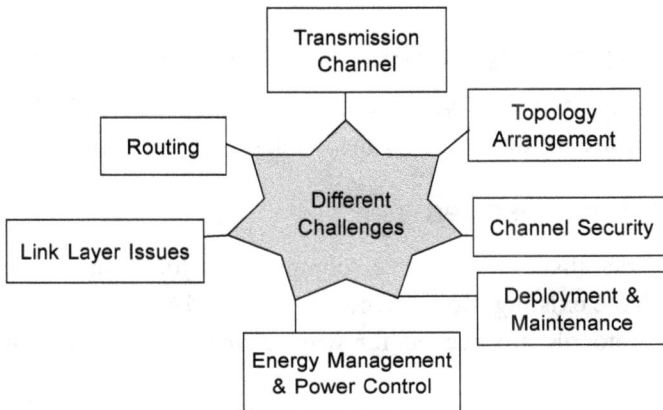

Fig. 6.5: Different Challenges in FANET

6.9.1 Transmission Channel

As aerial networks mostly provide a line of sight such the assortment of the proper band for communication becomes difficult in networks having multiple nodes. Likewise, to provide higher transfer rates this selection has to be carried out efficiently.

6.9.2 Topology Arrangement

One of the main issues in these networks is the organization of the nodes effectively. To improve the functioning of the networks. Recovery and rearrangement at the time of failures are certainly other important aspects of topology in these networks.

6.9.3 Channel Security

Denial of service (DOS), Flooding, a man in the middle attack (MIMA), masquerade attack, black holes, node impersonation, and heap management are some of the possible security threats in such networks which require effective strategies to manage any type of misuse in such network formations.

6.9.4 Deployment and Maintenance

The network should be easy to deploy and configure during network operations. The cost and time for deployment and maintenance should be extremely low.

6.9.5 Energy Management and Power Control

UAVs have a limitation of low energy backup. Thus, efficient designs and configurations are needed to lower the consumption of onboard energy units.

6.9.6 Link-Layer Issues

These networks involve high-level computing which cannot be managed properly with the existing Media Access Control (MAC) protocols. Therefore, new MAC protocols are needed for wide channel selection with enhanced security.

6.9.7 Routing

For UAV networks, effective and more strong routing protocols are needed that can provide higher transmission rates and minimum delays during operations, efficient route reconfigurations, fast recovery, better control over delays, and higher facility for the quality of services to the users.

6.10 LITERATURE REVIEW

T. Bekmezci 1 et.al., [2] is the first person who coined the word flying ad hoc networks (FANETs). In his research paper author explained various applications that are used in it. Extending the scalability of multi-UAV operations, reliable multi-UAV communication, etc. The author also explained FANET design characteristics, the difference between FANET and existing ad hoc networks. Various communication protocols have been discussed for FANETs.

T. W. Mclainl et.al., [3] are studied and presented their research for the cooperative control of UAV Rendezvous. Researchers are addressing the certain problem of cooperative rendezvous. In these findings, rendezvous benchmark problems are depicted and explained. This problem said when the three UAVs are flying with their assigned target at that time it may be possibilities to come under enemy radar system. There are two types of radar systems (1) Known (2) Pop-up. The information of the known radar is known by the UAVs at the time of mission start. In a Pop-up radar system, UAVs are only well aware when it comes under the range of this radar system.

M. H. Tareque et. al., [4] have discussed the utilization of unmanned aerial vehicles (UAV) which requires reducing the difficult tasks. Unmanned aerial vehicles (UAVs) requires coordination and cooperation with other UAVs to the performance task. In this case, multi-UAVs are used to carry out an intricate operation in a single operation. The most challenging problem for UAV conditions is reliability, security, and collision avoidance. At the last authors have explained communication is a difficult task in a multi-UAVs system and it is compared with the traditional ad hoc networks.

S. Raj, V. K. Panchal, and R. Chopra [5] have discussed that Flying ad hoc networks (FANETs) technology is increasingly used in the field of networking and it is continuously used for monitoring, surveillance, health care, etc. Communication is difficult between the flying nodes due to continuous changes in topology. To overcome this issue and to achieve effective communication in the flying nodes we can use the concept of one of the bird species called Hill Myna. These birds can explain to us a very intelligent way of communicating.

M. Bani et.al., [6] author is discussing characteristics, routing protocols, and mobility models used in flying ad hoc networks (FANETs). Mobility models are a challenging task in FANETs because of frequent changes in topology. Various mobility models have been discussed that solved the frequent change in topology. The mobility models are Random WayPoint, Gauss-Markov Mobility, Semi-Random Circular Movement, Mission Plane-Based, Pheromone-Based, and Paparazzi Mobility model. Furthermore, communication, cooperation, and collaboration are the most challenging design issues for multi-UAV systems. In this paper, ad-hoc networks between UAVs are surveyed as a separate network family, Flying Ad-hoc Networks (FANETs).

S. Raj, V. K. Panchal, and R. Chopra [7] explained the framework of the network used in flying ad hoc networks (FANET). The author has discussed the two categories of unmanned aerial vehicles (UAV). First is a single UAV can consist of 'n' number of UAVs where each node works independently without any types of intra and inter-network connection. Secondly, in a multi-UAV system, data sharing is important to transmission and control algorithms. The system contains various design problems in comparison to a single UAV. It solves many problems related to scrutiny, direction-finding as well as exploration.

R. W. Beard et.al., [8] discussed the cooperative and coordination rendezvous for FANETs. In this paper, the authors have focused on to target tracking system of UAVs. There are similar UAVs are flying over the sky to perform a complex task and after performing mission or complex tasks it will reach the same point. In the sky, unmanned aerial vehicles (UAVs) are flying from one point to another randomly. Due to randomly changing their position and topology, to find out the position and topology Voronoi maps are used.

Feng Luo et. al., [9] unmanned aerial vehicle (UAV have discussed there are various steps of communications requirements and also analyzed the groups of unmanned aerial vehicles (UAVs). According to the authors they have been discussing its application and characteristics of a distributed gateway selection solution that is based on a dynamic network partition. The mathematical model of the gateway selection problem in a UAV network was also analyzed.

A. Bujari et. al., [10] have discussed the various mobility models with their pros and cons in terms of different criteria, such as motion variation, randomization, collision avoidance, and network connectivity. The addition authors have clearly explained smooth turns and speed changes that could produce more authentically these randomized movements.

Y. Saleem et. al., [11] have discussed various IEEE bands such as IEEE L-Band, IEEE S-Band, and ISM band. However, they are focusing on the problem of a spectrum that is very important while using UAVs. Some spectrums are used for the unmanned aerial vehicle with the cognitive radiofrequency. This cognitive radiofrequency for unmanned aerial vehicle systems are integrated with different radio technologies.

S. Raj, V. K. Panchal, and R. Chopra [12] have discussed the three central nodes that are called by taking an example of one species called desert sparrows. The authors have been explained the clustering technique how communication intelligently happened. The boundary enclosing them is called a communication range. The desert sparrows are more intellectual having a sharp and precise understanding.

K.M. Polycarpou et. al., [13] suggested a search problem for UAVs to search a dynamic environment cooperatively. This is based on q-stepped path planning algorithms. Such algorithms are already in use in robotics and multi-agent systems.

S. Palazzi et. al., [14] suggested the high altitude platforms (HAPS) for UAV ad hoc networks. These are governed by satellites and are situated in the stratosphere sandwiched between UAVs above and satellites below. It is in direct contact with the satellite and the ground station. But the HAPS is more hypothetical than real. For now, HAPS-based hot spots are used for guidance and surveillance.

B. S. Iordanakis M. et. al. [15] suggested a routing protocol for aerial networks in ad hoc mode. This routing protocol is mainly for infrastructure-based routing, not for UAV networks. This protocol is based on the Ad hoc On-Demand Distance Vector (AODV) protocol, which is altered at the level of the MAC layer.

S. Raj, V. K. Panchal, and R. Chopra [16] authors have discussed the utmost aspects of routing protocols that are used in flying ad hoc networks. Most of the protocols used in FANETs are similar to those used in the previous wireless sensor networks such as MANET and VANET with few modifications to overcome their shortcomings. In the previous protocols, some of the limitations include scalability, energy consumption, etc. There needs to be continuous development in the field of routing protocols to adapt to these drawbacks. This may widen the area of applications in the field of wireless sensor networks.

C. Zang and S. Zang [17] proposed a clustering algorithm for UAVs networks. Also called mobility prediction algorithm this model is based on the calculation of link expiration time which tells the duration of connection existing between two nodes. A cluster head is selected based on the highest weighted nodes. This cluster is maintained for efficient transmission during the phase.

6.11 VARIOUS ROUTING PROTOCOLS FOR AD HOC NETWORK

Various routing protocols are used for the transmission of information. Routing is done in six different ways such as static protocol, proactive protocol, reactive protocol, hybrid protocol, geographical protocol, and hierarchical.

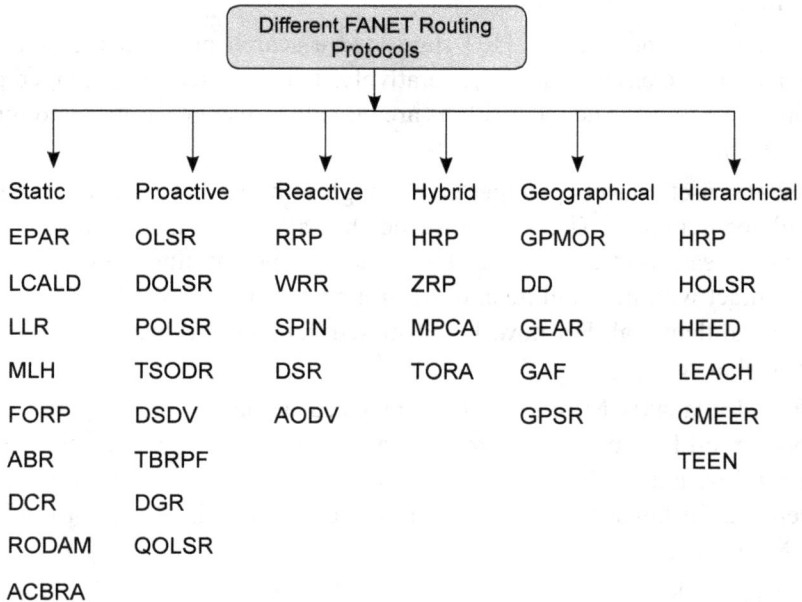

Different FANET Routing Protocols					
Static	Proactive	Reactive	Hybrid	Geographical	Hierarchical
EPAR	OLSR	RRP	HRP	GPMOR	HRP
LCALD	DOLSR	WRR	ZRP	DD	HOLSR
LLR	POLSR	SPIN	MPCA	GEAR	HEED
MLH	TSODR	DSR	TORA	GAF	LEACH
FORP	DSDV	AODV		GPSR	CMEER
ABR	TBRPF				TEEN
DCR	DGR				
RODAM	QOLSR				
ACBRA					

6.11.1 Static Protocol

M. Bani et.al., [6] have discussed the static routing protocol, In this protocol, the topology of a network is fixed and no changes can be made during the operation. Once the table is created for the routing, the information stored in the connected UAVs will remain the same as defined and no further changes or updates can be made. In case a failure occurs suddenly then no provision for updating the routing table dynamically.

Energy Power-Aware Routing (EPAR) Protocol

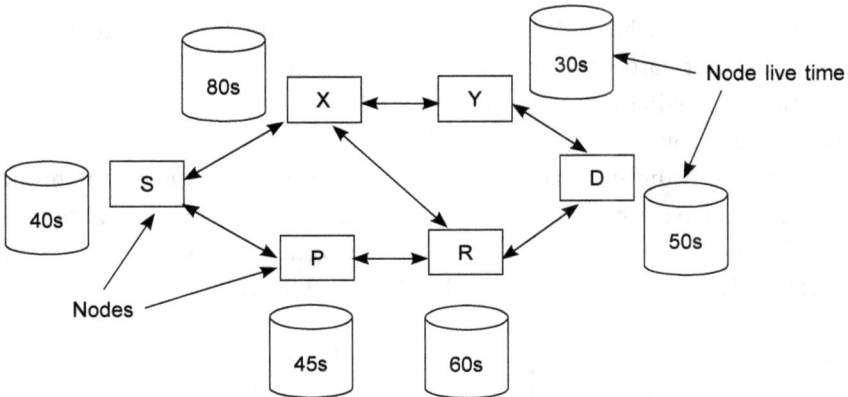

Fig. 6.6: Complete architecture of EPAR

S. Suman et.al., [18] have discussed the energy power-aware routing protocol. This protocol is used to find the lifetime prediction of the battery. EPAR protocol identifies the multiple paths in the intermediate routers to find the maximum energy or lifetime. It selects the path which has maximum lifetime using the EPAR algorithm.

Let's take the example in the given Fig. 6.6, S is represented as the sender node, and D is represented as the receiver node. EPAR algorithm finds, the path which has maximum lifetime from a sender node to receiver node. This algorithm has different ways from sender to receiver defined as below:

$$\frac{40}{S} + \frac{80}{X} + \frac{30}{Y} + \frac{50}{D} = 200 \qquad \ldots 1$$

$$\frac{40}{S} + \frac{45}{P} + \frac{60}{R} + \frac{50}{D} = 195 \qquad \ldots 2$$

$$\frac{40}{S} + \frac{80}{X} + \frac{60}{R} + \frac{50}{D} = 230 \qquad \ldots 3$$

$$\frac{40}{S} + \frac{45}{P} + \frac{60}{R} + \frac{80}{X} + \frac{30}{Y} + \frac{50}{D} = 305 \qquad \ldots 4$$

Now, EPAR find the maximum lifetime path from equation (4) which is 305.13

Load Carry and Load Delivery (LCALD) Protocol

M. Kaur et.al., [19] have discussed this protocol which is used to carry the load i.e. data or large information loaded on the UAVs and deliver it to the particular destination. The purpose of load carries and load delivery is to maximize throughput so that maximum data. The information from the ground to where the destination node is. This protocol is used for military purposes because a large amount of data is sent to the actual destination. The ground level or the source (SN) carries data and delivers it to the destination node (DN). Let's depict with the help of a diagram [20].

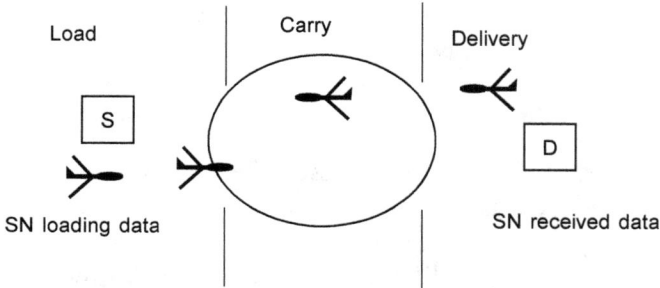

Fig. 6.7: Source to Destination Delivery of Data

Long Lifetime Route (LLR)

Z. Cheng and W. B. Heinzelman [21] has discussed this protocol used to discover the new path whenever a connection breaks. It suggests the best frequent route; the shortest path improves the overall performance. LLR reduces the connection discontinuation or path break. It could happen based on route lifetime distribution.

Route Lifetime Distribution

The route is made of different connected links in the network. The best method to find the best route is the shortest hop or intermediate nodes between sources to destination and this easily gets the lifetime of the route, which one is larger hop count or which is smaller. Consider the distance between sources to the destination node is L, and connection made via a node-link is N where N>L, nodes are connected via link source to destination, then calculate link distance using formula [22].

Multilevel Hierarchical Routing (MLH)

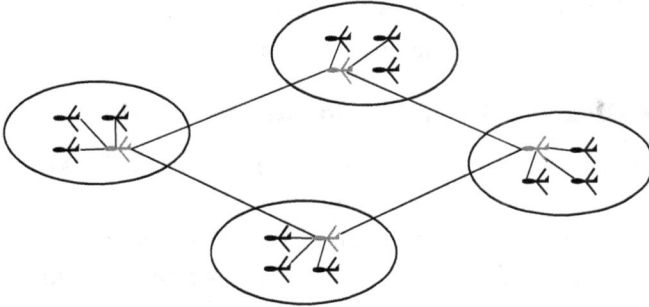

Fig.6.8: Multi-Level Hierarchical Routing

There are different bunches of UAVs flying in the sky and they make a cluster of nodes. They are connected and communicate in their specific region. Each region consists of a cluster head that communicates with the other regions via their cluster heads. In Figure 1.8 below the UAV shown in red color is the cluster head.

Flow Oriented Routing Protocol (FORP)

W. Su and M. Gerla [23] have first introduced this routing protocol. FORP is based on a multi-hoop handoff system, if one route disconnects and no other route is available then it reroutes the network. Another use of this protocol is to maintain the router information of the entire source and destination node which are active.

Associativity Based Routing (ABR) Protocol

S. Maakar and M. T. Scholar [24] have discussed the associativity-based routing protocol. This protocol is created on a query and reply base system for the search destination node. The source node sends the query to all the connected nodes in the network according to a priority-based system. It selects the consistent route first and then takes the better associativity preference [25].

Data-Centric Routing (DCR)

M. A. Khan et.al., [26]sensors and communication systems, the production of small UAVs (Unmanned Air Vehicles have discussed the data-centric routing protocol. Here routing is done depending on data characteristics and not on the IDs of the UAVs requesting it. The request from the ground station is sent to many UAVs each of which will decide whether to collect information or not to collect after that sends data to other UAVs nodes [6].

Routing On-Demand Acyclic Multipath (RODAM)

M. Mosko and C. E. Perkins [27] have designed the ROADAM protocol. All the routers attached in the network maintain the tables which have a list of the node distance, link, and cost of the table. The routing table contains the distance of all destination nodes as well as neighbor nodes and accordingly router updates the routing table as per the requirement. There is some point that the router must enter (i) destination nodes table entry (ii) updates regularly when required. Another main aim of RODAM protocol is to design a loop-free path from source to destination.

Ant Colony Based Routing Algorithm (ACBRA)

The algorithm of Ant colony optimization was given by Colorni and Dorigo, which was studied from the communication behavior of the ants in their colonies. The ants while moving, leave behind a chemical named pheromone in the path which is perceived by other ants and they follow the same path for a search of food. Thus, the pheromone guides the movement of a large number of ants. This phenomenon provides positive feedback to the algorithm which can increase the routing selection. When a route is taken by many ants, the probability of the route chosen by other ants becomes high [28].

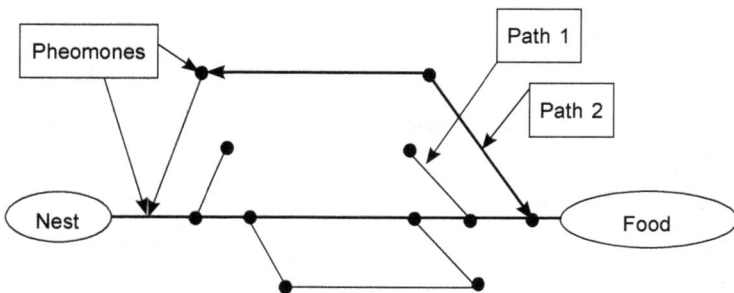

Fig. 6.9: Geographic Adaptive Fidelity (Virtual Gride)

In this figure, there are two paths path1 and path2 that represent the way where the ants find the food and for searching food the ant drop the pheromones in paths.

6.12 PROACTIVE PROTOCOL

In this protocol, the network maintains its route as well as its connected neighbor's node information. The routing tables information with a certain interval of time is refreshed periodically [25]. The drawback of this protocol is that it is not used for big networks and maintenance of the routing table for every node involved in such large networks.

Optimized Link State Routing (OLSR) Protocol

T.Clausen & P.Jacquet [29] was first introduced the OLSR protocol. The key concept was multipoint relay (MPR). MPR is the node that is selected during the broadcast of messages as flooding. Optimization is achieved in the network by reducing the flooding of messages from source to destination. MPR itself selects the node by one step neighbor to connect the source node with the destination node.

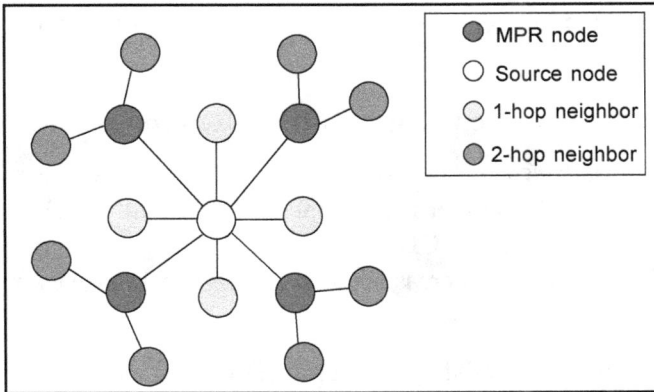

Fig. 6.10: Process of OLSR mechanism
Source(https://www.mdpi.com/574756)

Directional Optimized Link State Routing (DOLSR) Protocol

DOLSR protocol uses the Multi-point relay (MPR), which is a central node used to transmit information from one node to another. DOLSR is based on OLSR but has less number of relay points with the use of an Omni-directional antenna [26]sensors and communication systems, the production of small UAVs (Unmanned Air Vehicles. If the source knob has to transmit data to destination nodes that are calculated by compared formula Dmax/2 [30].

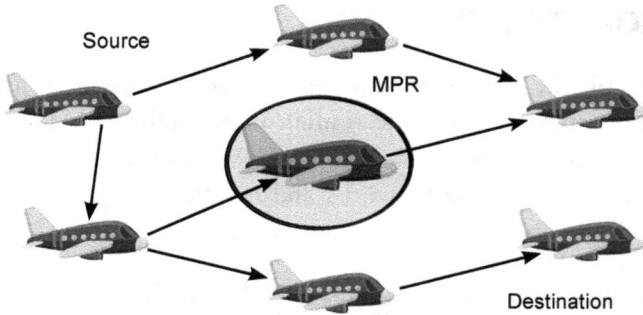

Fig.6.11: Directional Optimized Link State Routing

Predictive Optimized Link State Routing (POLSR) Protocol

Rosati et.al., [31] proposed, here routing information is obtained through a global positioning system (GPS). The relative speed between the two nodes is calculated using GPS and a higher quality link is chosen. The authors are explaining the concepts of relative speed when two nodes are highly moveable in the sky.

Time Slotted on Demand Routing (TSODR) Protocol

This algorithm is based on the division of time, as the packets are going to send from one node to another it will first check the path which must be free, and provide a time slot. In AODV, every packet before sending will contain a time slot. This process decreases the collision and improves effectiveness in communication.

Destination Sequence Distance Vector (DSDV) Protocol

DSDV is a step-by-step routing protocol where each connected node in the network requires a periodical update in the routing table. The distance vector idea is the concept of the Bellman-Ford routing algorithm. Every node contains the sequence number. The route with the highest sequence number is given the preference. This has the advantage of avoiding network loops.

Topology Broadcast Based on Reverse Path Forwarding (TBRPF) Protocol

A. Bujari et.al., [32] proposed this protocol that is designed in such a way that there is efficient dissemination of the packet. If there is any change in the link-state, it will quickly identify and reschedule the immediate computation which is appropriate for FANETs.

Delay Guaranteed Routing (DGR) Protocol

Delay guaranteed routing (DGR) protocol has created the concept of time division multiple access (TDMA) protocol. It is an integrated MAC and routing protocol. In this protocol, delivery effectively provides a delay guarantee. The transmission of data is based on time slots. DGR requires a short signal phase to get node location and then utilizes the vacant slot available to reduce the latency between two successive media access by sensor nodes [33].

Quality of Service OLSR (QOLSR) Protocol

H. Badis and K. Al Agha, [34] QOLSR is a wireless routing protocol that used wireless connectivity IEEE 802.11 that provides an enhancement quality. This protocol creates routing metrics where one or more nodes communicate with each other. Multi-point relay (MPR) is used as a forwarding packet and is responsible to mediate communication between connected nodes.

6.13 REACTIVE PROTOCOL

It is also known as an On-demand routing protocol, it discovers the path for the message, sends the information according to the need [19]. This routing protocol uses two message passing techniques. (i) Route request message (RREQM); In this, the source node (SN) sends the request over the network to the destination node (DN). (ii) Route reply message (RRP); In this protocol, the destination node (DN) sends the reply to the source node (SN) over the network as a result it maintains the same path mentioned earlier [35].

Reactive Routing Protocol (RRP)

The reactive routing protocol also called on-demand routing protocol (ODRP), represents no interaction takes place of two nodes than at this time no need to calculate the path between them. It is designed to reduce the problems of proactive routing protocol (PRP).

Wireless Routing Protocol (WRP)

This protocol is used for the maintenance of loop freedom. It requires every connected node to overhead at each nub in the network. There are four methods used to connect nubs (i) Distance table (DT), (ii) Routing table (RT), (iii) Link-cost table (LCT), (iv) Message re-transmission list (MRL) table [36] frequently changing network topology and the need for efficient dynamic routing protocols plays an important role. A variety of routing protocols targeted specifically at this environment have been developed and some performance simulations are made on numbers of routing protocols like Ad hoc On-Demand Distance Vector Routing (AODV.

Sensor Protocol for Information (SPIN)

According to J. Kulik et.al [37] have proposed this protocol is based on information dissemination through negotiation. SPIN is the data-centric routing protocol. It has the following assumptions:

1. The connected knob in networks are base station
2. The adjacent knob has the same data values.

Dynamic Source Routing (DSR)

L. O. Karaca and R. Sokullu have discussed [38] the dynamic source routing protocol. It is a convenient and effective routing protocol developed in the context of multi-hop networks where nodes (UAVs) are self-organized and self-configured. This protocol is based on two mechanisms first is Route discovery and the second is route maintenance.

1. **Route Discovery:** When a node helps to send information for which the route is not known, a route-finding process is initiated to find the route dynamically. A large number of route request packets are sent to the network. Each node receiving the request will rebroadcast it unless it has a destination route in its cache. Such a node will reply with a route reply that will be sent back to the source node.

2. **Route Maintenance:** This plays an important role while data sending between the source node to the destination node. If the network between source and destination has broken the source node is informed with a route error packet and this link is erased from the network.

Ad Hoc on Demand Distance Vector Routing (AODV)

In ad hoc on-demand distance vector routing the authors S. Das, C. Perkins, and E. Roye [39]low processing and memory overhead, low network utilization, and determines unicast routes to destinations within the ad hoc network. It uses destination sequence numbers to ensure loop freedom at all times (even in the face of anomalous delivery of routing control messages have discussed this protocol which is based on information of knob comprise next information for data flow. It deals with fast revision to dynamic links, short network processing, low network utilization, and retention overhead.

There are three types of messaging that happen in the AODV (i) Route Requests (RREQs) (ii) Route Reply (RREPs) and (iii) Route Errors (RERRs).

1. **Route Requests (RREQs):** When an IP packet transmits the source to the destination node it maintains the path and first sends the route request to the destination. The source code is responsible for the establishment of the route.

2. **Route Reply (RREPs):** The target node sends an acknowledgment to starting node as a confirmation that now ready to send a packet within the established network.

3. **Route Error (RERRs):** Sometimes due to a connection break at that time error is generated and the route itself sends the report to the router for the correction error.

6.14 HYBRID PROTOCOL

It is a combination of the above two protocols such as proactive and reactive protocols. The reactive protocol discovers the route in the extra time while the proactive protocol controls the message with huge overhead. So, the networks are divided into zones for an appropriate distinction between the two protocols discussed below.

Hybrid Routing Protocol (HRP)

According to J. Jun and M. L. Sichitiu [40] have explained this combines the previous protocols and is designed to overcome their shortcoming. HRP can reduce the large latency of the initial route discovery process in cases of reactive routing protocols, and also the overhead of control messages concerning proactive routing protocols. It works well for large networks. A network is divided into several zones where intra-zone routing is done through a proactive approach and inter-zone routing is performed with a reactive approach.

Zone Routing Protocol (ZRP)

According to Z. J. Haas and M. R. Pearlman [41], this hybrid routing protocol keeps the information of their connected neighbors only. It will work in the particular range that can be divided into zones and provide more effective routing to the connected nodes. The author explained the two zones in this protocol (a) Inter-zone routing (b) Intra-zone routing.

Mobility Prediction Clustering Algorithm (MPCA)

According to C. Zang and S. Zang [42] to overcome the issues related to existing algorithms in the network, a new algorithm based on weighted clustering is proposed known as MPCA. It is based on (a) link expiration time (b) dictionary of tri-structure.

Temporally-Ordered Routing Algorithm (TORA)

R. Sharma and D. K. Lobiyal [43] have explained here each UAV only updates data regarding neighboring UAVs. The important feature of this protocol is to limit flow control messages in an extremely dynamic environment to reduce fast responses to topographical changes

6.15 GEOGRAPHICAL BASED PROTOCOL

This protocol is based on the particular area where we find the details of the area to collect the information of a particular area. It is also based on the position and geographical details by which we find the exact location of the area and the position of the UAVs flying over the area.

Geographic Position Mobility Oriented Routing (GPMOR)

R. S. Raw et.al., [44] have explained the geographic position of mobility-oriented routing. In this routing, the position of the UAVs has changed geographically. The position of the UAVs is assumed and the data is sent to the destination nodes without discovering the route. The movement of the UAVs is based on the assigned range where it is deployed. It will take the pictures of the desired area and sent them to destination nodes.

Directed Diffusion (DD)

M. A. Matin and M. M. Islam [45] have explained the data-centric (DC) routing protocol. The interaction among the node is localized within a limited network neighborhood thus saving energy and increasing network lifetime. In this routing protocol, one node is located in middle to communicate to other nodes. The middle node is performed as a centralized node and used to transfer information to other nodes in a network.

Geographic and Energy- Aware Routing (GEAR)

A. Boukerche et.al., [46] have explained geographic and energy-aware routing. It is based on the location and needs all the information of connected nodes in the network. This protocol used GIS (Geographical information system) to find the location of particular sensor nodes in a network.

Geographic Adaptive Fidelity (GAF)

M. Maimour et.al., [47] have explained the geographic adaptive fidelity routing protocol. This algorithm is primarily designed for mobile ad hoc networks but may be applicable for ad hoc sensor networks. It is a hierarchical based routing protocol and clusters are based on the position or geographical location. The clusters are divided into zones and make a virtual grid for communication. The virtual grids are designed in such a way that every node of A wants to communicate with every node of B and vice versa. If the node has the same point in the grid is considered equivalent in regards to packet routing. The cluster head informs all the activities in the network to the base station.

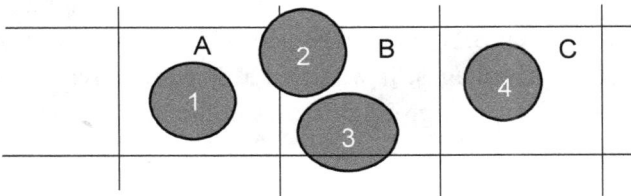

Fig. 6.12: Geographic Adaptive Fidelity (Virtual Gride)

In Fig. 6.12, node 1 communicate to node 2 and 3 similarly node 2 and 3 communicate to node 4 thus the node 2 and 3 lying in the same grid are considered equivalent and the rest are sleep node. GAF functions in three stages: discovery, activity, and sleep.

Greedy Perimeter Stateless Routing (GPSR) Protocol

J. A. Maxa et.al., [48] have explained the greedy perimeter stateless routing protocol. It is an innovative routing protocol for ad hoc networks that uses the location of the router and packet of destination and makes packet forwarding decisions. In this routing protocol, it makes greedy packet forwarding and decisions by information-connected neighbors in the topology.

6.16 HIERARCHICAL BASED PROTOCOL

This protocol is similar to a tree-like structure, one node is called the parent node, and other neighbor nodes are called a children node. This protocol is based on clustering concepts. Different clusters are used for the different mission areas. There are two clustering algorithm protocols used for FANETs. (i) Clustering head algorithm (ii) Mobility prediction clustering algorithm [35].

Hierarchical Routing Protocol (HRP)

G. Pei et.al., [49] have discussed the hierarchical routing protocol. This protocol is based on the cluster method. The networks are divided into a cluster, each cluster having a cluster head. This cluster head will gather information from the cluster and will transmit data to the base station. There is periodic re-election of CHs within clusters based on their residual energy. This balances the power consumption of each cluster.

Hierarchical Optimized Link State Routing (HOLSR)

According to L. Villasenor-Gonzalez et.al., [50], Hierarchical optimized link state routing (HOLSR) is an extension of OLSR, however hierarchical protocol has some advantages, it works in a dynamic environment with the cluster nodes. A cluster is a group of nodes collectively that work in a self-organized pattern.

Hybrid Energy-Efficient Distributed Clustering (HEED)

According to H. Jing and H. Aida [51], the nodes are based on the connectivity of clustering, and the clustering head gets the responsibility to connect all the nodes in the network. Cluster head may be increase as the area increases depending upon the requirements. Only the sensor nodes having high residual energy has the efficiency to become cluster head.

Low Energy Adaptive Clustering Hierarchy (LEACH)

T. Kang et al., [52] have explained the low energy adaptive clustering hierarchy. This algorithm is one of the most popular hierarchical routing protocols for sensor networks. LEACH algorithm is a cluster-based routing protocol based on the random formation of random election to find the head from the cluster. After that sensor node selects a random number between 1 to 0 if the sensor node gets value , less than the threshold value than the node become the head for the current session.

The threshold value can be calculated by:

$$T(n) = \left(\cfrac{P}{1 - P\left(r\,m\,\cfrac{1}{p}\right)} \right), \quad n \in G \qquad \qquad \text{... I}$$

$$0, \quad \text{othewise}$$

Where P = fraction nodes of cluster heads, r = current session or round, and G= set that is not a part of cluster head in last round. After the election of the cluster node, the cluster node will make a schedule of TDMA slot and assign the time of each node connected in the cluster.

Clustering Method for Energy Efficient Routing (CMEER)

According to T. Kang et al., [52] it is another technique to find cluster heads. In CMEER nodes will increase or decrease as per the requirement. The nodes itself consider being a candidate for cluster heads, using the above equation (I).

Threshold Sensitive Energy Efficient Sensor Network (TEEN)

A. Manjeshwar and D. P. Agrawal [53] have explained the threshold-sensitive energy-efficient sensor network protocol. It is targeted to every cluster connected to a network, in addition to every attribute, and the cluster heads. According to there are two threshold sets hard threshold (Ht) and soft threshold (St). In hard threshold, it's a value of sensitive attributes. In soft threshold, it is the value of triggered or target nodes.

SUMMARY

In this chapter, we have studied recently used technology Flying Ad Hoc Network (FANET). FANET is also known as Unmanned Aerial Vehicle (UAVs) and it is a subset of MANET and VANET. We have learned various standard communication protocols which are used for communication purposes. This chapter contains network architecture, classification, and challenges of FANET. In the last section, we studied various routing protocols used in the ad hoc network.

MULTIPLE CHOICE QUESTIONS (MCQS) WITH ANSWERS

Q1. What is a FANET

    (a) It is a small group of network

    (b) It is a large group of network

    (c) It is a mixed group of network

    (d) None of the above

Q2. What is the routing algorithm used in MANETs?

    (a) Shortest Path First

    (b) Routing Information Protocol

    (c) Distance Vector Protocol

    (d) Ad hoc On-demand Distance Vector Protocol

Q3. VANET stands for

    (a) Vehicular ad on network   (b) Vehicle ad hoc network

    (c) Vehicular ad hoc network   (d) None of the above

Q4. What is the type of network in which the routers themselves are mobile?

    (a) Wide Area Network   (b) Mobile Ad hoc Network

    (c) Mobile Network   (d) Local Area Network

Q5. MANET stands for

    (a) Mobile ad hoc network   (b) Mobility ad hoc network

    (c) Military ad hoc network   (d) None of the above

Q6 Which of the following is true for UAV networks

    (a) It is very complex

    (b) It has huge power requirements

    (c) Communication links break frequently

    (d) All of the above

Q7. SPIN stands for

    (a) Sensor Protocol for identification

    (b) Sensor Protocol for Information

    (c) Sensor Protocol for identity

    (d) None of the above

Q8. Which of these topologies in a UAV network has the highest chance of a single point of failure?

    (a) Star Topology   (b) Flat Mesh

    (c) Hierarchical Mesh   (d) Tree

Q9. UAV Stand for

    (a) Unmanned Aerial Network   (b) Unmanned Air Network

    (c) Unmanned Aero Network   (d) None of the above

Q10 UAV Networks can be used for

    (a) Relaying sensor data from the air and between ground points

    (b) Routing packets from UAV as well as ground-based systems

    (c) Cooperative surveillance

    (d) All of the above are true

Answers

1 (a)	2. (a)	3. (c)	4. (d)	5. (b)	6.(d)
7. (b)	8. (a)	9. (a)	10. (d)		

Abbreviations

FANET	Flying Ad Hoc Networks
EPAR	Energy Power-Aware Routing
OLSR	Optimized Link State Routing
HRP	Hybrid Routing Protocol
LCALD	Load Carry and Load Delivery
HOLSR	Hierarchical Optimized Link State Routing
MLH	Multilevel Hierarchical Routing
GEAR	Geographic and Energy- Aware Routing
FORP	Flow Oriented Routing Protocol
GPSR	Greedy Perimeter Stateless Routing
CMEER	Clustering Method for Energy Efficient Routing
ABR	Associativity Based Routing (ABR) Protocol
TEEN	Threshold Sensitive Energy Efficient sensor Network
DGPS	Differential GPS/Differential Global Positioning System
DOLSR	Directional Optimized Link State Routing Protocol

AGPS   Assisted GPS/Assisted Global Positioning System

AODV   Ad-Hoc On-Demand Distance Vector Routing

LEACH   Low Energy Adaptive Clustering Hierarchy

HEED   Hybrid Energy-Efficient Distributed

IMU   Inertial Measurement Unit

WSN   Wireless Sensor Network

DSR   Dynamic Source Routing

UAV   Unmanned Aerial Vehicle

LoS   Line of Sight

AP   Access Points

REFERENCES

[1]   S. Temel and I. Bekmezci, "LODMAC: Location oriented directional MAC protocol for FANETs," *Comput. Networks*, vol. 83, pp. 76–84, 2015, doi: 10.1016/j.comnet.2015.03.001.

[2]   T. Bekmezci and O. Sahingoz, "Flying Ad-Hoc Networks (FANETs): A Survey," *Ad Hoc Networks*, vol. 11, no. 3, pp. 1254–1270, 2013, doi: 10.1016/j.adhoc.2012.12.004.

[3]   T. W. Mclainl, P. R. Chandler, S. Rasmussen, and M. Pachter, "Cooperative Control of UAV Rendezvous," *Proc. Am. Control Conf. Arlingt.*, pp. 2309–2314, 2001, doi: 10.1109/ACC.2001.946096.

[4]   M. H. Tareque, M. S. Hossain, and M. Atiquzzaman, "On the Routing in Flying Ad hoc Networks," *Fed. Conf. Comput. Sci. Inf. Syst. (FedCSIS), 2015*, vol. 5, pp. 1–9, 2015, doi: 10.15439/2015F002.

[5]   S. Raj, V. K. Panchal, and R. Chopra, "Cooperative Rendezvous Optimization Routing Protocol for FANET," vol. 29, no. 5, pp. 13801–13806, 2020.

[6]   M. Bani and N. Alhuda, "Flying Ad-Hoc Networks: Routing Protocols, Mobility Models, Issues," *Int. J. Adv. Comput. Sci. Appl.*, vol. 7, no. 6, 2016, doi: 10.14569/IJACSA.2016.070621.

[7]   S. Raj, V. K. Panchal, and R. Chopra, "Bottomless Taxonomy of Cooperative Design for Flying Ad Hoc Network," *Int. J. Eng. Adv. Technol.*, vol. 9, no. 4, pp. 578–583, doi: 10.35940/ijeat.D6807.049420.

[8]   R. W. Beard, T. W. Mclain, M. A. Goodrich, and E. P. Anderson, "Unmanned Air Vehicles," vol. 18, no. 6, pp. 911–922, 2002.

[9]   F. Luo *et al.*, "A distributed gateway selection algorithm for UAV networks," *IEEE Trans. Emerg. Top. Comput.*, 2015, doi: 10.1109/TETC.2014.2382433.

[10]   A. Bujari, C. T. Calafate, J. C. Cano, P. Manzoni, C. E. Palazzi, and D. Ronzani, "Flying Ad-Hoc Network Application Scenarios and Mobility Models," *Int. J. Distrib. Sens. Networks*, vol. 13(10), no. 10, pp. 1–17, 2017, doi: 10.1177/1550147717738192.

[11]   Y. Saleem, M. H. Rehmani, and S. Zeadally, "Integration of Cognitive Radio Technology with Unmanned Aerial Vehicles: Issues, Opportunities, and Future Research Challenges," *J. Netw. Comput. Appl.*, vol. 50, pp. 15–31, 2015, [Online]. Available: http://dx.doi.org/10.1016/j.jnca.2014.12.002.

[12]   S. Raj, V. K. Panchal, and R. Chopra, "International Conference On Innovative Computing And Communication (ICICC-2020) Cooperative Optimization Algorithm Based on Desert Sparrow for FANETs Electronic copy available at : https://ssrn.com/abstract=3565250 International Conference On Innovative," pp. 1–6, 2020.

[13]   K. M. Polycarpou, M.M., Yang, Y., Passino, "A cooperative search framework for distributed agents, Intelligent Control,(ISIC'01).," in *Proceedings of the IEEE International Symposium*, 2001, pp. 1–6.

[14]   S. Palazzi, C.E., Roseti, C., Luglio, M., Gerla, M. and J. M.Y., Stepanek, "Enhancing transport layer capability in HAPS Satellite integrated architecture," *Wirel. Pers. Commun.*, vol. 3, pp. 339–356, 2005.

[15]   B. S. Iordanakis M, Yannis D, Karras K, Bogdos G, Dilintas G, Amirfeiz M, Colangelo G, "Ad-Hoc Routing Protocol for Aeronautical Mobile Ad-Hoc Networks," in *In Fifth International Symposium on Communication Systems, Networks and Digital Signal Processing (CSNDSP)*, 2006, pp. 1–5.

[16]   S. Raj, V. K. Panchal, and R. Chopra, "Classification of Routing Protocols Used for Flying Ad Hoc Networks (FANETs)," *Int. J. Futur. Gener. Commun. Netw.*, vol. 13, no. 4, pp. 1848–1859, 2020.

[17]   C. Zang and S. Zang, "Mobility Prediction Clustering Algorithm for UAV Networking," in *In GLOBECOM Workshops (GC Wkshps)*, 2011, pp. 1158–1161.

[18]   S. Suman, E. A. Agrawal, and P. A. K. Jaiswal, "EPARGA : A Resourceful Power Aware Routing Protocol for MANETs," *IJARCET*, vol. 5, no. 5, May, 2016.

[19]   M. Kaur, Simarjot, Talwar, "Routing Strategies in Flying Ad-Hoc Networks," *J. Netw. Commun. Emerg. Technol.*, vol. 6, no. 3, pp. 59–62, 2016.

[20]   S. Iyer, "Review of Flying Ad-hoc Networks (FANETs)," *Int. J. Recent Innov. Trends Comput. Commun.*, vol. 4, no. March, pp. 180–183, 2016.

[21]   Z. Cheng and W. B. Heinzelman, "Discovering long lifetime routes in mobile ad hoc networks," vol. 6, pp. 661–674, 2008, doi: 10.1016/j. adhoc.2007.06.001.

[22]   W. B. Heinzelman, "Exploring Long Lifetime Routing (LLR) in Ad Hoc Networks Categories and Subject Descriptors," pp. 203–210.

[23]   W. Su and M. Gerla, "IPv6 flow handoff in ad-hoc wireless networks using mobility prediction," *Proc. IEEE GLOBECOM*, pp. 271–275., doi: 10.1109/GLOCOM.1999.831647.

[24]   S. Maakar and M. T. Scholar, "Concept of Flying Ad-hoc Network : A Survey," no. April, pp. 178–182, 2015.

[25]   Z. Yang and A. Mohammed, *A Survey of Routing Protocols of Wireless Sensor Networks*. Shanghai, 2010.

[26]   M. A. Khan, A. Safi, I. M. Qureshi, and I. U. Khan, "Flying Ad-Hoc Networks (FANETs): A Review of Communication Architectures, and Routing Protocols," *IEEE*, pp. 1–9, 2017, doi: 10.1109/INTELLECT.2017.8277614.

[27]   M. Mosko and C. E. Perkins, "A new approach to on-demand loop-free routing in networks using sequence numbers," vol. 50, pp. 1599–1615, 2006, doi: 10.1016/j.comnet.2005.09.022.

[28]   C. Blum, "Beam-ACO — hybridizing ant colony optimization with beam search : an application to open shop scheduling," vol. 32, pp. 1565–1591, 2005, doi: 10.1016/j.cor.2003.11.018.

[29]   T. Clausen and P. Jacquet, "Optimized Link State Routing Protocol (OLSR) Status," pp. 1–75, 2003.

[30]   A. I. Alshabtat and L. Dong, "Low Latency Routing Algorithm for Unmanned Aerial Vehicles Ad-Hoc Networks," vol. 66110, no. 8, pp. 984–990, 2011.

[31]   S. Rosati, K. Kruzelecki, L. Traynard, and B. Rimoldi, "Speed-aware routing for UAV ad-hoc networks," *2013 IEEE Globecom Work. GC Wkshps 2013*, pp. 1367–1373, 2013, doi: 10.1109/GLOCOMW.2013.6825185.

[32]   A. Bujari, C. E. Palazzi, and D. Ronzani, "A Comparison of Stateless Position-based Packet Routing Algorithms for FANETs," *IEEE Trans. Mob. Comput.*, vol. 17, no. 11, 2018, doi: 10.1109/TMC.2018.2811490.

[33]   C. Shanti, S. Member, and A. Sahoo, "DGRAM : A Delay Guaranteed Routing and MAC Protocol for Wireless Sensor Networks," vol. 9, no. 10, pp. 1407–1423, 2010.

[34]   H. Badis and K. Al Agha, "QOLSR, QoS Routing for Ad Hoc Wireless Networks using OLSR," *Eur. Trans. Telecommun.*, vol. 16, no. 5, pp. 427–442, 2005, doi: 10.1002/ett.1067.

[35]   B. D. Soni, J. H. Jobanputra, and L. Saraswat, "A Comprehensive Survey on Communication Protocols for FANET," *Int. J. Sci. Res. Dev.*, no. Computer Networking| ISSN (online), pp. 31–34.

[36]   A. A. Radwan, T. M. Mahmoud, and E. H. Houssein, "Evaluation Comparison of Some Ad Hoc Networks Routing Protocols," *Egypt. Informatics J.*, vol. 12, no. 2, pp. 95–106, 2011, doi: 10.1016/j.eij.2011.04.001.

[37]   J. Kulik, W. Heinzelman, and H. Balakrishnan, "Negotiation-based protocols for disseminating information in wireless sensor networks," *Wirel. Networks*, vol. 8, no. 2–3, pp. 169–185, 2002, doi: 10.1023/A:1013715909417.

[38]   L. O. Karaca and R. Sokullu, *Smart Environments and Cross-Layer Design*. InTech Published, 2008.

[39]   S. Das C. Perkins, E. Roye, "Ad hoc On-Demand Distance Vector (AODV) Routing," pp. 1–37, 2003, doi: 10.17487/RFC3561.

[40]   J. Jun and M. L. Sichitiu, "MRP: Wireless mesh networks routing protocol," *Comput. Commun.*, vol. 31, no. 7, pp. 1413–1435, 2008, doi: 10.1016/j.comcom.2008.01.038.

[41]   Z. J. Haas and M. R. Pearlman, "The performance of query control schemes for the zone routing protocol," *Proc. 3rd Int. Work. Discret. Algorithms Methods Mob. Comput. Commun. DIALM 1999*, vol. 9, no. 4, pp. 23–29, 1999, doi: 10.1145/313239.313271.

[42]   C. Zang and S. Zang, "Mobility Prediction Clustering Algorithm for UAV Networking," no. 3, pp. 1158–1161, 2011.

[43]   R. Sharma and D. K. Lobiyal, "Proficiency Analysis of AODV, DSR and TORA Ad-hoc Routing Protocols for Energy Holes Problem in Wireless Sensor Networks," *Procedia Comput. Sci.*, vol. 57, pp. 1057–1066, 2015, doi: 10.1016/j.procs.2015.07.380.

[44]   R. S. Raw, D. K. Lobiyal, and S. Das, "An Analytical Approach to Position-Based Routing Protocol for Vehicular Ad Hoc Networks," pp. 147–156, 2012.

[45]   M. A. Matin and M. M. Islam, *Overview of Wireless Sensor Network*. Dhaka, Bangladesh: InTech, 2012.

[46]   A. Boukerche, B. Turgut, N. Aydin, M. Z. Ahmad, L. Bölöni, and D. Turgut, "Routing protocols in ad hoc networks: A survey," *Comput. Networks*, vol. 55, no. 13, pp. 3032–3080, 2011, doi: 10.1016/j.comnet.2011.05.010.

[47]   M. Maimour, H. Zeghilet, and F. Lepage, *Cluster-Based Routing Protocols for Energy Efficiency in Wireless Sensor Networks*. China: InTech, 2010.

[48]   J. A. Maxa, M. S. Ben Mahmoud, and N. Larrieu, "Survey on UAANET routing protocols and network security challenges," *Ad-Hoc Sens. Wirel. Networks*, vol. 37, no. 1–4, 2017, doi: 10.1080/09297040802385400.

[49]   G. Pei, M. Gerla, X. Hong, and C. C. Chiang, "A Wireless Hierarchical Routing Protocol with Group Mobility," *IEEE Wirel. Commun. Netw. Conf. WCNC*, vol. 3, pp. 1538–1542, 1999, doi: 10.1109/WCNC.1999.796996.

[50]   L. Villasenor-Gonzalez, Y. Ge, and L. Lamont, "HOLSR: A hierarchical Proactive Routing Mechanism for Mobile Ad Hoc Networks," *IEEE Commun. Mag.*, vol. 43, no. 7, pp. 118–125, 2005, doi: 10.1109/MCOM.2005.1470838.

[51]   H. Jing and H. Aida, *Cooperative Clustering Algorithms for Wireless Sensor Networks*. Tokyo, Japan: InTech, 2002.

[52]   T. Kang *et al.*, "A Clustering Method for Energy Efficient Routing in Wireless Sensor Networks," in *EHAC'07 Proceedings of the 6th WSEAS International Conference on Electronics, Hardware, Wireless and Optical Communications*, 2007, pp. 133–138, [Online]. Available: http://dl.acm.org/citation.cfm?id=1355643.1355667.

[53]   A. Manjeshwar and D. P. Agrawal, "TEEN : A Routing Protocol for Enhanced Efficiency in Wireless Sensor Networks," in *IEEE Xplore*, 2016, vol. 8, no. January 2001, pp. 1–7, doi: 10.1109/IPDPS.2001.925197.

EXPERIMENTS IN IoT–LAB

IoT PRACTICALS on Arduino and Raspberry Pi

Expt. No. 1: To get familiarization with Arduino/ Raspberry Pi and to perform the necessary software Installations.

Solutions: We will study installations one by one for both the kits. Let us start with Arduino Kit now.

Arduino Installation

Theory: Arduino IDE is an open-source IDE (Integrated Development Environment) that is used for uploading programs easily to a variety of Arduino boards, clones and compatibles.

Procedure: You can visit the Arduino website at *https://www.arduino. cc/* . The free software download is located at *https://www.arsuino.cc/en/ Main/Software*. Choose the option of **Windows Installer. Download the Executable Installable File.** When you are downloading, it might be different as the Arduino IDE is under continuous development. Once the download is completed, you will find the setup file in the Downloads directory. **Double click** to execute it. It may ask for the **admin credentials.** Enter the admin credentials. Click on "I Agree". And the Installation Options window will appear. Check all of the checkboxes and **click Next.** Then choose the directory where you wish the Arduino IDE is to be installed. Click **Install** and the installation starts.

When the installation is in progress, you will be prompted by a message 'Would you like to install this device software?' check the checkbox and click on Install button. Once the installation button finishes, click Close.

Thus, Arduino IDE is now installed on your computer. A small Arduino IDE icon appears on the desktop. Double click it and the splash screen appears. Then Arduino IDE starts working.

DOI: 10.1201/9781003728641-7

Raspberry Pi Installation

Theory: Raspberry Pi is one of the smaller computing boards available in the market. It is a small computing device, which is of the same size as a credit card. It can be used for a variety of applications like creating simple documents, learning programming, gaming, developing a temperature sensor, AR and VR.

Raspberry Pi is a single board computer measuring (85.60mm *56mm *21mm) with its own ARM processor, RAM, several other ports and peripherals and GPIO (General Purpose INPUT-OUTPUT) pins that facilitate the connection of electronic components. **Raspberry Pi** was first released in 2012. It has different models with process like $20, $25 and $35.programs are written in programming languages like Python, Scratch etc. it is capable of doing all those tasks that we want from a desktop computer. We can browse Internet too. Also, we can play high-definition video, make spreadsheets, word processing and playing games. Even **Raspberry Pi has several generations like Raspberry Pi 3 model B, Raspberry Pi 2 model B, Raspberry Pi zero.**

The basic set-up for **Raspberry Pi** includes HDMI cable, monitor, keyboard, mouse, 5V power adapter, LAN cable, 2GB micro-SD card. The official operating systems (OS) supported are Raspbian and NOOBS. Also note that other 3rd party OS like Ubuntu, Windows 10 core, Pinet and Risc OS are also supported by **Raspberry Pi**

Procedure: For downloading Raspian, the following steps are followed:

Step 1: Download latest Raspbian image from Raspberry Pi official website, *https://www.raspberrypi.org/downloads*.

Step 2: Unzip the file and end up with a .img file.

Step 3: Now write Raspbian OS in SD card. For that install "Win32 Disk Imager" software in Windows machine.

Step 4: Run Win32 Disk Manager.

Step 5: Plug SD card into your PC.

Step 6: Select the "Device".

Step 7: Browse the "Image File" (Raspbian Image).

Secure Shell (SSH) is a feature of Linux that allows you to effectively open a terminal session on your Raspberry Pi from the command line of your host computer. Recent versions of Raspbian do not enable SSH access by default. For enabling SSH, we follow these steps-

S1: Open command prompt and type **sudo raspi-config** and press enter key.

S2: Navigate to SSH in advanced option.

S3: Enable SSH.

In order to expand the file system, follow these steps:

S1: Open command prompt and type **sudo raspi-config** and press enter key.
S2: Navigate to Expand File System.
S3: Press enter key to expand it.

Note: Most commonly used programming languages in Raspberry Pi are Python, C, C++, Java, Scratch and Ruby. Any language that will compile for ARMV6 can be used with Raspberry Pi. Many applications developed using Raspberry Pi are media streamer, home automation, robots, Virtual Private Networks (VPNs), light weight web server with IoT etc.

A Breadboard with connections of LED.

Expt. No. 2: To interface LED/ Buzzer with Arduino/ Raspberry Pi and write a program to turn ON LED for 1 sec. after every 2 seconds.

First of all, let us work on **Arduino board.**

Theory: It uses Breadboards or solderless breadboards as the platforms for prototyping of electronic circuits. They are like emulators. If we have a breadboard and some electronic components then we can make the prototypes of electronic circuits without electrical wires or PCBs or even no soldering is needed.

The circuit diagram is shown next.

As shown in figure-1, a breadboard consists of a block of **plastic with many spring clips** held under the **perforations.** It is called as breadboard because it looks like bread. **The clips are known as the tie points or contact points.**

The contact points are used to hold and electrically connect the components. The contact points are arranged in the **blocks of strips.** As shown in figure-1 above, **that the strips are marked with + and – signs. They are also known as the power strips. Please note here that all of the contact points in a row is a block of terminal strip and are electrically connected.** These strips are usually connected to the power sources and provide power to the electrical components mounted on this breadboard. **The other types of blocks are known as the terminal strip blocks.** There are two blocks of terminal strips separated by a grove. **Also note that these grove acts as a passage for airflow for the ICs that are mounted on this breadboard. The contact points of the terminal strips are used to hold the electrical components and connect them electrically.** Unlike the power strips, the contact points in a column of a terminal strip are electrically connected. In the circuit diagram above, we can see the contact points labelled from A to J row-wise and from 0 to 60 column-wise. The group of contact points A0, B0, C0, D0 and E0 is electrically connected. **That is why the contact points in terminal strip are arranged in group of 5. This is also called as a full-sized breadboard.** Many other variants are also there like a 400 -point breadboard. Also, all of these breadboards have a common feature. All have a **self-adhesive strip on their rear side so that they can be placed securely when needed.**

Apparatus: Male-to-male jumper cables, female-to-female jumper cable, male-to-female jumper strip, resistors, LED.

Program:

```
// the set-up function runs once when you press reset or power the board.
        void setup( )
        {
        //initialize digital pin LED_BUILTIN as an output.
           pinMode(LED_BUILTIN, OUTPUT);

        }
// this loop function runs over and over again forever.
        void loop( )
        {
                digitalWrite(LED_BUILTIN, HIGH)          // turn LED on (HIGH)
                delay(1000);               //wait for a second
                digitalWrite(LED_BUILTIN, LOW)          //turn LED off (LOW)
                delay(1000);               //wait for a second

        }
```

We know that it is used to continuously blink the in-built LED. We can make an **external LED blink using the same program.**

You may connect the anode of the LED to Pin 13 of the board, also we connect the cathode to one of the GND pins of the breadboard say, using a 470 ohm resistor.

Results: When we prepare the circuit and power up the Arduino board then the LED starts blinking.

Modification to the circuit: Say, we want the LED to blink alternatively. **Note that this means that when a LED is ON then the other should be OFF and vice versa.** So, we must modify the code and the circuit also now.

Circuit Modification: Connect another LED to pin (say) 12 of the board through a 470 ohm resistor.

Code Modification:

```
            int led1 = 13;
            int led2 = 12;
    void setup( )
    {
        pinMode(led1, OUTPUT);
          pinMode(led2, OUTPUT);
    }
    void loop( )
     {
            //turn on led1, turn off led2
            digitalWrite(led1, HIGH);
            digitalWrite(led2, LOW);
            delay(1000);
            // turn on led2, turn off led1
            digitalWrite(led1, LOW);
            digitalWrite(led2, HIGH);
            delay(1000);

     }
```

In this program, we are configuring pin 12 and 13 as output. Then in loop( ), we are alternatively turning them ON and OFF. Power up the board. We will see the led lights blinking or flashing alternately.

Also shown in this figure, using FRITZING tool, we can control the traffic lights.

To flash three (3) LEDs consecutively in each iteration, we make some changes in the loop() functions as follows-

```
void loop( )
{
    for (int i=0; i < counter; i++)
    {
        flash (i, 60);
        if (i < counter)
        flash (i-1, 20);
        flash (i-2, 10);
    }
}
```

The Buzzer case:

Apparatus: Piezo-electric buzzer.

Circuit Diagram:

For this experiment, you need-

- *GPIO Breakout (optional)*
- *Breadboard*
- *Buzzer/piezo speaker*

And any Raspberry Pi board with Raspbian OS installed is always needed.

Program:

```
import RPi.GPIO as GPIO
import time
buzzerpin = 18
GPIO.setmode(GPIO.BCM)
GPIO.setup(buzzer_pin, GPIO.OUT)
def buzzer(pitch, duration):
period = 1.0 / pitch
delay = period / 2
cycles = int(duration * pitch)
for i in range (cycles):
GPIO.output(buzzerpin. True)
time.sleep(delay)
GPIO.output(buzzerpin, False)
time.sleep(delay)
while True:
pitch_s = input("Enter the Pitch (200 to 2000):")
pitch = float(pitch_s)
duration_s = input("Enter duration (secs): ")
duration = float(duration_s)
buzzer(pitch, duration)
```

Results:

When we run this program, it will first prompt you for the pitch in Hz and then the duration of the buzz in seconds.

Expt. No. 3: To interface Push Button/ Digital Sensor (IR/LDR) with Arduino/ Raspberry Pi and write a program to turn ON LED when push button is pressed or at the sensor detection.

Let us work on **Arduino board.**

Theory: Push buttons are special type of switches that fall under the category of **Momentary Switches. Note that this means that they close the circuit only when they are pushed.** Each push button has four legs/ contact points so that they can be easily used with the breadboard. Its electrical symbol is

Circuit Diagram:

Rig this circuit. **When the push button is in open state** (not pressed), the digital pin receives a constant yet a very small amount of current and its state is HIGH (1). **When we push the button,** the current takes the path of least resistance and flows to the ground through GND pin. Thus, the digital pin is LOW (0). So, this is how we can **detect a keypress.** The circuit is the hardware component. We need to program it with IDE.

Program:

We write a code now that shows that the LED will persist its state till the next keypress occurs. **This means that if the LED is glowing and you push and release the button then the LED will be OFF (0). Also note that when the LED is OFF and we again push and release the button, the LED will be ON again.**

```
// program constants defined
const int buttonPin = 12;
const int ledPin = 13;
//variables
int button State = 0;
int status = 0;
void setup( )
```

```
        {
            pinMode (ledPin, OUTPUT);
            pinMode (buttonPin, INPUT_PULLUP);
        }
        void loop( )
        {
            //Read button state
            buttonState = digitalRead(buttonPin);
            //if button is pressed...
            if (buttonState = = LOW)
            {
              //check if the LED is OFF
              if (status = = 0)
                {
                    digitalWrite(ledPin, HIGH);
                    status = 1;
                }
                else if (status = = 1)
                {
                        digitalWrite (ledPin, LOW);
                        status = 0;

                }
            }
            delay (200);
        }
```

Explanation: In this program, we have used a status variable to store the state of the circuit. The status variable is inverted every time we press the pushbutton and based on the status variable, we change the LED's state.

Expt. No. 4: To interface DHT11 sensor with Arduino/Raspberry Pi and write a program to print temperature and humidity readings.

We will interface DHT11 sensor with both one by one. Let us start with Arduino Kit now.

Arduino based DHT11 sensor interfacing:

Theory: DHT is a series of sensors that is used for measuring humidity and temperature. These sensors have a capacitive humidity sensor, a thermistor and an analogue to digital converter. **Note that these sensors output the digital signals corresponding to the humidity and the temperature values of the environment.** They are easy to be interfaced with the microcontroller chips like Arduino. The series is as follows:

- DHT11 – also known by the name RHT01.
- DHT21 – also known by the name RHT02, AM2301, HM2301.
- DHT22 – also known by the name RHT03, AM2302.
- DHT23 – also known by the name RHT04, AM2303.
- DHT44 – also known by the name RHT05.

Also note that all of these sensors have 4 pins and the names of these pins from left to right are as follows:

- **Pin 1: Vcc – to be connected to +5V** (3.3V to 5 volts).
- **Pin 2: OUT - output signal to be connected to the digital input.**
- **Pin 3: NC – Not Connected** (null).
- **Pin 4: GND – Ground Pin to be connected to GND.**

In this experiment, we will see the integration of sensors with Arduino board. Sensors are the electronic elements that sense the data. **It converts the physical quantity/ measurements into electrical signals.** They can be analog or digital. We are using DHT i.e., Digital Humidity and Temperature Sensor (DHT). Arduino supports a special library DHT for DHT11 and DHT22 sensors. This provides functions to read the temperature (dht.readTemperature()) and humidity (dht.readHumidity()) values from the data pin.

Rig The Circuit Following These Steps:

S1: Connect Pin 1 of the DHT to the Vcc (+3.3V) supply pin on the board.

S2: Pin 2/Data pin can be connected to any digital pin. Here, it is 12.

S3: Connect Pin 4 to the ground (GND) pin of the board.

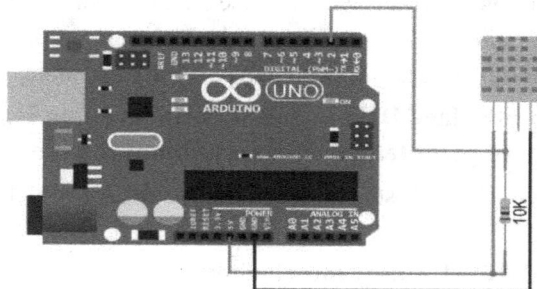

Circuit Diagram: We are using DHT11 or any other DHT sensor may be used. The connection scheme is same for all other sensors in the family.

We need to install the DHT sensor library. Go to Sketch → Include Library → Manage Library. Search for DHT sensor. Select the "DHT sensor library" and install it. Also, you can install **Adafruit Unified sensor library** from Manage Libraries in Sketch from menu-bar.

Program:

```
#include<DHT.h>
DHT dht (8, DHT11);    //initialize DHT sensor
float humidity; //stores humidity value
float temperature;         //stores temperature
void setup( )
  {
        Serial.begin(9600);
        dht.begin( );
  }
void loop( )
  {
//read data from the sensor and store it to variables- humidity and
temperature
humidity = dht.readHumidity( );
temperature = dht.readTemperature( );
//print temperature and humidity values to the serial monitor
Serial.print("Humidity: ");
Serial.print (humidity);
Serial.print("Temperature: ");
Serial.print (temperature);
Serial.println ("Celsius");
delay (2000);    //delay of 2 seconds
```

Connect the board to the PC. Select the port and board type. Verify and upload the code.

Results:

The readings are printed at a delay of 2 seconds as specified by the delay ( ) function.

Raspberry Pi based DHT11 Sensor Interfacing:

In this experiment, a DHT sensor senses the temperature and when the temperature goes above 30° C, a fan needs to be automatically turned on. To include the power of cloud to the projects in IoT, companies provide some platforms like Adafruit, Digital Oceans and Thing speak. So, we use Adafruit cloud in this experiment.

Apparatus: DHT sensor, 4.7ohm resistor, relay, Jumper wires, Raspberry Pi, a small fan.

Rig the Circuit. The following steps may be followed:

(i) For Sensor Interface with Raspberry Pi:

S1: Connect pin 1 of DHT sensor to 3.3V pin of Raspberry Pi.

S2: Connect pin 2 of DHT sensor to any input pins of Raspberry P. we can use pin-11 also.

S3: Connect pin 4 of DHT sensor to the GND pin of Raspberry Pi.

(ii) For Relay Interface with Raspberry Pi:

S1: Connect the Vcc pin of relay to the 5V supply pin of Raspberry Pi.

S2: Connect the GND pin of the relay to the GND pin of the Raspberry Pi.

S3: Connect the input or signal pin of relay to the assigned output pin of Raspberry Pi. We can also use pin-7.

(iii) Fan Interface with Raspberry Pi:

S1: Connect the Li-Po battery in series with the fan.

S2: NO terminal of the relay is connected to the positive terminal of the fan.

S3: Common terminal of the relay is connected to the positive terminal of the battery.

S4: Negative terminal of the battery is connected to the negative terminal of the fan.

Adafruit provides a library to work with the DHT22 sensor also. Install the library in Raspberry Pi. Get the details from github as follows-

git clone *https://github.com/adafruit/Adafruit_Python_DHT*

Go to the folder Adafruit_Python_DHT

cd Adafruit_Python_DHT

Install the library

      sudo python setup.py install

Now we are in a position to write the program in Python for interfacing say, DHT22, a Relay and a Fan with Raspberry Pi.

Program:

```
import RPi.GPIO as GPIO        # GPIO Library
from time import sleep
import Adafruit_DHT            # import Adadfruit library
$set the board for pin numbering
GPIO.setmode (GPIO.BOARD)
GPIO.set warnings (False)
# create an instance of the sensor type
 sensor = Adafruit_DHT.AM2302
print("Getting data from the sensor")
# humidity and temperature are two variables that store the values received
from the sensor
humidity, temperature = Adafruit_DHT.read_retry(sensor, 17)
print ("Temp = (0:0.1f) * c humidity = (1:0.1f%" .format(temperature,
humidity))
# set GPIO pin as output pin
GPIO.setup(13, GPIO.OUT)
if temperature > 50:
  GPIO.output (13, 0)    #relay is active Low
  print ("Relay is on")
  sleep (4);
  GPIO.output (13, 1)    #relay is turned off after delay of 4 seconds.
```

The result is that the fan is switched ON whenever the temperature is above the threshold value set in the code. Here, we have set the threshold value to 50.

Expt. No. 5: To interface a motor using relay with Arduino/ Raspberry Pi and write a program to turn ON motor when push button is pressed.

We will interface a motor with both one by one. Let us start with Arduino Kit now.

Arduino Based Motor Interfacing Using Relay

Theory: If it is a simple DC motor then we can use any motor with 5V to 7v voltage rating. We will use PWM output to control the speed of a DC motor.

Suppose that a motor is rated for 6V then when we supply 6V to it, we find that it rotates at its full speed. On the other hand, for 3V it rotates at half the speed. This is for analogue voltage. Arduino Uno's I/O pins are capable of operating at 5 volts. **Please note that when we set a PWM pin at 127, that is 50% duty cycle which is equivalent to delivering the amount of power that can be provided by a continuous 2.5V DC voltage.** This is how we can use the PWM to amount the power delivered to the motor, thereby controlling its speed. We cannot connect the motor directly to Arduino Uno as it may damage the motor if motor draws too much voltage from the I/O pins. Hence, we will use a PN2222 or 2N2222 NPN transistor as a switch and we will also use a 1N4007 diode to shield the I/O pins from the blowback voltage.

We have used the term Duty Cycle. Let us see what it means?

Duty Cycle: In general, the charging time constant is greater than the discharging time constant. Hence, at the output the waveform is not symmetric. **Please note that the high output remains for longer period than low output. And the ratio of high output period and low output period is defined by the term Duty Cycle. Duty cycle is defined as the ratio of ON time i.e., high output to the total time of one cycle.** Mathematically,

If W = time for output is high = T_{on}

T = time of one cycle.

D = Duty Cycle = W / T

So, $\%D = (W/ T) * 100\%$

Program (Arduino-based):

```
int motorPin = 3;
void setup( )
    {
            pinMode (motorPin, OUTPUT);
            Serial.begin (9600);
            Serial.println("DC Motor PWM Speed Testing…");
    }
void loop( )
    {
            analogWrite(motorPin, 63);
            delay(5000);
```

```
analogWrite(motorPin, 127);
            delay(5000);
analogWrite(motorPin, 255);
            delay(5000);

      }
```

In this program, we are operating the DC motor with various duty cycles. One the program is uploaded you will sense the difference between the speeds at various duty cycles. **Also note that if you reverse the connections of the motor power pins then the motor rotation direction will also change.**

This was a simple DC motor. What if we want to use a servo motor with Arduino?

I. Using a Servo Motor with Arduino

Theory: We say that Servo motors are the special motors that use PWM-Pulse Width Modulation. Unlike DC motors, using servo motors we can control the precise angle for which the motor rotates. Also, we can control the angular velocity and the resulting linear velocity of the motor rotation. Even its direction can be controlled. This needs PWM.

Circuit Diagram and Waveforms:

There are 3 -wires in the servo motor. Black is the GND, Red is the power supply and Yellow for signal. Arduino provides different libraries for different actuators. Servo library is the library containing functions to operate the servo motor.

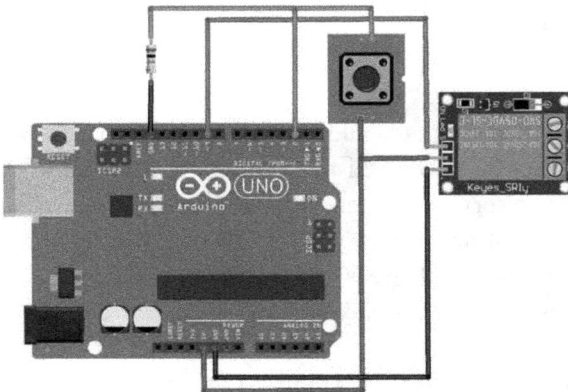

Connections: It shows three connections—Vcc, GND and PWM. Connect the PWM pin to Arduino's digital I/O PWM pin. Connect Power pins to +5V and GND of Arduino as shown in the circuit diagram.

Program: The servo motor can be controlled by writing the code for PWM. But the Arduino IDE comes with a Servo library for the operations on servo motors. We create an instance of the class Servo. The instance must be attached to the pin before being used in the program. Write() functions takes the degree value and rotates the motor accordingly. Connect the board to the PC.

```
#include <Servo.h>
Servo myservo;
int angle = 0;
void setup ( )
{
        myservo.attach(3);
}
void loop ( )
{
        for (angle = 0; angle <= 180; angle++)
        {
          myservo.write(angle);
           delay (10);
        }
for (angle = 180; angle >= 0; angle- - )
          {
           myservo.write(angle);
            delay(10);
          }
```

Result: We import the library and create an object for Servo motor. In the setup() module, attach() is called to associate servo with a PWM pin of the Arduino board. The servo can rotate till 180 degrees. The write() module takes angle as an argument and sets servo to that angle. This program moves the servo motor from 0 to 180 degrees and then back to 0 degrees. The motor turns 0, 90 and 180 degrees with a delay of 1 second each.

II. Using a Servo Motor with Raspberry Pi

Apparatus: 5V servo motor, Breadboard, jumper wires, 1K-ohm resistor, 5v 1A power supply.

Theory: Servo motors are used in remote control vehicles and robotics. Most servo motors are not continuous. This means that they cannot rotate all the way around rather just over an angle of about 180 degrees. The position of the servo motor is set by the length of a pulse. **Note that the servo expects to receive a pulse at least every 20 ms. If that pulse is high for 1 ms, the servo angle will be zero. If it is 1.5 ms, it will be at its center position and if it is 2 ms, it will be at 180 degrees.**

Circuit Diagram and Waveforms:

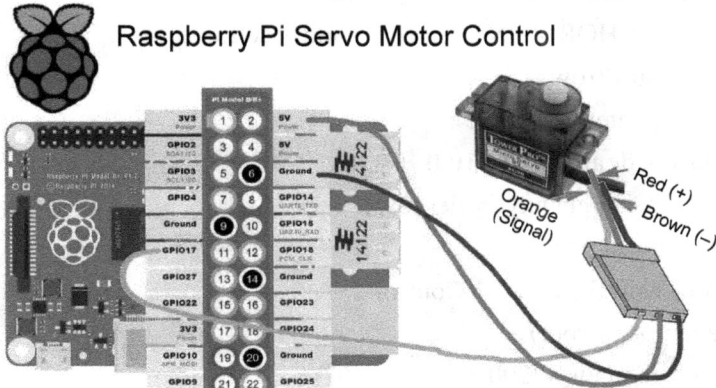

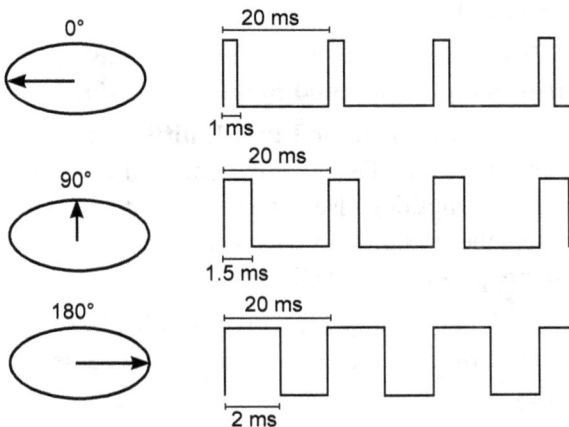

Raspberry Pi Servo Motor Control

Program:

```
from Tkinter import *
import RPi.GPIO as GPIO
import time
GPIO.setmode(GPIO.BCM)
GPIO.setmode(18, GPIO.OUT)
```

```
pwm = GPIO.PWM(18,100)
pwm.start(5)
class App:
def_init_(self, master):
frame = Frame(master)
frame.pack( )
scale = Scale(frame, from_=0, to = 180,
orient = HORIZONTAL, command = self.update)
scale.grid(row = 0)
def update(self, angle):
duty = float(angle) / 10.0  + 2.0
pwm.ChangeDutyCycle(duty)
root = Tk( )
root.wm_title('Servo Control')
app = App(root)
root.geometry("200 * 50 + 0 + 0")
root.mainloop( )
```

Expt. No. 6: To interface OLED with Arduino/ Raspberry Pi and write a program to print temperature and humidity readings on it.

Theory: OLED stands for Organic Light Emitting Diode. There are many manufacturers that package LEDs into a bar graph. It can have any number of LEDs. LED bar graph is nothing else but a number of LEDs bunched together. It is used to represent the strength of various physical measurements like noise, temperature, volume, pressure, humidity etc.

- **Apparatus:** Arduino Uno, jumper wires, LM35 Temperature Sensor, Arduino Uno or any other Arduino board, DHT22 sensor, Breadboard, OLED Display.

Circuit: The following is the circuit that interface an OLED to Arduino chip.

Connections Made:
- Connect DHT22 positive pin + (VCC) to Arduino pin +5V
- Connect DHT22 negative pin - (GND) to Arduino pin GND
- Connect DHT22 pin (Out) to Arduino digital pin (7)
- Connect OLED Display pin[VCC] to Arduino pin[5V]

- Connect OLED Display pin[GND] to Arduino pin[GND]
- Connect OLED Display pin[SDA] to Arduino pin[SDA]
- Connect OLED Display pin[SCL] to Arduino pin[SCL]

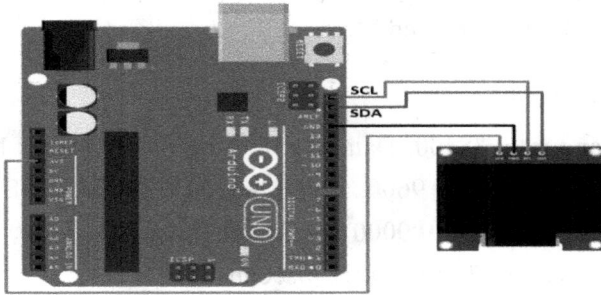

We can use LED bar display for temperature sensing. We need to use map() function of Arduino C to map the temperature values to their LED count on the LED bar display. This way, we can create a digital thermometer.

Program: It has already been given in experiments earlier.

Even OLED interfacing with Raspberry Pi has been discussed earlier.

Expt. No. 7: To interface Bluetooth with Arduino/ Raspberry Pi and write a program to send sensor data to the smartphone using Bluetooth.

Expt. No. 8: To interface Bluetooth with Arduino/ Raspberry Pi and write a program to turn LED ON/OFF when '1' / '0' is received from the smartphone using Bluetooth.

Solutions: Both experiments are related and hence single solution is given below.

Apparatus: LCD, HC-05, Arduino Uno, resistor valued between 220Ω–1KΩ).

Theory: HC-05 module is used to utilize Bluetooth SPP (Serial Port Protocol) module. Serial Port Bluetooth module is fully qualified Bluetooth V2.0 plus Enhanced Data Rate (EDR), 3Mpbs modulation with 2.4GHz radio handset and baseband. It may be arranged as a master or as a slave. This module has 2 methods—operation, Command Mode.

HC-05 Specifications

- Default baud rate: 38400, Data bits: 8, Stop bit: 1, Parity: No parity.
- Baud rate supported is: 9600, 19200, 38400, 230400, 460800.
- Auto-pairing INCODE: "0000" as default.
- Auto-reconnect in 30 mins after disconnection.
- Low power 1.8V operation, 1.8 to 3.6 V I/O.
- Frequency: 2.4GHz, ISM (Industrial Scientific and Medical) band.
- Modulation used: GFSK (Gaussian Frequency Shift Keying).

Interfacing HC-05 Bluetooth Module and Mobile Application

We are trying to interface a HC-05 Bluetooth module and communicate through a mobile application, say Android. The circuit diagram below shows the connections of HC-05 Bluetooth module with 5 LEDs connected on pins 8, 9, 10, 11 and 12 which is toggled when the user interacts by generating a desired message which sets a desired LED to ON or OFF state via communications through Android application and HC-05 Bluetooth module. This shows how to get an input from an Android application and process the inputs. You can compile the code given in this experiment and upload it to Arduino Uno board to observe at the desired output.

There are three main parts to this project. An Android smartphone, a Bluetooth transceiver, and an Arduino.

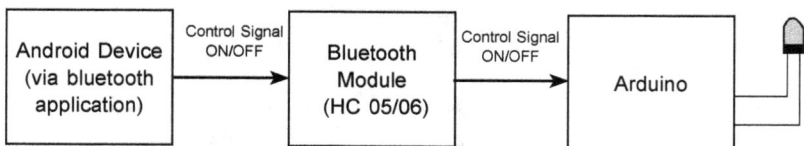

HC 05/06 works on serial communication. The Android app is designed to send serial data to the Arduino Bluetooth module when a button is pressed on the app. The Arduino Bluetooth module at the other end receives the data and sends it to the Arduino through the TX pin of the Bluetooth module (Connected to RX pin of Arduino). The code uploaded to the Arduino checks the received data and compares it. If the received data is 1, the LED turns ON. The LED turns OFF when the received data is 0. You can open the serial monitor and watch the received data while connecting.

Connections

1. Rig the circuit.
2. Write the desired program C.
3. Compile the code of interfacing and upload it to Arduino Uno board.
4. Install Bluetooth SPP Manager Android APP on your mobile.
5. Turn ON Bluetooth. Make it discoverable.
6. Connect to HC-05 Bluetooth module by pairing it.
7. Type number "1" in the message area and click on send. LED 1 should turn ON.
8. Type number "1" again and LED -1 should turn OFF.
9. Repeat this for other numbers also.

Circuit Diagram

Connecting the Arduino Bluetooth Hardware

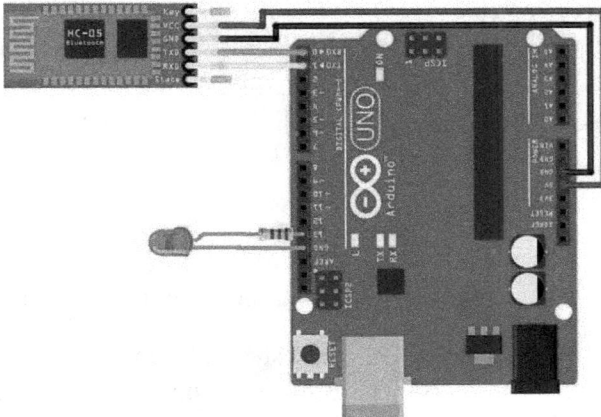

Arduino Pins | Bluetooth Pins

$$RX \text{ (Pin 0)} \longrightarrow TX$$
$$TX \text{ (Pin 1)} \longrightarrow RX$$
$$5V \longrightarrow VCC$$
$$GND \longrightarrow GND$$

Connect an LED positive to pin 13 of the Arduino *through a resistance* (valued between 220Ω–1KΩ). Connect its negative to GND, and your circuit is complete.

Uploading the Sketch to Arduino

```
char data = 0;          //Variable for storing received data
void setup()
{
Serial.begin(9600);     //Sets the data rate in bits per second (baud) for serial
data transmission
pinMode(13, OUTPUT);    //Sets digital pin 13 as output pin
}
void loop()
{
if(Serial.available() > 0)  // Send data only when you receive data:
{
data = Serial.read();   //Read the incoming data and store it into variable data
Serial.print(data);     //Print Value inside data in Serial monitor
Serial.print("\n");     //New line
if(data == '1')         //Checks whether value of data is equal to 1
digitalWrite(13, HIGH);  //If value is 1 then LED turns ON
else if(data == '0')    //Checks whether value of data is equal to 0
digitalWrite(13, LOW);  //If value is 0 then LED turns OFF
}


}
```

Upload the given sketch to Arduino using the Arduino IDE software.

Precautions: The R_X (pin 0) of Arduino should be connected to T_X pin of the Bluetooth module. The T_X (pin-1) of Arduino should be connected to R_X pin of Bluetooth module. When uploading program to Arduino, remove the pins connected to T_X and R_X of Arduino.

Results

The code uploaded to the Arduino checks the received data and compares it. If the received data is 1, the LED turns ON. The LED turns OFF when the received data is 0. You can open the serial monitor and watch the received data while connecting

Expt. No. 9: Write a program on Arduino/ Raspberry Pi to upload temperature and humidity data to ThingSpeak cloud.

Theory

Let us first of all see what is Things Speak?

As we Know that today cloud computing and its services need a global access to data so as to provide results at a faster rate. So many companies provide cloud computing access for free and adaptable interfaces. Some of these platforms are **Adafruit, Digital Oceans and Thing Speak.**

This practical collects the temperature data and logs it to a public IoT platform named as ThingSpeak. This platform provides a structured way of accessing the data. Also, it links the logged data with the social network platform i.e., Twitter. This allows receiving tweets for the user-defined conditions.

The block diagram representation for this experiment is-

Apparatus: ESP-8266 board, Application Board and Arduino Uno board.

We have already seen the Arduino board and its pin configuration. Let us now see what is this ESP-8266 board?

ESP-8266 Board

Interfacing of ESP-8266 with Arduino

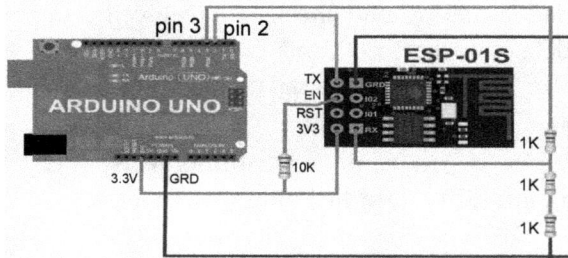

Connections:

The following connections should be made:

Arduino Pins	ESP-8266 Pins
Pin 2	TX
Pin 3	RX

Arduino Pins	Application Board Pins
+5v	+5v
GND	GND
AO	LM35

ESP-8266 Pins	Application Board Pins
+5v	+5v
GND	GND

Procedure:

S1: ThingSpeak is a public IoT platform that is maintained by a company named as **MathWorks.** If you have to use this platform the you must create a Mathworks account first. For this follows these sub-steps:

1. Go to *www.thingspeak.com*
2. Click on "Sign Up" from the menu at top.
3. Create an account with a suitable email id and password.
4. Mathworks will then send you a verification email. Do it.
5. Thus, an account in MathWorks is created.

S2: Create a new channel: Go to *www.thingspeak.com* and sign in using the email and password that you created above. Click on channels→ New

Channel. A channel is where we can monitor and log data. Enter channel details like "Name", "Description" and "Field1". Save the channel. Note down the channel ID and Write API Key somewhere.

S3: Execute Sketch.

S4: Wtach Temperature Logger: Observe the temperature on Thinspeak Temperature Logger's Private View.

S5: Make the channel public. By default, the channel i.e., Temperature Logger is private.

Program:

```
// Temperature Logger—ThingSpeak
 #include<SoftwareSerial.h>
#include<stdlib.h>
#define DEBUG true
//replace with your channel's API key
String apiKey = "8A6GHP378421P74L"


// now connect pin 2 to Tx of serial USB and Pin 3 to Rx of serial USB
SoftwareSerial ser (2, 3);          //Rx, Tx
void setup( )
//enable debug serial
Serial.begin (9600);
//enable software serial
ser.begin (9600);
//reset ESP8266
sendData ("AT + RST\r\n", 2000, DEBUG);
//configure as access point as well as station
sendData ("AT + CWMODE=3\r\n", 1000, DEBUG);
//connect to your access point, enter your SSID and pwd
sendData ("AT + CWJAP= \UTkorde\", \"XXXXXX\" \r\n", 5000, DEBUG);
delay(3000);
sendData ( "AT + CIFSR\r\n", 3000, DEBUG); //get ip address
delay(1000);
sendData ( "AT + CIPMUX = 0 \r\n", 2000, DEBUG); // single connect
}
```

```
void loop( )
  {
          //read values from LM35
          //read 10 values for averaging
          int val = 0;

          for (int i = 0; i < 10; i++)
            {
                    val += analogRead (lm35Pin);
                    delay (500);
            }
          // convert to temp
          // temp value is in 0-1023 range
          // LM35 outputs 10mV/degree C i.e., 1 volt = 100° C
          //Temp = (avg_val / 1023) * 5 Volts * 100 degrees / Volt
                float temp = val * 50.0f / 1023.0f;
          //convert temperature to string
          String strTemp = String (temp, 1);
Serial.println (strTemp);
//TCP CONNECTION
String cmd = "AT + CIPSTART=\"TCP\", \"";
cmd + = "184.106.153.149";      //api.thinspeak.com
cmd+ = "\", 80";
ser.println (cmd);
if (ser.find ("Error") )
  {
          Serial.println("AT+CISTART error");
          return;
  }
//prepare GET string
String getStr = "GET/update? api_key=";
getStr += apiKey;
```

```
getStr += "&field1="
getStr += String(strTemp);
getStr += "\r\n\r\n";
//send data length
cmd = "AT+CIPSEND=";
cmd+= String (getStr.length( ) );
ser.println (cmd);
if (ser.find (">"))
 {
    ser.print (getStr);
 }
else
{
        ser.println ("AT + CIPCLOSE");
        //alert the user
        Serial.println ("AT + CIPCLOSE");
}
//thinkspeak needs 15 seconds delay between updates
delay (16000);
}

String sendData (String command, const int timeout, boolean debug)
 {
    //send the character read to ESP8266
 ser.print(command);
long int time = millis( );
while ((time + timeout) > millis ())
 {
        while (ser.available())
         {
             //read next character
            char c = ser.read( );
```

```
            response += c;
        }
    }
if (debug)
    {
        Serial.print (response);
    }
    return response;
}
```

Results/Output (om running sketch):

Ready message is shown on the display monitor, AT commands are shown on the display monitor, IP address of ESP-8266 module is shown on the display monitor. Also the temperature values are shown on the display monitor and the temperature values are logged on to ThingSpeak channel. The output waveforms are shown below.

Expt. No. 10: Write a program on Arduino/ Raspberry Pi to retrieve temperature and humidity data to ThingSpeak cloud.

(The students are advised to modify the above experiment and do this experiment yourself).

Expt. No. 11: Write a program on Arduino/ Raspberry Pi to install MySQL on Arduino/Raspberry Pi and perform basic SQL queries.

Please follow the following steps to know how to install MYSQL server on Raspberry Pi or to know how to install MariaDB server on Raspberry Pi.

1. Please open the Raspberry Pi terminal.
2. Execute the following command to update the existing packages.

sudo apt-get update

3. Now execute the following to install MySQL server which is shown below. While installing if it is asking do you want to continue then please enter y and hit enter

sudo apt-get install mysql-server

4. Now please execute the following command for secure installation which is shown below.

sudo mysql_secure_installation

5. Please hit Enter for current root password.

6. Now enter y and hit Enter for setting a new password

7. Now enter New password.

8. Now please enter y to remove anonymous user and hit Enter.

9. Now please enter y to disallow remote login .

10. Please enter y to remove test databases.

11. Please enter y to reload privileges tables.

12. Now please execute the following command to login into the database and

   Enter the password which you have entered in step 7.

sudo mysql -u root -p

13. Execute the following command to see databases present in the mysql database.

show databases;

14. Execute the following to create Demo database in mysql server which is shown below.

CREATE DATABASE Demo;

15. Now please execute the following to go in Demo database

USE Demo;

16. Please execute the following command to create database user

CREATE USER 'admin'@'localhost' IDENTIFIED BY 'admin';

17. Execute the following command to grant all privileges

GRANT ALL PRIVILEGES ON Demo.* TO 'admin'@'localhost';

18. Now execute the following command save all the changes

FLUSH PRIVILEGES;

19. Now please execute the following command to come out of database.

Quit

20. Execute the following command to restart the MYSQL server

sudo service mysql restart

How to insert and fetch data from MySQL database?

Please follow the following steps to insert and fetch from the MySQL database:

1. Open the Raspberry Pi terminal.

2. Execute the following command to login to the database and enter the password which is shown below.

sudo mysql -u root -p

3. Execute the following command to use Demo database which is shown above.

USE Demo;

4. Execute the following command to create login table which has two columns i.e., is username and password which is shown above.

create table login (username varchar(25), password varchar(25));

5. Execute the following command to insert data into login table which is shown below.

insert into login values('admin','admin123');

6. To see the inserted values please execute the following command which is shown below

select * from login;

Expt. No. 12: To publish temperature data to MQTT broker.

The functions of all the devices have already been discussed. Let us now see the circuitry and the apparatus required.

Apparatus

Temperature and humidity sensor, Arduino Uno, jumper cables, LED.

Theory: MQTT stands for Message Queuing Telemetry Transport protocol. It is a light weight protocol. By light weight it means that it demands minimal resources for its functioning. IoT prefers to use this type of protocol due to resource constraints. MQTT follows the publish-subscribe pattern.

The overall process is as shown below:

Circuit Diagram: The circuit diagram to upload sensor data to ThingSpeak cloud/ NodeMCU is shown below.

Procedure:

S1: The sensor senses the data and pushes it to the ThingSpeak cloud through NodeMCU that is one of the nodes. And this node is called as **Publisher.**

S2: The transmission process is taken care by MQTT protocol.

S3: ThingSpeak cloud service provider acts as a broker. It takes care of the subscribers provided with suitable messages.

The temperature and humidity sensor will read the data. This data will be sent to the NodeMCU and further to the ThingSpeak cloud. **This process of publishing data to the cloud is known as Publishing.**

INDEX

For Product Safety Concerns and Information please contact our EU
representative GPSR@taylorandfrancis.com
Taylor & Francis Verlag GmbH, Kaufingerstraße 24, 80331 München, Germany